Jeff Andler opens his h....... ....s.
In this record of his pe   :e
and recoil, but above   of
a man and his commi......... .. .. and productive communicator of the Gospel and I am honored to call him my friend. I encourage you to read this book and be ready to see that for all of us, "It gets even better."

—DR. ROY D. MASON
President, Global Evangelism Ministries

"It Gets Even Better," is a candid reminder that the believer's journey will include ups and downs, good days and bad, and laughter and tears. Jeff Andler gives a heartfelt picture of his spiritual journey, which beautifully illustrates how God is at work to give His very best to all of His children.

—DR. STEVE GANDY
Pastor, Arlington Baptist Church Mint Hill, NC

Not only have I read the book, I've watched the author's passion for the Word of God and its application in his life for 22 years. Whoever you are, sit down with this book and see how to rise from the ashes of pain and rejection—and learn to soar!

—JACKLYN A. SIMPSON
Associate Vice Chancellor and
Director of Housing and Residence Life,
University of North Carolina, Charlotte

When Jeff Andler combines his skill as a story-teller, his raw honesty, and his deep commitment to scripture, the result is a book that will engage you in a path that travels from difficult struggles to liberating freedom. Abiding in the grip of Biblical truth, he shows you how to leave the past behind and defeat pain before it defeats you.

—K. ALLAN BLUME,
Editor/President, North Carolina Biblical Recorder

IT GETS EVEN BETTER

FROM THE BOTTOM TO THE BEST IS NOT THAT FAR

JEFFERY P. ANDLER

CROSSBOOKS

CrossBooks™
A Division of LifeWay
1663 Liberty Drive
Bloomington, IN 47403
www.crossbooks.com
Phone: 1-866-879-0502

© 2014 Jeffery P. Andler. All rights reserved.

No part of this book may be reproduced, stored in a retrieval system, or transmitted by any means without the written permission of the author.

Scripture quotations taken from the New American Standard Bible, Copyright © 1960, 1962, 1963, 1968, 1971, 1972, 1973, 1975, 1977, 1995 by The Lockman Foundation. Used by permission." (www.Lockman.org)

First published by CrossBooks 07/18/2014

ISBN: 978-1-4627-3891-5 (sc)
ISBN: 978-1-4627-3893-9 (hc)
ISBN: 978-1-4627-3892-2 (e)

Library of Congress Control Number: 2014911439

Printed in the United States of America.

This book is printed on acid-free paper.

Any people depicted in stock imagery provided by Thinkstock are models, and such images are being used for illustrative purposes only. Certain stock imagery © Thinkstock.

Because of the dynamic nature of the Internet, any web addresses or links contained in this book may have changed since publication and may no longer be valid. The views expressed in this work are solely those of the author and do not necessarily reflect the views of the publisher, and the publisher hereby disclaims any responsibility for them.

Dedicated to Lynne, my wife and best friend,
who has been beside me through it all

CONTENTS

Foreword ix
Preface xi

1—Begin at the Bottom 1
2—Enough for a Lifetime 10
3—Rising from the Ashes 20
4—Little Flowers and Lodges, Part 1 32
5—Little Flowers and Lodges, Part 2 43
6—Live at the Lodge 56
7—Dressed to Kill! 67
8—Busting the Concrete 81
9—Invitation to the World 100
10—A Voice from the Past 112
11—When Life Went South 131
12—Prison Break 143
13—Not Afraid of the Dark 159
14—Into the Night 171
15—No Bag for Your Journey 183
16—Not All Fun and Games 195
17—Full Circle 212
18—Not Finished Until He Is 227

Notes 233

FOREWORD

Have you ever had a wart on your nose and didn't want it there? Has your house ever burned down? Perhaps you couldn't get into college. Has there been a time when you wondered if you deserved something that was happening to you? Did you lose your job? Can you never seem to satisfy everyone? Are there times you feel as if you appear foolish? Have you ever felt, or do you now feel, destroyed, worthless, helpless, crushed and defeated? Do you wonder how you'll ever get past this mess? Are you wondering what to do next?

Even if your dilemma is not listed above, don't worry – whatever it is I can assure you – "IT GETS EVEN BETTER!"

Really! I read this book for myself, Bobby H. Welch, and immediately I said, "It Gets Even Better!"

I have known Jeff Andler for a long time and followed him through the years. As you read, you will trust, appreciate, and desire to thank him for sharing in such a unique way, things which can make life even better for you and yours. I have even suggested to him that he consider an edition of this book for teenagers and children, because the lesson it teaches is for everyone. READ ON! It's about to start getting better for you!

Remember, as you read—and as Jeff reminds us, whatever has happened to you is not nearly as important as what has happened since then. Like so many others, you may find yourself in the lowest place ever. The following pages cause us to realize that your present place is truly unique! It may not feel like a good place to *be,* but it is a great place to *begin.* Not a good place to *stay,* but a great place to *start!*

So get started toward that new place for you, where "It Gets Even Better!"

With You In His Certain Victory!

Dr. Bobby H. Welch

(Dr. Welch is the former pastor of the First Baptist Church, Daytona Beach, FL, past president of the Southern Baptist Convention, and creator of the Faith Evangelism series; He is currently the Associate Executive Director for Church Growth of the Tennessee Baptist Convention)

PREFACE

It's about Time!

I suppose it would be considered by many as an inner-city ministry. It was definitely in the "undesirable" part of town. It was where the most indigent and outcast people lived, where the crime rate was the highest, the living conditions the worst, and the educational achievement the lowest. Even the smell was offensive in the area, thanks to the smokestacks of the local paper mill rising above it. Yet for the better part of fifty years, the Bay Harbor area of Panama City, Florida, was where my mother directed a Christian benevolence ministry. As you might imagine, the rest of our family was involved as well.

Day after day and year after year my dad, brothers, sister and I were exposed to a variety of experiences associated with her work. Some were hilarious, some sad, some tragic, some downright astounding, and some even dangerous. Remaining family and friends still talk about those experiences, and they can bring the same level of laughter or disbelief as they did decades ago. Many times our mom would end a day by saying, "Now I've seen everything!" only to have the next day end with, "I *thought* I had seen everything!" We all listened as she described her adventures, usually with wide eyes and dropped jaws.

There were more than just the inevitable experiences we had come to expect in that environment. I also watched the times when my mother endured difficulties that resulted from the bureaucracy related to the work. Unfortunately common, there were those who had little personal contact or involvement but had the authority to make decisions that affected her service.

I especially remember as a high school senior when this issue escalated to the point my mother found herself in a position to make choices that would reveal and confirm her character. She could maintain a position, be assured of finances, and remain in the good graces of those who had influence without involvement. Or she could take steps that would likely abandon those political conveniences in favor of taking the direction best for the ministry and the needs of the community, with which she was so close. The first choice would keep her in familiar territory, comfortable but compromising. The second choice would move her into a life-altering and previously untried approach to ministry, though it was the only way to preserve her desired effectiveness.

It was no surprise to those who knew her that she chose the latter, with very little deliberation. It meant she would lose face with some but would embark on a new journey of faith with the Savior. It meant she would turn her back on the conditional and, therefore, questionable security offered by people and begin to rely totally on the security that is promised by God. It meant the high spiritual values she had always rightfully verbalized would be tested and then fully realized.

What it did not mean was that the days following her courageous and correct decision would be filled with fanfare and ease. Quite the opposite was true. As is quite often the case, she initially observed disappointment, a measure of humiliation, and a time of isolation. As I would learn personally in the years since, these are not necessarily negative experiences. In fact, they are probably imperative and will definitely prove to be invaluable.

You see, when we experience unprecedented disappointment in people around us, it can indelibly impress on us that people must never be the object of our spiritual faith and trust. While humiliation is unpleasant and embarrassing, it can permanently remind us of our ultimate weakness and our need for One greater and stronger. And though isolation is loneliness, it is when that One can speak to us and work in us in the clearest and most undistracted ways—if we submit to the opportunity and His authority. Yes, I now know I was indeed privileged decades ago to have been exposed to a variety of experiences that have remained with me to motivate and inspire.

Throughout the years I have described, there was another comment from our mom that we probably heard more than any other as she reacted to the events of her day: "I have to write all of this down one day," or, "I ought to write a book." Everyone familiar with her work agreed, especially those who were eyewitnesses to her uncommon experiences. "If you do not do that," they would say, "you'll never be able to remember all of these things, and neither will anyone else."

Perhaps you have correctly concluded that she never accomplished that goal. As far as I know, she never began to pursue it. The priority of daily dedication to the people she served—providing clothes and groceries for a family; getting electricity or water restored to a rundown home; planning weekday Bible classes, Sunday afternoon worship services, and coordinating volunteers—did not allow the time required to produce a written record of her ministry.

The number of those who remain and remember that time is shrinking. Our father died as a young man in his late fifties, Mom passed on in 2009, and even our brother, John Jr., left us abruptly in 2012. Others who could accurately recall the testimony of Mom's life and ministry are scattered or very advanced in years.

I can foresee the time when I may endeavor to produce a record of the unique history to which I've referred. For now, however, her example is what has compelled me to record the experiences we have been afforded in my own family's life and ministry, especially those of recent years.

God called me into ministry in 1971. Thirty-one years later, He brought me through significant changes in philosophy and practice that resulted in a ministry life overflowing with its own incredible adventures. It is almost uncanny how my own experience mirrors that of my mother, both in initial difficulty and struggle, determined yet life-changing choices, and resulting faith. There were even similarities in our ages, stages of life, and children's ages.

Just a year or so into that time, I began to echo the familiar words of my mother: "I have to write all of this down!" I also remembered she went to her grave having never done so and I was determined not to do the same. My new venture into a new faith-based ministry was young, but we had already seen examples of God's presence and provision in ways simple yet exciting. You will see how, over time, these blessings grew in magnitude and scope. But at the time, God used the humble provisions of life to confirm His leading, and I considered each to be worthy of remembering.

In 2003 I began to write what I guess could be called a "book." I had never written a book before. I recall writing instructions in high school and college, but those were just enough to get me through term papers and other assignments. No matter, though, because my goal was to simply leave a history of experiences lived and lessons learned for family and loved ones to share—if even *they* would be interested.

It seemed like as soon as I began, my progress slowed as I sensed the Lord impressing a thought upon me. "This journey has just begun. "Take your time. You are going to learn much and, therefore, have much more to tell later." I had just gotten started and was already postponing progress.

I never dismissed from my mind the desire to resume recording our ever-increasing experiences. But just like Mom, the growing demands of ministry and life in general kept the plan waiting. "Just like Mom," I would repeat to myself, "I need to be writing this down. I need to return to that book thing." Even though the desire was there, I knew there would have to be a change in my schedule and responsibilities that would free me to dedicate the time required. I wasn't sure what that was going to be, or what I wanted it to be for that matter. I am eternally grateful for the multiple gifts and abilities God so kindly bestowed on me. I am equally grateful for our ministry that He has developed, which affords the opportunity to use and enjoy them all. So the question was not, "What do I give up?" but, "What do I even *want* to give up?"

Many times I rationalized the day will come when I am older and no longer physically able to keep my present pace of ministry. *Then* I can settle in and reminisce in written word to my heart's content. That didn't ring true in my spirit, as I was reminded, "Do not boast yourself of tomorrow" (Proverbs 27:1), and, "You do not know what your life will be like tomorrow" (James 4:14). I struggled to see how any one of the important ministries God gave me should be sacrificed for something that might be more *my* idea than His. So I pressed onward. Ten years passed; 2013 arrived, and life was moving on as usual.

I cannot say that God deliberately brought about developments in my life or if He just allowed them, but it is interesting how circumstances arose that interrupted my activity and left me time to think and listen to Him a little more closely. Not long ago, while busy serving in ways that the Scripture directs, something occurred in my life that interfered, shut me down, and gave me no choice but to sit quietly.

Sitting quietly would be a distinct change and challenge, for almost everything in my ministry involved my voice. From childhood, I was involved in choirs, was a voice major in college and seminary, thirty years a church music and worship pastor, and a frequent preacher and speaker. Even when I was not using my voice, plans and preparations were being made that require my voice. I was humbly grateful for the gift God had given me and always endeavored to exercise proper vocal care in hopes of keeping it useful for as long as possible.

However, on Mother's Day in 2013, a change began. I awoke feeling fine, but by the end of our morning worship service, I felt a bit run down. By the time we could get some lunch and reach our home, I was running a fever that exceeded 103 degrees by late afternoon. It remained at that level for several hours, though there were no other detectable symptoms. Within twenty-four hours, the fever had disappeared, my energy returned, and I seemed to feel normal. *Very odd indeed,* I thought. I pursued the activities of the week, all of which involved my voice. I experienced no vocal difficulty or fatigue, and the mysterious Mother's Day incident was forgotten.

On Friday, my wife and I hosted a cookout for the senior adults from our church and neighborhood. All went well. Talking, singing, laughing—no problems. About the time the crowd began to disperse, however, I began to notice the need to repeatedly clear my throat and was experiencing a sudden hoarseness. The problem worsened by the minute, and within an hour after the initial symptom, I could not speak above a whisper. An examination by my doctor revealed the problem would not be quickly solved. Subsequent tests determined the Mother's Day fever was caused by a mysterious virus that apparently affected the nerves to my vocal cords. Instead of toned and straight, they were left bowed, sagging, and for the time being, useless.

I was assured my voice would be restored but was told to expect progress to be slow. I immediately began therapy that would last into the fall. Until the strength of the vocal cords could be restored, speaking normally would be hindered, and singing was out of the question. This certainly was not the course of events I would have chosen for myself. But I did not panic and set about to keep ministry responsibilities covered without the use of my voice.

At our retirement center church, we were in a study I did not want to interrupt before scheduling substitute speakers. I decided to script my sermons and let our team members present these as I continued my responsibilities at the piano. After a few weeks, a team member and dear friend named Ted said, "You know, I've always enjoyed hearing you speak, but I think I enjoy your writing even more. You should consider writing more in the future." Ted did not know it, but the weeks since my voice troubles began, and the sermons I had written, had me thinking about that very subject. I had not forgotten my plan to record some of our experiences. It was beginning to dawn on me that perhaps circumstances were, in fact, creating the opportunity. A thought that I expressed more than once to others now occurred to me: *God's interruptions, whether caused or allowed, are usually God's opportunities.*

As I will share in more detail later, we had experiences that taught us the truth of God always working for our good. I never grew discouraged in my sudden change of pace. In fact, I grew excited to anticipate exactly what God might want to accomplish. I turned my attention to expressing His work through me without the use of something to which we all had grown so accustomed—my voice.

There was no doubt that my life had developed a set of patterns. Patterns that were good, productive, enjoyable, and probably comfortable. But no matter how positive, even these kinds of patterns may eventually qualify as ruts. So what did I do? With some extra time on my hands, the desire still in my mind, and the nudge from a friend, I located the old floppy disk that held the work I began ten years earlier. *I'd really like my voice back,* I thought, *but while I'm working on that, I may as well make use of the time doing something that I've been wanting to do. Something Mom wanted to do and never did. I don't know how long it will take for my voice to return, but if I just get started on this project, I'll stay with it regardless.*

In the pages that follow, my desire for you is twofold. First, I would be honored to have you share our excitement as you experience our testimony of God's amazing dealing, provision, and blessing in our lives. But there is something more, something deeper. Over the years, as I have shared many of these experiences with patient listeners, it has been common to see amazed reactions before the story ended. Knowing they have not yet heard the exciting climax that remains, I have often continued by saying, "Hang on, it gets even better!"

By definition, the word "better" means, "of higher quality," or, "in a superior manner." To say something is better automatically indicates that whatever preceded it was in some way inferior by comparison. That is exactly the principle we experienced as God brought us from a fairly predictable life of Christian service, through very difficult and faith-testing upheaval, and into new levels of spiritual freedom, usefulness, and peace. For us, life was okay, then became suddenly devastating, and then became eternally better… and better… and better. My desire is that you can say the same about your own experience, if you do not already.

Are things going along okay for you? It can be better. Are you enduring difficulties that have you distracted, confused, and frustrated? It can be better. No matter what your present state, it can get even better!

So here I go. Here *we* go. We'll step back in time and resume the work that began a decade ago. And I suppose it's about time!

CHAPTER 1

BEGIN AT THE BOTTOM

It's not what you want to hear. It's not what you think you need to hear, though it comes from those you know to be well meaning. You know they are trying their best to comfort, encourage, and empathize. But all their efforts to do so just further reveal the fact they are clueless. Taken alone, the manner in which they speak indicates they have no idea of the depth of the hurt and helplessness you feel. They may be family members, close friends, or mere acquaintances. But at this point your level of trust toward the entire human race has received severe damage from your recent experience. It is irrelevant, therefore, *who* is speaking because your wound is still raw enough that any words from anyone are more irritating than soothing, more ignorant than insightful. Their attempts to comfort you almost bring an inner rage rather than reassurance. Depending on your personality and state of mind, you might be able to manage to respond politely with a weak smile, a phony gesture of appreciation, or an insincere acknowledgment of their "understanding." Intellectually, you know they are trying, but emotionally, you know their efforts are not working. What you would really like to do is tell them to… well, never mind.

To what well-meaning verbal attempts am I referring? You know, something like, "Well look at it this way, when you've hit bottom, there's nowhere to go but up," or, "God sometimes puts you on your back, so you will look up at Him." When they get "spiritual" about it, you might really want to go off because comments like the latter seem to suggest that something about your life actually caused you to deserve what you are experiencing. And how in the world could that be true?

After all, you've been a believer since childhood, weren't terribly wayward as a teenager, and you've been a faithful husband and father. You've been an example of service in your church and quoted all the right Scripture verses at just the right times to just the right people. You've been careful to use every God-given ability to the fullest for Him, and as your reward for this life of diligence, He was surely going to protect you from the very hell that has devastated you. But that's not even close to what has happened. In fact, you are convinced He stood aside and let you bear the full force of the attack.

You're in pain, but still aware enough to cringe at the thoughts invading your mind. Yet they are there. "I don't want to hear about God. He is the very One who could've prevented this, but He didn't. Where was God when I needed Him to rescue me? Why did He let this happen to me? After all I've done for Him, why?"

You never thought the day would come when you would think—or heaven forbid, say—words such as these. But you have, and you begin to realize you've hit a low point in your life that only happens to other people. God is testing your once rock-solid faith to its breaking point. All the wise counsel you've given in the past does not seem to be helping you, and now the insights offered by others feel like empty platitudes. You'd really prefer to do without them.

Do the preceding circumstances fit a past point in your life? Have they stumbled upon you and insensitively mirrored your present state? If the answer to these questions is no, I breathe a sigh of relief on your behalf—for now. Even so, I also offer a gentle admonition to continue reading because the day is likely to come when that answer will change. Something digested from these pages may then be able to squeeze its way into your conflicted mind as a reminder of hope.

If the answer to either question is yes, first of all, I offer you my deepest sympathy and empathy. Although it may seem like I am telling your story, it is my own experience I share in these pages. Though the pain has faded into insignificance, my memory of the experience is still clear. Therefore, I encourage you to continue reading in hope the following pages bring the encouragement and motivation you need to help you transform your struggle into a painless memory as well. Though impossible to imagine while in the stress of difficulty, I now know—and you can too—this is a real and exciting possibility.

For me, it has become a real and exciting reality. Faith will indeed be strengthened. Priorities will be joyfully rearranged or possibly transformed altogether. The God of Light we question in our darkness will raise us to levels of love, trust, and surrender never before imagined. The result will be a complete joy and freedom never before experienced.

Most unlikely of all is the fact that the quality of life reached after the devastating experience can actually bring about the *genuine* practice of Paul's admonition, "in all things give thanks" (Ephesians 5:20). The realization will come that without past defeat, present victory would not be a daily way of life. Perhaps most amazingly of all is that the deeper the wound, the faster these things can become true! By the way, we will also reach the point of recalling the words of our previously mentioned comforters and belatedly feel the warm gratitude toward them they deserve. Although their attempts to comfort may have seemed futile at the time, they did care enough to try, and their "insights" are now proving to be true.

You have surely concluded that I have passed through some dark valley from which I saw no escape. And you would be correct. I hope, however, that you are not the overly curious type whose appetite for a detailed account of my experience has been piqued. I am afraid you will be disappointed. Since it is my desire for these pages to encourage, inspire, and give hope, I see no point in possibly causing you to relive your hurt by dragging you through mine. After all, whatever happened to us *then* is not nearly as important as what has happened to us *since* then. Whatever attacks, injuries, or humiliation came our way, they are in the past, a cold, rigid territory that cannot be relived or minutely altered. We must choose to leave it behind, or we shall remain its prisoner and victim. That means we will continue in the bitterness it inflicted. Who needs that? Who *wants* that?

I will, however, begin with the state in which I found myself immediately after my devastating storm—when there were days that felt as cold and dark as the storm itself. This was a time when new questions bombarded my cluttered mind that was busy trying to sift through my emotional wreckage. It was a time when I hoped to find something that would bring sense to my experience.

"What do I do now?" "Why did this happen to me?" "What did I do to cause this?" Yes, I remember that time vividly... filled with confusion, doubts, loneliness, and destroyed confidence. It was not a good place in which to *stay*, but I know now it was a great place from which to *start*. Read that last sentence again.

While I cannot say this is true of everyone's trials, I do recall the experience I endured reached a climax followed by a specific ending point. I was strangely relieved to know it was finally over but not before it left me feeling stripped of all dignity, self-worth, confidence, reputation, determination, and… well, you get the idea. And if dealing with those feelings were not difficult enough, add to it the keen awareness that I had been forced into a point of starting over in life—in my late forties with a wife, a son in college, and a daughter headed there in a year—with absolutely no idea of how to begin.

A few of my friends who stayed by my side during and after the ordeal offered me encouragement: "With your abilities and experience, you'll have opportunities to serve all over the place." While grateful for their confidence, I somehow sensed deep down that I should not hold my breath until it happened. That too was a new experience, because ever since feeling God's call to the ministry as a teenager, I had been fortunate to be the one who was pursued by people offering opportunities to serve.

My wise mother told me shortly after my call to ministry, "Son, if God has truly called you, you do not need to look for 'jobs.' Just serve Him with all you've got and keep your nose clean, and jobs will look for you." That philosophy had worked like a charm for over thirty years, but I saw no way for it to come to my rescue after this defeat. Do you see the depth of my hurt? It even had me questioning my mother's time-tested and heretofore proven wisdom.

I would quickly find that Mom was not the only one I would question. For probably the first time in my life, I had serious questions and doubts about myself. While I hoped I had never been an insufferable egotist in the eyes of others, self-confidence had never really been my problem.

Through the years, God had been gracious in allowing me various abilities. I diligently developed each of them to the fullest extent possible, so they could be used for His glory. I went to college on music scholarships and received multiple awards and honors, both musical and academic. I enjoyed success in the churches I served. Almost any idea I came up with (always believing it was from the heart of God) seemed to be accompanied by the road map to accurately bring it about. Along with the ideas and dreams seemed to be the knack for drawing into my vision others who could eagerly help get the job done. For thirty-plus years, it was really true that "with God all things were possible." If I could dream it, it could be done!

Not anymore. In the past, I had known setbacks and challenges here and there, but this experience dropped me hard and fast, shattering a lifetime of self-confidence into a million pieces. This man who was always so sure of where he was supposed to be going, so sure of how to get there, and so sure of taking others with him, was now confused as to his next step and quite convinced there was no one in line to join him.

I remember thinking that even if I returned to familiar areas of ministry, I would not know what to do or how to do it. I questioned and criticized a lifetime of music ability and experience. *I must not have been all that capable or I wouldn't be here alone wondering what to do next.* I questioned and doubted my recent and brief experience as a pastor. *What made me think I could do that? What a fool I must look like.* I was embarrassed and questioned the example I was to others. *What must these people think of me? I must be a joke to them.* I was convinced that if anyone knew I still existed, and if they had anything to say about me at all, I would not want to hear it.

I identified totally with David, who said, "I have become a reproach, especially to my neighbors, and an object of dread to my acquaintances; those who see me in the street flee from me. I am forgotten as a dead man... I became a byword to them" (Psalms 33:11–12; 69:11). No, things were not literally that drastic, but they were in *my* mind. I was down on myself, I was down on the situation, I was just down. Way down.

Not only did I question and doubt myself, I began to question and doubt others. Previously a fairly trusting and open individual, I decided to shut down every portal of my soul to prevent any emotional entrance by anyone. I spared myself the slightest hint of a future experience that might bear resemblance to the one I had just endured.

Though I willingly continued to engage in the company of those I considered to be my remaining friends, I admit their complete trustworthiness was also held in question. I kept a safe, self-preserving distance emotionally and conversationally. After all, my experience had not been the result of some physical affliction, natural disaster, or the plot of one that might have been considered an enemy. It had involved people I would not have expected to be involved.

Don't think me too naïve, for I had not lived to be forty-something without ever being disappointed or seeing others similarly devastated. This longtime music minister knew the phrase of the old hymn, "I Am Resolved:" "Friends may oppose me, foes may beset me." But that truth had never reached this level for me personally. My feelings once again were echoed in the words of David, "For it is not an enemy who reproaches me, then I could bear it; Nor is it one who hates me who exalts himself against me, then I could hide myself from him. But it is you, a man my equal, my companion and familiar friend. We who had sweet fellowship together, and walked in the house of God in the throng" (Psalm 55:12–14).

As far as I was concerned, if it could happen once, it could happen again, and I was taking no chances. Needless to say, even in a crowd I felt pretty isolated and lonely. I didn't care for the loneliness, but for the time being, it was a price I was willing to pay to have the "security" it afforded.

Finally—and the most relentlessly disturbing of all—I questioned and doubted God. My walk with the Lord had never really been in question. For years I began each day in the study of His Word and spending time in prayer. As indicated, the ministries I was involved in over the years seemed to have His blessing upon them, or so it appeared. As a result, I suppose I may have thought I had the spiritual formulas figured out. Sure, there were the inevitable inconveniences and minor obstacles, usually overcome with steadfastness and a willingness to work. But until now there had never been a spirit-crushing defeat that left me feeling destroyed, worthless, and helpless.

I recall the first "morning after." I arose as always, dressed, and ate a little something. But that's where the similarities with most other mornings of the past three decades ended. As I said earlier, it had been my faithful practice to begin each day with the Lord. *Why should I bother with that?* I wondered. *What good will it do? In fact, what good has it done? It certainly did not prevent what has happened to me.*

You may correctly conclude I had no desire that day, or for many days to come, to continue in the habit I had known for almost a lifetime. As far as I was concerned, God let me down big time, and it didn't really matter if I spoke to Him or if He spoke to me. All I would say to Him anyway would be an expression of anger. And I was sure there was nothing He could say to me that would be of interest. For the first time in my life, I was not on speaking terms with God, and I didn't care. But thank the Lord old habits, in this case a good one, die hard.

Though I had no idea what the Bible could say to me that morning, something in me knew if I gave in to the despair and turned my back for even a few days, I may head down a dark road from which there could be a point of no return. So I picked up my Bible, turned to where I had left off in my recent study, and went through the motions of time with God. It was empty and dry.

I continued my day as I always had, out the door to walk the streets of my neighborhood in prayer. Talk about a bust. I tried to mumble something but gave up almost immediately, saying nothing more and hearing nothing in return. It quickly became apparent that God was obliging my desire to not hear from Him. This man, who had for so long lived to be an example of spiritual tenacity and endurance, was settling into a life of bewildered spiritual silence. Again, a new experience. Silence had never been my style of communication and function in any relationship on the human or spiritual levels.

Silence would not be my style for long this time around either, for one trait in my life that was not destroyed by my experience was dissatisfaction with unresolved conflict in relationships. Though I was angry with God, I had not been so foolish as to entertain the thought I no longer loved Him. So after not many days, as He knew I would do, I was the first to break the silence between us. At first, my words mainly consisted of the usual questions. "Why has this happened to me?" I would have loved an answer, but nothing.

"I've served you faithfully through the years." Nothing.

"What did I do to deserve this?" Nothing.

"You could've done something to prevent this." Nothing.

"So why didn't you?" Nothing.

"You know I can't sit and do nothing." Nothing.

"You made me to be active and productive." Nothing.

"I'll go crazy and drive my family crazy too." Nothing.

"What am I supposed to do now?" Nothing.

"Why won't you say something?" Nothing. Nothing. *Nothing!*

You'll recall I had been just fine with God's silence earlier. I was now finding that while He was with me, cared for me, and hurt with me, He was not at the beck and call of my roller-coaster emotions, obliged to speak only when I was in the mood to listen. I also became aware, and have learned to understand at deeper levels since then, that He is not threatened by my questions or my anger.

As this one-sided pattern continued, I began to be concerned with the obvious issues of a father and husband. The expenses of college, home and family had not been sympathetically placed on hold. I could not—and did not wish to—avoid giving thought to those needs.

My wife, Lynne, worked two days a week as a dental hygienist. We had saved her income over the years for our children's education and for occasional fun money. Now it was our sole income, at least for the time being. It was at this point some very new questions troubled my mind. I had never been averse to any honest work, but other than ministry, I had no experience that would attract a position much above entry level. The last I had heard, not many places were looking for forty-something-year-old rookies. What would I do to support my family?

I had friends in various administrative fields who might help me out with a maintenance or handyman position. I was comfortable with tools, there wouldn't be a lot of stress involved, and stress-free was right up my alley at the time. But when I tried to pick up the phone, there again was that interruption inside. You remember, the same "something" that warned me not to miss my time in God's Word and prayer? That same voice told me if I turned my back on what had been the focus of my life for over thirty years, my life may be no more than a joke to all I'd ever influenced. *But*

I can't go back into a ministry position, I thought. *It was in ministry that I was so recently and thoroughly devastated.*

So there I was again, stalemated in the conflict of inner debates, not quite knowing what to do next. The phone wasn't ringing, the offers weren't coming, clear answers were not in view. The house was quiet, though my mind was not. But no one heard that noise but me and my God, who wasn't responding. It was as low as low had ever been for me. Sitting on the bottom. Not a good place to *be*, but a great place to *begin*. Not a good place to *stay*, but a great place to *start*.

Now hang on. It gets better!

CHAPTER 2

ENOUGH FOR A LIFETIME

What is God up to? The more I questioned, the more strangely and stubbornly quiet He seemed to be. About the time I began to wonder if my spiritual exile was to be permanent, a spark of rational thought found its way to my mind.

For years I had attempted to instill in others what I had learned to be the crucial element in knowing the will of God—to know the Word of God. "God's Word *is* God's will," was a conviction I verbalized so many times I lost count. Then that "something" inside let me know it was time to practice what I preached. All my independent attempts at reason had produced nothing, so it was time to go to God's Word. Really *go* to it and not just go through the motions with it.

I became aware that while it may seem like God is sometimes silent, He is in fact always speaking, as long as His Word is available to us. How many times had I told others the foremost and clearest way God speaks to us is through His revealed Word? In my difficulty, I had let that slip my troubled mind. It's a little embarrassing to admit it took me awhile to reach this point. However, the experience does help me better understand when I witness people who do not see things clearly or find answers very quickly while in the throes of a crisis.

I must pause at this point to testify I did begin to recognize the little something inside was not a something but a Someone—God, the Holy Spirit—who still dwelt within my wounded heart. Just about everything else had been driven out, but He remained in spite of the carnage.

It was He who deflected my attempt to disregard my daily time with Him. It was He who would not allow me to pursue an occupational direction that abandoned His call on my life. And it was He who reminded me the advice I had given others was now needed in my own experience.

He had been there all along. It is interesting how we as God's children can quickly claim He is not speaking when the real problem is we are not listening, or that He simply is not saying what we want to hear. What I have previously referred to as God's silence was probably not silence at all but my deafness. Yes, it was deafness due to pain and probably a little self-pity, which I felt was justified, but deafness just the same.

My circumstances would've gone from bad to worse if God had not lovingly helped me overcome them. And it dawned on me that He was perfectly willing for me to make the right choices along my road to recovery without realizing it was He who was helping me make them. He was willing to forfeit the immediate credit He was due for quietly guiding me into those choices. His concern was my spiritual survival and, therefore, could accept my delay in consciously giving Him the glory for His role in the process. He knew, as in all things, His time would come. And He loved me enough in my situation to be willing to wait. He really *is* so good.

Having brought me to this point, our heavenly Father continued to make Himself evident in the fact that my retreat to the Scriptures did not require an intense search through the printed pages. In other words, it was not even necessary for me to open my Bible. As it had happened so often in past moments of need, the promise of Jesus once again became a reality. "But the Helper, the Holy Spirit, whom the Father will send in My name, He will teach you all things, and bring to your remembrance all that I have said to you" (John 14:26). As promised, the Spirit began to take my mind to verses that were needed to address my situation and put me on a path that would leave it behind. These were not obscure, out of the way verses that would be considered little known yet profound biblical treasures. No, they were the fairly familiar and frequently used. I found myself in well-traveled scriptural territory, reviewing words I thought I had understood and applied in my life for many years. I soon came to experience them fully for the first time.

The first was Christ's admonition from the Sermon on the Mount: "But seek ye first the kingdom of God and His righteousness, and all these things will be added to you" (Matthew 6:33). In verses 19–24, Jesus warned against the overemphasis on earthly treasures, which would inevitably take full occupation of our hearts and enslave our spirits.

As if reading the minds of His hillside audience, He immediately addressed what would probably have been their response and ours. How are we to care for our lives if we do not emphasize money? "Do not be anxious for your life, as to what you shall eat, or what you shall drink; nor for your body, as to what you shall put on" (Matthew 6:25). I like how the King James Version translates the opening phrase by using the words "take no thought." Many times, in an effort to ease the mind of a friend, we often reassure them by saying, "Don't give it a second thought." In teaching us to trust Him for the needs of our lives, Jesus said not to give them a *first* thought. That must have been seen as radical advice by that crowd, about as radical as it stills seems today.

In Matthew 10:9–10, when Jesus officially called and commissioned His disciples, they found He would privately confirm what He publicly preached when He gave them explicit instructions to "not acquire gold, or silver, or copper for your money belts, or a bag for your journey." When we're living for Him, these issues are simply not to enter our minds.

I had lived by these principles for years, hadn't I? I was in full-time ministry and felt I had obeyed God's call on my life. I was always diligent to be where I was supposed to be, doing what I was supposed to be doing, and when it was supposed to be done. I had always been diligent to set the right example, hadn't I? He had kept His end of the Matthew 6:33 deal by putting me in a nice church position, where I could pick up a paycheck every week or two. He even threw in added benefits like retirement plans, medical insurance, and more. This Matthew 6:33 "thing" had really not been that hard, and for me and mine, it always seemed to be wrapped up in a tidy little system (and I still believe He can choose to care for us through conventional methods if He so desires).

Like everyone, we occasionally experienced times that were financially tight, but God had always come through to get us to the next payday. But now I was sitting and staring into emptiness with none of these securities looking back at me... except for One. God was the only part of the past equation of my life's security that was still part of the present. I nervously began to realize I was about to be required to practice a level of faith and trust in Him not previously experienced.

I pause once again at this point to emphasize a truth I'm sure we all believe. But it's one I see few come to totally realize and consistently practice. In this life, there is nothing that should be considered secure if it can be lost or taken away by any person or circumstance, including death. I am convinced if those things from which we try to draw our security are not going to remain constant and consistent into eternity, we would do well to avoid leaning upon them now. If we do not, we will probably live to see the day when they will disappoint us and leave our hopes unfulfilled.

As previously noted, Jesus warned against setting our sights too keenly on the things of this life when He stressed, "Do not lay up for yourselves treasures upon earth, where moth and rust corrupt, and thieves break through and steal. But lay up for yourselves treasure in Heaven, where moth and rust do not corrupt, and where thieves do not break through and steal" (Matthew 6:19–20).

We may depend on wealth, but who has not heard of wealth being erased by business failure or economic disaster? We may depend on possessions and property, but who has not heard of these being robbed or ruined by theft, fire, or flood? We may depend on position that was rightfully acquired through hard work and diligence, but who has not heard of position being lost to a younger, ambitious, more energetic, and possibly conniving individual? We may even depend on relationships with family and friends, but who of us has not heard of these disintegrating due to misunderstanding and conflict, or being abruptly ended by the hand of death?

If we are honest, many of us would have to admit we do not like thinking this way. But the truth of the matter is—and always has been—that whatever experience of collapsing security we have seen in the life of another can potentially happen to us. God and His Word are the only securities we will stand upon for all eternity and, therefore, should be the only foundations that receive our faith and trust today. We must join David's perspective when he said, "God only is my Rock and my salvation" (Psalm 62:6). In short, since He is all we really *have*, He is all we really *need*.

My wife and I had disciplined ourselves through the years to live within our means, avoid debt, and to save a little along the way. Now simple mathematics reminded us that living without some measurable income would quickly eat away at what reserves we had and leave us in a financially precarious position. Though opportunities were not knocking at my door, I knew the bill collectors would not be so kind as to follow that example.

In facing this concern, the radical invasion of the Matthew 6:33 principle into my life did not bring with it a readily clear picture of how it was to be fulfilled. Prioritizing "the kingdom of God and His righteousness" was not a new concept to me, but to do so with absolutely no conceivable means of support certainly was. I would soon learn God was taking me through a process that would wean me from the visible and explainable to the point of trusting Him who is "immortal, invisible, the only wise God" (1 Timothy 6:16).

My purpose was to see *only* those things important to God and His kingdom in such a captivating way that the incidental things needed to support my existence would be utterly overwhelmed. They would be overruled into insignificance—and finally unconsciousness. Quite simply, my mind was to be filled each day with His higher kingdom purposes to the extent there was no time or space for me to give the first thought to my survival or comfort. For the first time in my life, these were to be *totally* God's concern. I would also totally learn for the first time that He is much better at handling them than I could ever be.

After using Matthew 6:33 to focus my concentration on "the kingdom of God and His righteousness," and to abandon concern for my needs, the Spirit "called to my remembrance" more of what I had long since learned. He revealed exactly what this kingdom focus should involve. Specifically, He took me to a later portion of the gospel of Matthew, chapter 25, verses 35-36, "I was hungry and you gave Me something to eat; I was thirsty and you gave Me drink; I was a stranger and you invited me in; naked, and you clothed Me; I was sick, and you visited Me; I was in prison and you came to me."

This well-known account of Christ's description of the division of "the sheep and the goats" is clearly an event in the future judgment. However, it is also made clear the rewards given at that time are determined by one's diligence regarding the issues presented. Issues God obviously holds as priorities for us in this present life. <u>Priorities that will actually eliminate the possibility of self-distraction if genuinely and consistently pursued.</u>

I had read these words many times and heard them as the emphasis of many sermons. But their significance began to become more personal as I once again heard Jesus say, "to the extent that you did it to one of these brothers of Mine, even the least of them, you did it to Me" (verses 40, 45). It was strange how I'd missed the impact of His admonition for so long. "You did it to them, you did it to Me. You neglected them, you neglected Me" (paraphrase mine). Even the use of the words "Me" and "Mine" in the form of a proper name was a fresh observation that Jesus took these matters not only very seriously but also very personally.

Had I been neglecting what was so important to the Lord? I had grown up in my family's ministry, which was located in an area of our town where needs were obvious. I had helped pack and deliver boxes of food, clothing, and gifts at Christmas and other times, though probably more a result of parental coaxing than personal concern.

I must admit the concentration of my church ministry had not allowed time for these things on a consistent basis. I knew the poor and hurting were out there, but it seemed there simply weren't hours left in my average day to involve myself in their plight. My calling to a life of serving the Lord via church work had seen to that. Planning and implementing various music rehearsals; planning and leading multiple worship services; planning and preaching the necessary sermons; the constant pursuit of new people for our ministry and the endless task of "chasing" those we already had; attending staff meetings, and so on, left me dry and spent at the end of each day. Someone else would have to tend to the remaining needs of the world. I was doing my part as a motivator of God's people, and I was only one person, comfortable with the realization God didn't expect me to meet all the needs of humankind singlehandedly.

However, I looked into these verses anew and afresh with the awareness my part no longer existed as I had known it. I realized what Jesus verbalized as important to Himself did not even include most of what had been so important to me.

As we go further into the transformation of my priorities, I present one more Scripture the Spirit called to my remembrance. He had turned my mind to those who were ill, indigent, impoverished, and imprisoned, but there was an area or two remaining in the world around me He did not want me to ignore. I had left a study of the book of James incomplete in the position I had recently vacated, so He didn't have a problem reminding me of chapter 1, verse 27: "This is pure and undefiled religion in the sight of our God and Father, to visit the orphans and widows in their distress, and to keep oneself unspotted by the world." Keeping myself "unspotted" had not been my problem. But once again, the inclusion of orphans and widows on a regular basis was another story.

Here I was with plenty of time on my hands. No church position to dominate my time or my mind, and the Spirit of God using the Word of God to begin to show me how He would occupy all three. Could He be responding so quickly to my impassioned prayer that He not leave me idly unproductive? Possibly, but the arena in which all this could take place was still a mystery. It was becoming obvious that He was simply calling me to be obedient to the centuries-old mandates outlined in His Word, but how? Where? With whom?

Then came the inevitable inner debates that occur in one experiencing a break from lifelong thoughts and practices in the area of Christian ministry. *Okay, Lord,* I thought, *if I am to involve myself with those who are sick, lonely, captive, elderly, and so on, what about the practice of deliberate evangelism and soul-winning? I mean, social ministry is fine, but what I really need to be doing is sharing the plan of salvation and bringing people to a decision for Christ, right?* After all, that's what I had always done and had seen a great deal of response (response yes, though I now know true conversions are another matter). I had enjoyed ministry in a few churches where evangelism was a high priority, and numerical growth and baptisms were realized.

Yet in all of this, the Spirit reminded me that while secular agencies deal with people strictly on a worldly, human, physical, and even emotional level, a true Christian ministry does not. As I began to consider the challenges of Matthew 25 and James 1:27 more extensively, I found responding to them would begin at one level in the lives of others and naturally progress to another. The great motivation of my life and ministry—evangelism—would not be neglected.

Allow me to elaborate. Jesus said, "I was hungry, and you gave me something to eat" (Matthew 25:35). When we see the "least of these" around us suffer physical hunger, the appropriate initial response should be the provision of food. It is doubtful someone will clearly hear the gospel message in his soul above the cry of hunger in his stomach. However, we know mankind suffers from more than one type of hunger. Yes, there is the recurring hunger of the body, for which physical food provides temporary relief. But there is the more eternally damaging hunger of the soul. Jesus addressed this hunger when He said, "I am the bread of life; he who comes to me shall not hunger and he who believes in me shall never thirst" (John 6:35).

To consistently deal with physical hunger, we must provide many meals. To deal with spiritual hunger, we need to provide only One, the Bread of Life, Jesus Christ. There are many of the "least of these" around us who suffer from physical hunger. We must feed them. *All* of the "least of these" around us suffer from spiritual hunger. We must feed them. We must deal with the physical and the spiritual because both make up the individual. Jesus responded to both. Neither can be ignored. It is a task within itself to last a lifetime. We have bread and the Bread of Life to share, and when we do, we minister to Christ Himself.

Jesus said, "I was thirsty and you gave me something to drink" (Matthew 25:35). When we see the "least of these" around us who suffer from physical thirst, our appropriate initial response is the simplest of acts: the offer of a cup of water. It is unlikely a person will hear the gospel message in his soul above the dry echo in his throat. However, we know mankind suffers from more than one kind of thirst. There is the recurring thirst of the body, for which liquid provides only temporary relief. There is also the thirst of the soul, which Jesus addressed when He said, "whoever drinks of the water that I shall give him shall never thirst" (John 4:14).

To deal with physical thirst, many drinks will be required. To deal with spiritual thirst, only one drink is needed, the living water, Jesus Christ. There are many of the "least of these" around who suffer from physical thirst. We must give them water. All of the "least of these" around us suffer from spiritual thirst. We must give them the Water of Life. We must respond to both because the individual is both physical and spiritual. Jesus responded to both. Neither can be ignored. A task within itself to last a lifetime. We have water and the Water of Life to share, and when we do, we minister to Christ Himself.

Jesus said, "I was in prison, and you came to me" (Matthew 25:36). Seeing the "least of these" around us who are imprisoned will require a little more effort. They are not readily visible. Still, we know they are there, so we will have to go to them. Perhaps that is why Jesus said, "you *came* to me." When we go to them, we will find our presence provides them one important thing the state prison system is unable to provide: moments of relief from their desperate loneliness induced by confinement (more on this in a later chapter).

We know mankind suffers from more than one kind of bondage. There is the obvious bondage of incarceration, for which our loving visits provide temporary relief. But there is the potentially eternal bondage of the soul to sin. Paul addressed this in Galatians 4:3–4, 7: "So also we, while we were yet children, were held in bondage under the elemental things of the world. But when the fullness of time came, God sent forth His Son… Therefore you are no longer a slave, but a son; and if a son, then an heir through God."

To even partially relieve the loneliness of those who are in physical prisons, multiple and consistent visits are required. To bring total freedom from the prison of sin, we need only to introduce the One who will come as a permanent resident and "cellmate," Jesus Christ. He reassures them, and all of us, "If therefore the Son make you free, you shall be free indeed" (John 8:36).

There are many of the "least of these" in our society hidden in a prison, away from sight. We must go to them. All of the "least of these" around us are prisoners to sin, which holds them in their own personal bondage. We must go to them. Those imprisoned within physical confinement may eventually leave that prison. Those imprisoned in sin will not unless we go to them. We must respond to both because prisons are both physical and spiritual. Jesus responded to both. Neither can be ignored. A task within itself to last a lifetime. We have the friendship, the Friend, and the freedom to share. And when we do, we minister to Christ Himself.

You see the point God was driving home into my heart, and now hopefully yours. Whether we're responding to the hungry, the thirsty, the stranger, the naked, the sick, the prisoner, the orphan, or the widow, there is a physical and spiritual application to each. Neither can be ignored.

God brought familiar Scripture to my heart in new ways, and it was time to get busy. I knew there was an abundance of these individuals in the world. I also knew I would not have to go far to find them. I still did not know how my needs would be met in all of this, but at the time, I seemed to be more concerned with the need to productively live God's call in my life.

It seemed He spoke to me and said, "Jeff, I called you to ministry first, not a church. I called you to people, not a position. I called you to service, not a salary, and I've just given you more than enough to keep you busy for the rest of your life." I knew it was time for a new step of faith that would be expressed in my next words to the Lord. "Okay, Lord, I'll serve you by serving others, for pay or for free, and if we starve, we starve." I can't be sure, but it almost seemed as if I heard Him softly reply, "That's what I've been waiting to hear."

Where to begin? Who to call? "The needs are everywhere," He said, "and you don't have to go very far to start. Why not begin close to home? What about that retirement center just down the street from your neighborhood?" I had passed it every day for several years on the way to and from my church job. I got in the car to go and check it out.

Hold on. It gets even better!

CHAPTER 3

RISING FROM THE ASHES

Before we reach the retirement facility, I hope you don't mind if we take a quick detour. You see, once developments began to take place, many things happened during the same days and weeks, and this will help me share them in as orderly a fashion as possible.

I take this detour to show I was not alone in my restoration. Yes, God was with me, but so were others He strategically placed in my life. A couple of months before the climax of my trials, I received a call from a young pastor who was serving a church not far from our home. His name is Eric. I had ridden by his church many times over the years. It was a traditional looking place—red bricks, white columns, steeple, and all. I knew it had been there a long time, but I did not know much about it, except to notice when the pastor's name would change on the marquis in front.

I had met Eric only once, two years earlier. I had visited to courteously inform him of our new church start not far from his, and to assure him we had no plan of raiding his flock to build our own. He now invited me to visit over lunch, and I readily accepted. I don't turn down many meals.

I don't recall why he requested this meeting, but I do remember it began a valuable friendship. I was facing difficult problems, and as ministers often do, we traded stories and insights about common trials and tried to encourage one another. He became a special friend in the last weeks of a negative time in my life. He also played a part in bringing about a quick beginning to my restoration.

As our friendship grew, I had kept Eric familiar with the progress of my trials, leading to the climactic fall into my dark place. Soon afterwards, he called to see if I would do him a favor. "My wife and I are going on vacation in about a month," he said, "and we'll be gone over two Sundays." Immediately my mind went in the direction I felt sure he was heading. *He's going to ask me to fill in for him,* I thought. *No way. How do I get out of this?* Now I'm not right all the time, but I was that time. Then he said it. "I need you to speak for me on those Sundays. We have a morning and evening service, so you'll be filling in four times."

My mind was already racing with dread. You recall I said I felt stripped of all confidence. *What do I have to say that those people want to hear? This church is just a few miles down the road from where life blew up in my face. Like it or not, church business becomes everybody's business; they have heard about what happened to me. And probably versions that are nowhere near the real story. How can I stand in front of them, or anybody?*

I obviously did not want to accept his invitation, but what could be my excuse? Not conflicts in schedule. The phone wasn't ringing, remember? I certainly couldn't predict sickness. Then that same prodding that would not allow me to ignore my daily time in the Bible and prayer manifested Himself again, replacing my thoughts with His. *Turn this down, and you risk sinking deeper into your present state of mind.* Knowing I was not to be let off the hook by God or Eric, I agreed to be his pulpit supply for those first two Sundays in April 2002.

This ought to be special, I thought sarcastically. *Why did I agree to do this?* It was only days after my life had dropped out from under me. The way I felt convinced me I would be on display more than anything else, exposed and embarrassed. Then I sensed the Lord impressing my spirit: *Are those words from Me?* I immediately knew the answer. As I had reminded countless others over the years, God is *not* the accuser, and He is *not* the voice of discouragement and defeat in our lives. *Okay, so I'm going to preach in this church for two Sundays. What in the world am I going to say?*

The answer was not long in coming. In fact, that very night, as I lay in my bed, God did again what He had earlier done to put me on the road to reassurance. He brought the familiar to my mind. Specifically, it was one of my favorite verses of Scripture, Isaiah 40:31: "Yet they that wait upon the Lord shall gain new strength; they will mount up with wings like eagles, they will run and not get tired, they will walk and not become weary."

Several years before, I was passing through a trying period when the pastor of our church asked if I would like to speak in his place during an upcoming Sunday evening service. Though I was the music minister, I was always glad to have a preaching opportunity. I spoke from that verse of Scripture, using the imagery of the eagle to illustrate what Isaiah was saying to the child of God. My approach was certainly not original, but it struck a chord with me and many people that night. God was bringing it to mind again. Was the "eagle sermon" (as it was known among family and friends) to be one of the four shared at Pastor Eric's church? It was certainly appropriate to my situation at the time and would no doubt apply to many who would be listening, as does every principle in God's Word.

Yes, I would share from Isaiah 40:31, but as the next few days of prayer and study revealed, it would not be one of the four sermons; it would be all of them. *Four messages from one verse! Never done that before,* I thought. But as I discovered in the following days because so much had happened in my life, because so much happens in the lives of all people, God would have no problem having much to say through a verse that says so much. I would also find He would be saying it all mainly to *me*.

The first Sunday arrived, and my family and I drove into the parking lot, still nervous about showing my face. Several of our faithful friends who stood beside us in our trial also came and marched themselves to the front rows as a show of support. God love them. Many people kindly introduced themselves to this guest, who they already recognized. One of the deacons asked me if I would accompany them to a room behind the sanctuary, where they prayed each week. I agreed and began to follow him. One of our friends in attendance saw and quickly joined us. "I didn't want you to go alone," he whispered privately. I knew he sensed my lack of confidence, though we had only known each other for a few months.

We reached the room several minutes before the service, and took a seat, waiting for others to arrive. I sat quietly, contemplating the unfamiliar faces surrounding me, save one—my friend Ben. Then it happened. Maybe the deacon was trying to be nice. Maybe he was trying to be hospitable by making conversation with the guest preacher. Maybe he was fishing for some juicy information to satisfy his curiosity. Whatever the motive, he looked at me and asked, "Jeff, what exactly happened at your last church that turned out so badly?"

No way! Did this guy really ask that—in front of a room full of strangers? Attention was fixed on me, waiting for an answer. Did he think I had a prayer of giving an adequate response in the inadequate time we had? Did he think I even *wanted* to respond, to relive before an unfamiliar audience what I was struggling to forget? Did he really ask that just moments before I was to preach the Word for the first time in weeks? My reason for wanting to reject Pastor Eric's invitation was being realized. I felt as if I was on display, had been the topic of previous discussion, and was now being publicly interrogated.

Thank God for my friend Ben and his sensitivity in not permitting me to go into that room alone. He did not give me time to answer before coming to my rescue. I cannot remember exactly what he said, but I recall he smiled, made a comment that defused the situation, and redirected it to another day and time. I breathed a sigh of relief. Then we prayed and entered the service.

It was a fairly traditional church, and we sang many of the great old hymns I had known since childhood. A lifetime of singing these songs eliminated my need for printed assistance, and I found myself singing heartily as I always used to—switching from bass to tenor on alternating stanzas. The familiar lyrics began to be applied to me in new ways that morning, and every now and then, I felt tears welling in my eyes. I hoped none would spill onto my face because that would be a display open to the interpretation of any who happened to glance in my direction. I was still too fragile in my own mind to have any of that. I do not recall if that indeed happened, but it doesn't matter, because now I don't really care.

As the singing continued, the Lord seemed to be having a personal ministry session with just me. I felt the energy of my spirit rising. My enthusiasm for the purpose in being there was also rising, and thoughts of my morning message seemed to flood my mind. The eagerness to stand and share the truths I studied was building inside me, to the point I was ready to explode. Could this be? Could the man who so sheepishly exited his car in the parking lot not an hour earlier be so quickly transformed into an excited guest speaker? Could the one who narrowly escaped complete embarrassment in the prayer room just a few minutes ago be brought to this level of anticipation?

Before you get the idea I was suddenly this bold and self-confident preacher, I must quickly say none of this was happening due to *my* determination. I was once again experiencing the reality of another scriptural promise I had known so well: "For we do not have a high priest who cannot sympathize with our weaknesses, but One who has been tempted [tried, tested] in all things as we are, yet without sin. Let us therefore draw near with confidence to the throne of grace, that we may receive mercy and may find grace to help in time of need (Hebrews 4:15–16).

It was my time of need. I was to stand before people as an instrument of God's truth. I suppose that due to my recent circumstances, it felt like it was my first time. He did not need me to be confident in myself, but He did want me to speak with confidence in His Word. Though I did not realize it then, I know now that I had "drawn near" to Him as best I could, and He was keeping His promise to give "help in the time of need." That time had come. Not in the car while driving to that church. Not in the parking lot as I nervously walked into the building. But as I was on the edge of stepping onto the church stage and taking my place at the pulpit. It was "time," and the "help" came.

In the days prior, I probably did not think I had "drawn near" to Him. I certainly did not feel I had drawn near to Him with "confidence." I was insecure and, at best, lacked confidence. I was still questioning myself and God as a result of recent circumstances. However, in retrospect, I feel perhaps I had drawn near to Him in ways I previously did not think would qualify as being genuine or acceptable in order for God to keep His promise. What do I mean?

While it is true I did not approach Him during that time with overwhelming spiritual enthusiasm, I had not turned my back on Him. While I was dealing with being upset and disappointed in Him, I had not turned a deaf ear to Him. And while it may not have felt like the quality time I had known in the past, I did continue to expose myself to His Word daily and have a semblance of a prayer time. Though walking with God was not the pleasurable experience it once was, I did keep walking as best I knew how, anger, confusion, humiliation, and all. Maybe I was like Peter in John 6:67–68. After being deserted by so many professed disciples, Jesus turned to the twelve and asked, "You do not want to go away also do you?" As was often the case, Peter took the role of spokesman and answered, "Lord, to whom shall we go? You have words of eternal life."

Please do not misunderstand the spirit in which I say this. I am not boasting at this point. I did not feel like following God. I did not feel like reading my Bible. I did not feel like praying. I did not feel like preaching. But like Peter, and I do not know all the reasons for his answer to Jesus, I simply did not know anything else to do. And frankly, though following the Lord had not been pleasant lately, I was afraid to venture into any other direction. As I similarly suggested in chapter 1, if walking *with* God could be this tough, how bad might things become if I walked *away* from Him?

You may not agree with my perspective on Hebrews 4:16, but perhaps staying focused on God when it was hard somehow qualified as "drawing near" in His eyes. That trudging through the daily practices of exposure to His voice, even though the dividends were unsatisfying, qualified as having "confidence."

No, I wasn't feeling very confident about Him at the time, but I also would not allow myself to steer my confidence in another direction. So bless Him, God did not require me to feel everything I was doing. But in His mercy, He gave me credit for doing it. It's almost as if He said, "Okay, we've put this guy through the fire. We've hurt him and made him mad and confused. But it looks like we're not going to drive him away. We're proving whether he's the real deal. He hasn't been warm and fuzzy, but he hasn't turned his back. So let's bless him with grace in this hour of need."

So often we, as God's children, place conditions on how we are to live out the principles of His Word. How we're supposed to feel, speak, or act in order for them to be effective. I've come to believe God is much more touched and responsive when He sees us being clumsily steadfast when it's the hardest. When we're honestly genuine as opposed to spiritually polished. When we seek to "draw near" to Him because He seems far away.

We may be hurting, perplexed, and even angry, but as previously stated, He is not offended, insulted, or threatened. He knows it all before we come. In more than one instance He has told us clearly in His Word what we are to do. I found if we simply do what we're told, He will simply do what He promises. And because He is all good, it will all turn out good for us (Romans 8:28).

When the time for the sermon came, I stepped to the pulpit and faced the congregation for the first time. It was an attractive sanctuary, traditional on the inside as it was on the outside. There was an empty balcony across the back, and on the main floor, the congregation numbered just over 150. I made opening comments and told a joke that received a hearty laugh. It seemed like they would be a warm and receptive crowd. Then I turned their attention to Isaiah chapter 40 and began the first of my four "eagle" sermons.

It is not necessary to recall exactly what I said in this or the following three sermons. All I need to say is that as I began to speak, something continued to return to life in me. The more I spoke, the more I was energized. I felt an increasing freedom and power I thought was gone and did not expect. By the time the service ended, I felt as if I had been raised from the lingering depths of disappointment to a renewed purpose. In the course of an hour or so, I could tell I was on the fast track to recovery.

There were still unanswered questions about the future, but I left that church parking lot a different person than had arrived. I would find this was only the beginning of the process of my renewal.

We returned that evening. Even in those days it was becoming increasingly rare for churches to hold Sunday evening services, but this one still did. We arrived early enough to greet people and have time to fellowship as they entered, another strong indication I was feeling more like the "old me." The music minister was a man named Larry, with a smiling personality and thick, white hair that rolled like sea waves over his head. As I noticed the group of approximately thirty beginning to take their seats at the front of a side section of pews, he stepped toward me, smiled, and said enthusiastically, "Wow, you really pack 'em in!"

"Really?" I responded as I contemplated the small congregation that looked like a "BB in a boxcar," a phrase I had learned from a former pastor in describing a crowd that was too small for their room.

"You sure do. On Sunday evenings, we usually have only about half this many."

For years I was accustomed to very large crowds. At my former church, most of our Sunday school classes were larger than the crowd at this service. Our choir was larger. Our orchestra was larger. I kept silent about all of that irrelevance, for in light of my recent situation, I found his words extremely encouraging. I began the evening with my spirit lifted once again. Our small congregation enjoyed heartfelt singing, and I continued my series from Isaiah 40:31. The renewed life and power I experienced that morning also continued.

What a change! A week earlier I was doing my best to avoid being with people or even being seen by them. But during the next week, I was actually excited about my return the next Sunday. Excited about the fresh insights God was teaching me from His Word and about being together again with His church.

During the week between the two Sundays, something happened that further bolstered my spirit. I had gone into a grocery store, and as I passed through the checkout, the young cashier looked at me and asked, "Didn't you speak at our church this past Sunday?"

After confirming the identity of the church, I answered, "Yes, I did."

"I enjoyed that so much," she said unashamedly before everyone. "You shared a lot that was a help to me.

"Thank you," I said. "You have no idea how much that means to me."

"Oh yeah," she continued, "after Sunday morning, I came back Sunday night. I don't usually attend on Sunday nights."

"I'm so glad you were encouraged. I hope we will see you again this Sunday."

"You sure will," she declared. "I'll be there, and I've already invited a friend to come with me."

"My goodness, you have made my day," I said, restraining myself from reaching across the counter and hugging her neck. I walked to my car, but I felt like my feet were not touching the ground.

We did return the next Sunday, and what a day it turned out to be. As we began the morning service, I turned from the front pew and looked at the congregation behind me. I felt like the father in a familiar Christmas poem, but silently expressed my reaction with altered words:

> *And what to my wondering eyes should appear*
> *But a great crowd of people now gathering here!* [1]

The main floor was comfortably filled to capacity, and the previously bare balcony was almost full. Now to be fair, the previous Sunday was a day that is notorious to church leaders—the change to daylight savings time. If you fail to reset your clock on Saturday evening, you're going to be an hour late to your Sunday morning destination. I didn't speculate with anyone the reasons for the congregation's increase in size. All I knew was something all preachers may as well admit: we love a crowd. I was grateful I had not driven away the previous congregation or discouraged them from inviting others.

Engaging in the musical worship once again energized me, and the sermon was again blessed with God's freedom and power. Like the eagle presented in the Scripture verse, I felt like I was taking wing and beginning to soar. I had experienced freedom and energy before, but this had a new sense to it. I could not explain it, but I could already tell this was flying in a new way.

I always thought I had strength, but Isaiah was talking about "renewed strength." At the risk of redundancy, I say again that my past strength had been drained and depleted. I was totally in His hands now, and He was giving me a "renewed strength" that would replace that which I had lost. A strength that doesn't just motivate to do, but liberates to be.

The music minister and his wife invited our family to join them after the service for lunch in their home, and we gladly accepted. We enjoyed a sumptuous meal and relaxed fellowship. Then Larry asked, "Jeff, why don't you sing something in the service tonight, either by yourself or with me?" I nodded. "If you do not mind, just arrive a little early, and we can put it together."

That evening we were in for more pleasant surprises. As the people gathered, the "pack 'em in" crowd of about thirty the Sunday evening before had grown to over one hundred. We were all delighted, and the regulars were visibly elated beyond words. Larry and I sang a simple medley of hymns, and my voice seemed to feel stronger and clearer than it had in a long time. I felt the same energy and freedom in singing that I had in my speaking. God was "renewing my strength" in every way.

By this time, I could feel myself already leaving the recent hurt and devastation behind as irrelevant. When the service ended, and we were saying our words of thanks and farewell, it was almost sad to think that our brief yet life-saving experience at this church was coming to an end. But it wasn't. Not just yet.

While still squeezing in a couple of last good-bye hugs and handshakes, a sixty-something-year-old couple approached Lynne and me. "I need a minute to ask you a question," the man said.

"Sure," I replied.

"This summer," he began, "we are going with a large group of people on a mission project to Romania. There are over eighty of us, and we will be divided into four teams. Each team needs a pastor. The team my wife and I will serve with does not yet have a pastor. Eric has gone with us in the past but cannot be with us this year. I wanted to extend the invitation to you. If you would like to go as our team pastor, I will cover half your expenses if you think you can raise the rest."

"I would love to do that," I answered eagerly. "I grew up traveling with an air force dad and have also been on several short-term mission projects with past churches."

"That's great," he said, "but would you like time to think and pray about it?"

"No sir, I don't," I said. "You see, I don't need to pray about this because this is an answer to prayer!"

He did not know it, but you recall from earlier chapters how I had expressed concern to God that I not be left idle and unproductive. I knew now that every opportunity to participate in His priorities were answered prayers and opened doors.

As believers, we need to grasp the truth that when we are faced with an opportunity to respond to something God's Word reveals as His will, it is not a call to prayer. It is a call to action. In fact, we have adopted a practice in our ministry. When a call or invitation comes, if our spiritual gifts and abilities can meet the need, if the requested calendar date is clear, and if God provides necessary funds, the answer is yes. For over twelve years, that approach has worked quite well.

I fear believers are not always sensitive to the fact that the pious response to opportunities of "Let me pray about it" may just be a delay of doing what God wants done. Whether intentional or unintentional, the result is often procrastination and ultimately, the neglect of God's will in our lives as revealed in His Word.

One of the faithful friends who attended all four services those two weeks made an observation shortly after our experience. Her name is Jackie. To merely call her a faithful friend is quite inadequate, because her loyalty and steadfast friendship to our family through the years has been unparalleled. She is one of those rare people you allow to become a part of almost every area of your life. You know, they help raise your kids, babysit your pets, exchange gifts for Christmas and birthdays, and even help split and stack your firewood! I've always heard it said no one is indispensable, but I'm pretty sure Jackie is the exception. She is that kind of friend.

"I saw you rise like the phoenix from the ashes," she said then and has said many times in the years since. "I knew how hurt you were, how low you had fallen, and on those two Sundays, I watched you literally rise out of all of it. It was an amazing thing to see. I have never witnessed anything like it before and probably never will again. You came back to life, and I'll always be glad I was there to see it." Though she used the mythological bird to describe the experience, I know she was talking about an eagle.

Jackie was right. I did rise from my ashes but not in my own strength and determination. I was lifted by Another. I have heard stories of those who profess no faith in God, hit rock bottom, pull themselves up by the bootstraps, start over, reinvent themselves, and somehow end up even more successful. Human beings may find it within themselves to overcome human difficulties. They may rise above defeat and boast of victory while others applaud them. They are admired and envied by adoring fans. I do not begrudge them that. But when their life ends, nothing is left.

It Gets Even Better

What we're talking about here is not just life but *spiritual* life. Not just earthly character but *eternal* character. My walk with God had been challenged, my faith had been shaken, my spiritual confidence gone. Spiritual crises will not be overcome apart from the One who imparts the Spirit to the believer. He either brings about or allows the crisis, so He will be the One who will lift us from it. When He does, we experience new levels of insight that enrich every area of our lives and extend into eternity.

In this life we can be sure there is an ash heap waiting for all of us. We can rise from it in our own strength or be lifted from it by His. Both may seem to have results, but the latter is better. No, the latter is best. The latter is eternal.

My now longtime friend Pastor Eric left that church a few months later for a new ministry, and I have not had the opportunity to return there. However, I will never forget those two Sundays at that church near our home. It will always be a special place to me. Every time I ride by or sit at the traffic light opposite its steeple, I have fond and warm memories. I will never forget how God used the opportunity to lift me from the low point of defeat to a new outlook for the future, though I still had no idea what that future looked like. He used every part of that positive experience to say, "I am not finished with you yet. Just keep moving." So keep moving I did.

Hold on, it gets even better.

CHAPTER 4

LITTLE FLOWERS AND LODGES, PART 1

I now resume the approach to my original destination when I left our home that day—an assisted-living facility called the Little Flower. An unusual name, and I had no idea of its meaning. Years earlier, I watched it being built as I drove to and from my office at the mega-church, where I served in Charlotte, North Carolina.

Before you get the wrong impression as to why I slipped in the term "mega-church," I did so for reason of contrast. I pulled into the small parking lot of the Little Flower, a care center for declining senior adults. This entire complex could fit in the parking lot of my former church a dozen times or more. This was a place where I was unknown and the people inside were unknown to me. Though I had no doubt I was doing the right thing, I was still struggling with being reduced to this humble state. For eleven years I was the music minister at one of the largest churches in our country. I led a three hundred-member choir and orchestra. I had name and often face recognition among those familiar with church life in our city. Now here I was, once known, now unknown; once prominent, now a "peon"; once with notoriety, now a nobody. At least in *my* mind. Opportunities had always pursued me, but there I stood, sheepishly extending my hand to ring the doorbell of the Little Flower. "Ding dong."

This was all very new to me, indeed. But I learned it was exactly what our Lord wanted me to do in attitude as well as action. To be willing to become unimportant in the world and in my own eyes in order to become important to those who are largely neglected. To forsake church activity when it hinders the pursuit of kingdom activity.

The door opened, and standing before me was something, I mean someone, I was not expecting. Before I spill the beans, I must remind you I was a lifelong Baptist boy. Don't misunderstand; I do not believe we Baptists have a monopoly on Jesus Christ or that we are the only ones who will grace heaven's golden streets. But I was Baptist through and through. I told you a little about my mother, but I did not tell she was Baptist. I recall asking her one time what she would be if she were not Baptist, and without blinking, she said, "I'd be ashamed!" I never quite shared her level of commitment to the denominational label, but the Baptist church had been the environment in which I had learned and lived my Christian faith. I do not regret that heritage. That being true, while I was never hostile or closed to people of other denominations, I probably never learned how to comfortably interact with them. I never had to, due to my confined environment.

So who answered the door of the Little Flower? An elderly and petite nun. My above average powers of deductive reasoning immediately brought me to the unspoken conclusion, *This place is Catholic!* Now my mind can often race with inaudible conversations as I try to size up a situation and decide what to do next. It did that day. *What do I do now? Will I be comfortable in this environment? I'm not Catholic; will they want me here? Do I want to be here?* My first venture in pursuing my new commitment to God had me out of my comfort zone, but I knew I was to continue with the plan.

"Hello, my name is Jeff," I began. "I'm sort of between jobs and have some time on my hands. I wonder if you need someone to help with anything around here."

"Well, what are your interests?" she asked sweetly.

"First of all, I am a musician. I like to sing."

"You need to meet our activities director. She will definitely want to know about you. Please come in and follow me."

The once important Jeff Andler. Once on staff in a big Baptist church. Now being led by a non-Baptist, 100 percent Catholic nun through a strange environment to meet another stranger, probably another Catholic. She introduced me to Kelly, a smiling, bubbling lady about my age who never met a stranger. Yes she was Catholic, and I liked her immediately.

"We have an activity where you could be such a help," she beamed. She told me of a Thursday afternoon sing-along. An elderly nonresident named Mary came to play every week, and for almost an hour, they sang old songs popular in their day. And guess what? Mary was the organist at a nearby Catholic church. I liked her immediately too. That lady could play every Broadway tune, love song, and simple ditty from the old days, all from memory. I wondered how when I saw the accentuated bend in her upper back from osteoporosis and her gnarled arthritic hands. Those hands also trembled, as did her aging voice, which quickly revealed her Long Island, New York, background.

"It would be so great if you could come on Thursday afternoons and sing with them," Kelly said. "It will mean a lot to the residents, and your voice would be a huge help to Miss Mary."

"Sit and sing?" That was a far cry from what I was accustomed to, but I knew the answer. I had nothing but time on my hands, and I was beginning at the bottom. "I'll be glad to," I said. "I'll see you Thursday afternoon."

For the next few weeks, for the next few months, for the next few years—more than twelve now— there I was on Thursdays, doing my best to encourage Little Flower residents to join in singing by setting the example. It wasn't easy at first, because I did not know most of the songs. Miss Mary wasn't playing my Baptist hymn repertoire. No, I had to learn every show tune and every "Golden Age of Hollywood" song imaginable, but I must say, I had a good time doing it.

It didn't take long, however, for me to wonder as I turned into the parking lot, *What am I doing? I'm having a good time, they're having a good time. But what good am I doing?* I was not getting the chance to share the gospel, which is what a good Baptist boy should do. Nor were my new Catholic friends likely to ask me to do so. I was not even singing any of the great old songs of the faith. And because I was not in charge, I was in no position to impact the content of our time together. Should I be doing something else? God gave me no peace to make a change, so my Thursday afternoon schedule continued.

I also found walking into that environment every week inherently involved more than sitting and singing. I'm not sure who planned it, but the residents were always served their afternoon snack in the middle of our sing-along. Miss Mary would break from the music and usually share some tidbit of trivia about a Broadway musical or a specific song, and she was always interesting. Not being one to remain idle, I helped distribute the goodies, which usually led to assisting someone juggle cookies, Kool-Aid, and a songbook. Inevitably, I suppose, many weeks I found myself kneeling on the floor, wiping spills when our juggling was unsuccessful. Such a menial task was certainly a change for me, but it was not at all unfamiliar. My first part-time job as a teenager was as a janitor at my mom's ministry facility.

There was more. One Thursday after our sing-along, I exited as usual by the back porch, which faced a pick-up area in the parking lot. One of the residents was sitting there, visibly agitated. I spoke to her by name and asked why she was troubled. She was waiting for her son to come, but he was running a little late (actually very little, but enough to worry his mother, who was in early dementia). *I have things to do,* I thought, but I could not justify any of them as more pressing than the need before me. I had met her son on numerous occasions and knew he would arrive, but she was not so confident.

"Would you like me to wait with you until your son gets here?" I asked.

"Oh, that would be so nice," she said, beginning to smile through her shaky voice, a few tears, and wringing hands.

I sat beside her. We talked, shared family information, and laughed. In seconds, her entire demeanor changed. Within minutes, her son arrived, and we put her in the car next to him, happy as a lark.

I remember thinking as I got in my own car to leave, *Wow, I feel as fulfilled, warm, and satisfied as I did after any Christmas or Easter pageant I used to lead—and with a lot less stress and effort.* I was learning that pursuing the things important to God fulfills and energizes our lives rather than draining us, as do so many of the activities we create in His name.

After I was at Little Flower for several months, Kelly informed me that Miss Mary was leaving soon to travel with family up north. She would be away for one month. "We need you to fill in for Miss Mary," she said. "It will be four Thursdays."

"I'll be glad to do what I can," I replied, "but there's one problem. I do not play the piano very well, and I cannot play *any* of the songs Mary can." As a voice major in college and seminary, I was required to have a certain level of proficiency on the keyboard, but nothing that qualified me to be Miss Mary "junior." I played piano privately for my own enjoyment or when I was composing and arranging pieces for our choir and orchestra, but I never played in front of an audience. I could rarely complete a selection without glaring mistakes, even if I had written it. I could read music, of course, but I could not get those notes on the page to my fingers in an acceptable fashion. I did not want to say no, but this was getting way out of my league.

Remember I told you Kelly never met a stranger? Well she also never took no for an answer. No panicked explanation or plea could get through to her. "Anything you do will be fine," she said. "If you can't play, just sing the songs a cappella with them."

A cappella! The musician and performer in me began to balk at the thought. Singing those songs without piano after being accustomed to Miss Mary's accompaniment would be disastrous—okay, mainly to me.

Knowing I would be embarrassed to tears by my piano playing, I agreed to fill in anyway. I took a copy of the lyric sheets home—no music; Mary didn't need it, remember? I made a list of about a dozen of the easiest tunes I could hear in my head. You know, top-forty stuff like "Take Me Out to the Ball Game," "In the Good Old Summertime," and "Let Me Call You Sweetheart." Every day I practiced the daylights out of those songs, but there was still a problem. Miss Mary filled about an hour every week in our sing-along, and my entire repertoire was about forty-five minutes short. I dug out funny stories from my files, jokes from old *Reader's Digest* magazines, and anything else I could find to fill the time. I suppose I could have shortened our time together, but I did not want them to feel cheated.

The first Thursday came, when I was to debut. I led a song or two and then read a funny story. Another song or two, another story or a few jokes. We were having a good time, but I could tell I would run out of material before running out of time. Then, unexpectedly, one of the ladies raised her hand and asked permission to speak. "Of course," I said, having no idea what we were about to hear, but happy it would help fill the time.

"You are always so happy," she declared. "Why are you always so happy?"

As stated earlier, for months I had wondered where this Little Flower involvement was going. Would I ever be free to share specifically with them of my faith and my motivation for being there? Now it looked like the opportunity was being dropped in my lap. "I'll be glad to tell you why I am happy," I said.

I quickly gathered my thoughts, so I could share concisely yet adequately of my Christ-centered purpose for life. At almost the exact time I began to speak, that sweet little nun appeared at the back of the room and leaned against the wall, listening. I wasn't particularly intimidated, but I did wonder how she would react and how my words would be received.

I began, "You see, I am happy, though 'happy' might not be the best word to use. Some days I do not feel happy, but every day I have joy. Being happy is usually determined by how we feel at the time, depending on our circumstances. But the joy I have inside remains the same. And I find that the more I understand this joy, the less often life can make me unhappy. What gives me this joy?" Pointing to the crucifix on the wall above me, I continued, "All around this place, we are reminded of the One called Jesus Christ, who died on the cross for us. While that seemed like a tragic event, it was what He did to take away our sin that separates us from Him." Pointing again at the crucifix, I said, "We must remember that He did not remain on that cross or in the grave. He rose again that *we* might be forgiven and have everlasting life with God in heaven, which is why we were created."

About this time, the nun was making her way toward me and finally stood silently by my side. I did not know why, but I was on a roll, so I did not stop.

"Many years ago," I said, "I learned of Jesus and what He did for me on the cross and why. As a boy, I realized my sinfulness and that I needed a Savior. I asked God to forgive me and invited Jesus into my life. He has lived in me ever since, teaching me how to please Him and giving me this joy that you call happiness." At this point the little sister stepped closer and wrapped her arms around my waist. "I'm *happy* because I have *joy*," I concluded, "and I have *joy* because I have *Jesus*. And you can have Him too."

Seeing I had finished my comments, the sister looked at the group, smiled, and said as she squeezed me affectionately, "Aren't we glad God brought him to us!"

The door was now completely open. From that point on, they knew who and what I was, and they are just fine with it. They are ready to hear of my trips abroad and other details of our ministry. On a couple of occasions, they have had bazaars and shared proceeds with our ministry. And there have been numerous occasions when, following the death of a resident—after the family has had the funeral mass at their Catholic church—I have been invited to lead a memorial service at the Little Flower with the confined residents. At each of these, the gospel is always shared and made clear. That's right, a born and bred Baptist boy leading services at a Catholic facility.

Best of all, we have seen residents and some staff alike realize the priority of a relationship *with* God over a religion *about* God and come to saving faith *in* God. In this experience, God has impressed upon my heart that when we consistently live the love of Christ, people will more likely listen when we talk about Him.

Our weekly songfests continued to primarily feature the old-time hits, but Miss Mary began to include "How Great Thou Art," "Amazing Grace," or other well-known hymns of the faith. She would always ask me to sing the verses as a solo. She knew I was familiar with them, while many of the residents were not.

After suffering a stroke, Miss Mary became a resident of the Little Flower in the summer of 2005. While in rehabilitation for several weeks, I was asked to handle the weekly sing-along, piano and all. I stepped aside when she returned to her Thursday afternoon duties and continued for the next few years. Thanksgiving night of 2009, she passed away quietly in her sleep. My skills at the piano had increased over time, and once she was gone, her baton was passed to me. I am "Mr. Sing-Along" to this day.

Playing the piano with an audience is one more thing that was once foreign to me but is now a normal, enjoyable, and expected part of my life. Soon I would be involved on a weekly or monthly basis in several other senior adult facilities in our area.

All of this came to pass largely due to a Baptist boy's weekly visits to a Catholic assisted-living facility and the influence of an elderly church organist named Mary. In this experience, God was teaching me that "My thoughts are not your thoughts, neither are your ways My ways" (Isaiah 55:8), especially in regard to how He would broaden my usefulness to Him and others. He can use *what* He chooses, *where* He chooses, *whom* He chooses, *when* He chooses, and *how* He chooses to work in our lives. The process will likely challenge and change our tried and true ideas.

Before we leave Little Flower, there is one more experience I must share. Soon after I became involved there, I could not help but notice a young man on the staff. His name was Tim. There were several reasons why he caught my attention. First, he appeared to be about the age of our son, and I thought it was interesting to see a young man of his age employed at this kind of facility. Surely this was just a step on his way to the fulfillment of a greater plan, but he seemed to love being there. I could tell the residents were perfectly comfortable with him. He treated them with patience and compassion, coupled with genuine enthusiasm. A nice-looking lad with a constantly bright smile, he was up and down the hallways, tending to his duties, and would pass our sing-along area many times during a typical Thursday afternoon. He was Catholic too, and I liked him immediately also, though we hadn't even met.

Finally, our paths crossed as I was leaving one day. I extended my hand and introduced myself. "Oh yeah, I've seen you at the sing-along," he said. "We really appreciate you helping out. We don't get a lot of men as volunteers."

Every week after becoming acquainted, we met with a smile and a handshake that evolved into the chest butt hug we guys often do. I was old enough to be his father, but we were very comfortable with each other. I had a feeling his genuine personality deserved the credit for that as much or more than mine. We enjoyed our relationship and occasional conversations.

I wanted to speak with Tim about his relationship with Christ, but in an environment that would be nonthreatening to him. Finally, we agreed to meet for lunch at a nearby sandwich shop. It was my plan to treat him, but when I arrived, he had gotten there first and already ordered and paid for his meal. I told you I liked this guy! We sat, ate, and talked quite comfortably about all sorts of things. As time passed, I knew I needed to turn the conversation to my intended purpose.

"Tim," I said, "there is another reason why I asked you to meet me today. I want to ask you a question if you do not mind. Some folks might consider it personal."

"Shoot," he said.

"Well, you don't really know me, and you may not know anything about what I believe and what is important to me, but—"

"Stop right there," he interrupted.

My mind quickly reacted by wondering what was coming next. Was I going to be shut down before I began?

"You say that I don't know what you believe. That's not true. I know exactly what you believe. We *all* know what you believe."

"What do you mean?" I asked.

"I've watched you come into the Little Flower every week. I've watched how you sit beside the residents and sing and smile like you're singing to *them*. I've watched you help with their songbooks and spills, and I've watched you make them laugh. I know what you believe because I watch how you live. You're a Christian. You believe in God, and you live what you believe. I can see it. We all see it."

"That's very encouraging to hear you say. But may I say, recognizing that in me or just being aware of what a Christian should look like is not enough for *you*. What do *you* believe?"

Tim shared with me that he believed in Christ as the Savior and that he had assurance of eternal life. We continued to enjoy a pleasant relationship, but in time, Tim took a position at a facility some distance away. I heard he got married but have lost further contact.

In sharing this experience, I must again stress it is not my purpose to bring attention to me personally. It is to show people recognize the character of Christ when it is lived consistently and genuinely before them. As believers, we do have the responsibility to verbally "confess Christ before men" (Matthew

10:32) and "confess with our mouths the Lord Jesus Christ" (Romans 10:9). Many times we must carefully and wisely make those opportunities. But the opportunity to *live* Jesus Christ before others is constant and will serve as undeniable evidence that supports our witness when we do speak.

"God has set eternity in the heart of every man," Solomon tells us in Ecclesiastes 3:10. And Paul reminds us in Romans 1:19–20, "that which is known about God is evident," and, "since the creation of the world His invisible attributes, His eternal power and divine nature have been clearly seen, being understood through what has been made, so that they are without excuse."

People know. No, not all people know God, but because of what He has created in us, people recognize His character and attributes in those who do. That is the very reason they are either drawn to that character or rebel against it. If there were no spiritual awareness, there would be no spiritual reaction.

You see, though I had always understood the need for my behavior to support my words, my experience was to create the opportunity to verbally evangelize as soon as possible. While that may occasionally have positive results, God used the Little Flower to show me that a Jesus *lived* will much more often become a Jesus truly *shared* and a Jesus readily *received*.

The Little Flower. Where did they get that name? In the Catholic faith history there is a figure known as Saint Thérèse of Lisieux. She was known for her love of flowers and her choice to serve in little-known, menial places of service. She did not aspire to have a prominent position. Like the flowers she loved, she felt God was pleased to have her "blossom" wherever she was. She became known and remembered as "the Little Flower."

I am not Catholic, but I am reminded in all this that my desire as a believer is not to be achievement and ambition in the world or even the church. It is to be available to blossom where needed, regardless of perceived status. The world is not in need of another Christian celebrity or spiritual superhero, but it could sure use a lot more little flowers.

"Whoever wishes to become great among you shall be your servant, and whoever wishes to be first among you shall be your slave" (Matthew 20:26–27). And that is something we can all be, if we want to be, and if we are willing to be.

Our ministry team shares Christmas at the Little Flower"

CHAPTER 5

LITTLE FLOWERS AND LODGES, PART 2

I've always heard that when you live in a small town, you'd better watch what you say because word gets around. Charlotte, North Carolina, is not a small town, but I found word gets around here too, especially in the network of senior adult facilities.

I had only been involved at the Little Flower for a few weeks when I went to a local hospital to pray with a friend before his surgery. Harold is a very capable guitarist, who played faithfully in our former church orchestra and remained a steadfast friend during our recent trials. When I arrived I found he had been taken to surgery early, so I joined his wife, Marge, in the waiting area. She was accompanied by her sister, Trish, and immediately introduced us. We had enjoyed relaxed conversation for a while when Trish directed her comments specifically toward me. "I understand that you're involved at the Little Flower on Lawyer's Road," she said. "Doing music or something like that. Is that right?"

"Yes I am," I answered, immediately curious as to how she could have known that and why it would be of interest to her. "Why do you ask?"

"Well, it just so happens I am the activities director at a retirement community called Wilora Lake Lodge. Are you familiar with it?"

"Yes, I know where it is located," I said. It was another facility I was familiar with but had no time to investigate previously, again due to my demanding church duties. It was a few blocks off the beaten path, definitely not readily in view. If I had not taken the time to discover what was behind the door of the Little Flower, which was built before my eyes, it stood to reason this out-of-the-way retirement home had no chance of getting my attention. That was about to change, and so was my life.

I knew by now that Trish had likely been made familiar with my situation as it was known to Harold and Marge and, therefore, also knew I had time on my hands. Again, my keen powers of deduction brought me to the conclusion that another opportunity was about to present itself. Wow, I should've been a police detective.

She began to explain. "At the Wilora Lake Lodge complex, there are actually three facilities. There's the main building, the Lodge, a four-story apartment building that houses independent seniors. Many of them still drive, do their own shopping, travel to Sunday church services, and so on. Behind the lodge but attached to it is the Cove. It is our assisted-living facility. Located behind the Cove and the Lodge is the Healthcare Center. It is separate from the other two and provides full care."

I listened and nodded, waiting for her to reach her obvious purpose. "I am responsible for activities at the Lodge and the Cove," she continued. "Since you have an interest in senior adults, I wanted to let you know we need another volunteer to come to the Cove once a month and lead a brief Bible study or devotional time."

Here I was again, with time on my hands and no reason to turn down an invitation that was another answer to my prayer to remain productive. Keep in mind this was still very early in my ministry transformation, and while God had indeed impressed James 1:27 ("visit the fatherless and the widows") upon my mind, I was not yet completely aware I had a special interest in senior adults. However, the calendar was clear on the third Wednesday afternoon of each month, my abilities would meet the need, and no financial support was necessary. So my answer? Yes, of course. I had begun my involvement at the Little Flower in mid-March and would begin at the Cove in mid-April.

As I arrived and met Trish on my first Wednesday afternoon, I heard great old hymns being beautifully played on the piano. For all I knew it could have been a recording. As we approached their meeting room, Trish said, "By the way, we have a lady named Jean who comes to play on Wednesdays. You'll take over when she is finished." When we entered the room, a lady several years my senior looked up at us from the piano, her face with a welcoming smile. I couldn't tell if her countenance was a result of the sheer joy of playing or a greeting to the "new guy," so I decided it was both. She was all over the eighty-eight keys with ease and grace. I could tell there was nowhere she would have rather been at that moment. I liked her immediately too.

My eyes circled the room, watching many of the residents mouthing the words to hymn favorites. It wasn't long before I joined in. *Wow,* I thought, *another lady who plays the piano. One plays old songs I don't know, and one plays old songs I do know.*

Jean finally ended her concert, prematurely in my view, and Trish introduced me to the group. So began my monthly visit to the Cove, which continues to this day. Just a year or so into my visits, Jean had to discontinue her commitment at the piano, and guess what? Yep, yours truly took over that role too. Since I was familiar with the type of songs Jean provided, I was able to reach a comfort level a bit faster than at the Little Flower. Now, as the years have passed and my playing has continued to develop, I do a combination of sacred and secular oldies there and at all the facilities I visit.

Not much time passed before Trish approached me with yet another offer. "The folks at the Cove have really enjoyed you being with them," she said.

"Thanks," I replied. "I enjoy being with them too."

"We-l-l-l," she went on, "we've been trying to have a lunch activity in the Lodge dining room on the first Monday of each month, but it hasn't been going all that well. I call it Soup, Salad, and Scripture. I've been trying to lead it, but I'm not a minister, and I'm not a speaker. I think if we had the right person it would be successful. Is that something you think you would want to do? If so, we would be glad to provide lunch for you, and the residents who attend will pay a modest price. We generally serve a buffet that often consists of our Sunday buffet leftovers. You can eat with the residents and then share a Bible devotional like you do at the Cove."

The calendar was clear, my abilities would meet the need, and no financial support was necessary. In fact, a meal was included, and it was not only free but delicious. I was also beginning to discern Trish was not only concerned

full schedule of activities from which to choose. She
n to as much spiritual input as possible in the waning
o my answer? Yes, of course.

Little Flower and the Cove, my Monday Soup, Salad,
'ilora Lake Lodge continues. We've shared from the
Beatitudes in Matthew chapter 5, the model prayer in Matthew 6, many of Christ's parables, and much more. One aspect of this ministry I enjoy is that many residents who do not profess a specific faith will come for the economical buffet. They often forget it will be followed by a spiritual emphasis. They find themselves faced with the choice of leaving the room or tolerating Bible study. Being from a generation that probably valued proper etiquette and consideration on a higher level than today, it has been rare to see anyone exercise the nerve required to excuse themselves and leave me standing there. Some have learned to be absent on the first Mondays, but most found we do not bite or even bark, and continued to attend, even if only for the low-priced, high-quality meal. I obviously do not mind why they attend. I am just glad to have them exposed to God's Word.

As the next several weeks passed, my relationship with Trish and the folks at Wilora Lake Lodge and the Cove progressed quickly and comfortably. Trish had not approached me with additional requests, but one day during a conversation, I was impressed to ask something of her. I was a little early for one of my visits, and we sat in a large and attractively furnished living room just inside the Lodge entrance.

I do not recall everything we discussed, but we did talk about the grateful spirit shown by the residents for *any* attention they were given. "It's not hard to tell they appreciate what your staff does here," I said, "and what we as volunteers do as well." Then I added, "I see many activities you have here during the week, but let me ask, do you have a Sunday morning worship service?" I'm not sure if I was asking because I specifically wanted to provide such a service or just curious. At the time, my Sunday mornings were not occupied with a regular church responsibility as they had been for decades.

"We do not," she said. "We have a gentleman who comes to teach a Sunday school class in the Wilora Room, down the hall. They meet at 9:15 and end at 10:00 or so. Those who attend then visit here in the living room or return to their apartments. We have never had anyone or any group step forward and offer to hold a service."

I only paused for a second or two before I felt free to respond, "Would you like one?" There was a part of me that wondered if I should put myself in the position of creating expectation in Trish so quickly. I knew I was asking a question that hinted at a suggestion. I now believe there was a bigger part of me that knew I needed to return to a Sunday morning schedule of assembling with God's people (Hebrews 10:25).

"We'd love one," she said enthusiastically. "Are you offering?"

"Well maybe," I said. "As you know, my schedule is in the development stage. My Sunday mornings are clear right now, and there is a need here. This could be something we might be able to do. What would it take to make it happen?"

"Well," she said, "there are some concerns that would need to be understood before we commit to something like this. For one, if we begin a Sunday service, it must be consistent, like in any church. One reason we have never attempted to do this is that few groups can make a weekly commitment. Many of our residents feel as if their lives have experienced enough upheaval and insecurity. If we have a service, it must be consistent week after week. We cannot hold a church service one Sunday and then not the next."

I certainly understood her reasoning, but it never occurred to me that we would have such a self-defeating approach, or why anyone would. I reassured her. "If we do this, it will be consistent. My wife and I will be here every Sunday unless away or sick, and then we'll have someone here to carry on. It will also be my plan to have someone to lead music and even those who will provide special music as often as possible. I promise, if we do this, we will do it right, and the residents can count on it every week."

Needless to say, Trish was positive in her reaction but expressed one more detail. "The time and location of the service will need to be coordinated," she said. "This living room is the only space large enough to hold a service, and it is right by the door of our dining room. We have no Sunday morning activities scheduled here, but the first lunch seating is at 11:30 a.m. The service would have to end before then. Believe me, when it's time for lunch, some residents will not be mindful of a church service that is still in progress."

My years of coordinating church events kicked in, and we decided on a plan. If the Sunday school class dismissed at 10:00, we could begin the service at 10:15 and endeavor to end an hour later. I believe it was late June or very early July at this point, so we set the first Sunday of August 2002 as our beginning. Trish would begin the promotion at the Lodge and the Cove, while I informed friends who wanted to continue a ministry relationship with me.

We held the first service on Sunday, August 4. Let me introduce you to our team, beginning with the original group. You met my friend Harold earlier, who came with his guitar and audio system and helped with the music. He stayed with us for about two years but then decided to become involved again in the orchestra of a church near his home.

Our college-age son, Jeremy, also attended every Sunday and played the drums on the old hymns and gospel songs we sang; bless him. Our daughter, Lyndsey, was with us and helped bring some of the folks who attended from the Cove, which was down a very long hallway from our worship area. Lynne and I deeply appreciated the loyalty demonstrated by Jeremy and Lyndsey and regularly assured them we would understand if they wanted to investigate involvement in a church environment more suited to college students' needs. They remained for some time but eventually landed in a church about twenty minutes from our home, where they became very involved in music and worship ministry. That was a new experience for Lynne and me, to have our children serving in a church different from ours. We made the adjustment quite easily, as we remembered there comes the time when all children must leave the nest.

You met our friend Ben. He was with us for the first several years, until his family moved a distance from Charlotte that made it impractical for him to continue. Ben was as regular as clockwork and very comfortable with the people. He would fill in for me on occasion when I had to be away. He had a full white beard, which made him a natural to dress as Santa Claus our first Christmas season, when we began the tradition of providing gifts for the residents every year.

Another of the original team was Debbie, a fortyish young lady who had cerebral palsy. She used a walker and could not speak clearly, which required that she use a device to allow her to type words and then played back what was written. Debbie had been a member of our mega-church, where I had the opportunity to be a friend to her. I always made it a point to speak to her, give her a hug, and even tease her. I never treated her like she was disabled. In fact, I treated her pretty much as I did everyone. I guess she became pretty attached because when she found out we were holding services at Wilora Lake, she found a way to be there every week. If she could not attend, I would receive a call the night before, informing me through a special telephone operator. She obviously could not contribute in the ways others did, but she was there at the entry area, smiling and kindly gesturing to greet the folks as they arrived. They loved her. She considered that *her* Sunday morning job, so much so, if I received one of those Saturday evening calls, it included the instruction to have someone "take her place." After several years, Debbie also moved to an area that made it impossible for her to continue being with us. We and all the people who remember her still miss her.

As for our team members who remain today, I am happy to say first of all that my wife, Lynne, is still with us. Each week she helps folks from the Cove make the long trek to the Lodge living room. This may involve just walking slowly beside someone or steering a wheelchair. Lynne has a gentle and genuine way that makes folks feel very comfortable and safe. They are proud to refer to her as "our pastor's wife."

Our friend Jackie also remains at our side. If you met her, you would understand why I say she "bounces" and even "pounces" on whatever need presents itself, from helping Lynne to getting extra chairs to adjusting the thermostat. Jackie is bubbly and energetic, and she is a natural with people. They have no choice but to love her. If they didn't, she would find a way to win them over.

Next are Ted and Joyce, a couple we have known and admired for over twenty years. They are both involved in the Sunday school class and have developed a very meaningful relationship with that group. Ted often serves as substitute teacher for the class, and he also leads a Wednesday afternoon Bible study. He and Joyce are very dedicated to the folks at the Lodge, frequently returning on Sunday evenings to lead fellowships and share refreshments, as well as being involved in other weekday activities. Joyce leads our singing on Sunday mornings and is known by some as "Joyce the Voice." Whether speaking or singing, she has a clear and powerful voice that projects and captivates. She is a tremendous musical asset to this and other areas of our ministry.

Finally, there are Jim and his wife, Kathy. Jim is a gentle, witty servant who helps arrange chairs, copies the song sheets for worship, and even sees that Joyce and I have a cup of water each week to keep our voices hydrated. I don't think Jim considers himself a strong singer, but when Joyce is away, he will step to the microphone and help lead the singing. A true servant. Recurring health issues prevent Kathy from being with us regularly, but she prepares the master song lyric sheet every week and sends it with Jim for copying.

You can see God organized just the right combination of people and personalities for this special ministry. This is something we have seen Him do in every ministry direction He has led.

We even gave our little church a name, The Wilora Lake Fellowship. Lynne, Jackie, Jim, and I arrive around 9:00 each Sunday morning to prepare the seating, audio system, and lyric sheets. Though I have practiced all week and that morning before leaving home, I go to the piano and rehearse the morning song selections once more. We take a few minutes to enjoy a little fellowship and laughter before breaking up to greet those who arrive early.

As the service time draws nearer, most of our team is at the entry area as a growing stream of residents comes down the long hallway from their apartments and the Sunday school class. Our deliberate human barricade makes it virtually impossible for anyone to pass without sharing ample smiles, handshakes, hugs, and maybe a kiss (we let the latter be *their* choice). We have found that when we begin every Sunday like this, every Sunday is off to a good start at Wilora Lake.

Our little church is a diverse group, with folks from many different faiths. This is the South, so you know we have Baptists. We also have our share of Methodists, Presbyterians, Lutherans, Catholics, and Pentecostals. Some time ago our service attracted a dear lady of the Mormon faith. She is excited to be with us and regularly expresses her gratitude for the preaching and teaching of God's Word. After attending for more than a year, she indicated trusting Christ as her Savior at the close of a service.

In addition to diverse faiths, we have had worshipping with us those of varying backgrounds. These have included African American, Oriental, and Hispanic, in addition to Caucasian.

Ours is a growing congregation, and it is common to welcome a new face or two almost weekly. However, though usually filled to capacity, we do not outgrow our facility. Why? It is a sad fact in this environment, we say farewell to folks on a somewhat regular basis. Some may be transferred to a different facility due to a change in care, finances, or family location. We also see those who decline in body and are no longer able to attend. We see those who decline in mind and are no longer willing to attend, often due to fear or confusion.

Finally, there are those who pass from this life, some with warning and some without. It has been a recurring experience to return from a mission trip, vacation, or arrive on a Sunday morning as usual to find one whose smile warmed us the week before has vacated this earth. One who retired to bed to get a night's rest, only to awaken to eternal rest. One who had a sudden stroke, heart attack, or aneurysm moments after laughing with other residents at the dinner table. One who was finally given relief and release after a long and debilitating battle with disease.

This is the part of our ministry that we do not like. In fact, only a small handful of residents who were with us in 2002 remain to this day, and we are keenly aware their countdown is in play. But while we are always saddened at the temporary separation from these loved ones, our joy is often heightened at their home-going. More than once we have had to allow sorrow to give way to gratitude as we realized the one who struggled with blindness could now see. Another in constantly discouraging pain was now free. All who strained under the sheer weight of old age and physical deterioration were once again young and strong. Yes, being in this environment week after week, year after year has taught us that we *will* grieve, though we "do not grieve as do the rest who have no hope" (1 Thessalonians 4:13).

When we began at Wilora Lake, I had the naïve idea that it would just be this "sweet little ministry, lovin' on old folks." I could not have been more mistaken. Since 2002 we have met some of the dearest saints of God that could possibly exist anywhere. They have become an unprecedented source of encouragement and joy to each member of our team. Those who have visited as musical guests or in some other capacity commonly remark, "There is a unique and wonderful ministry here." Most desire to return, and some who cannot be with us every week have found a way to visit on a more infrequent basis.

It is far from patronization or platitude when I repeatedly tell our folks, "Since coming to Wilora Lake, I look forward to Sunday mornings more than at any time in my life." And why shouldn't I? There is an atmosphere of love and acceptance. There is an absence of selfishness, politics, and agendas. There is a team of believers who just want to serve, joining weekly with a larger group who are visibly and verbally thankful for the opportunity to worship, fellowship, and learn.

I'm convinced this experience has created an environment just shy of heaven itself. Every moment is special and uplifting—like our welcome time, when a chorus is played at the piano; those who are able to move about exchange greetings with each other, and with those who must remain seated; at Christmastime, Mother's Day, and Father's Day when our ministry shares gifts that are generally small and inexpensive, yet hold priceless value to the givers and the receivers; when we distribute miniature flags around the Fourth of July and see everyone wave them enthusiastically as we sing "America the Beautiful," "God Bless America," or even a medley of "You're a Grand Old Flag" and "Yankee Doodle Dandy" (while being aware of the troubles that plague our country).

Many times a Baptist, Presbyterian, Lutheran, Pentecostal, Catholic, Methodist, or Mormon resident has passed through the exit line and said, "Pastor Jeff, I have been in church all of my life, but I am learning more about the Bible now than ever before." I typically respond by saying, "I just repeat what I hear. He tells me, and I tell you." I frequently remind them of my mother's words, "You're never too old to learn," and, "When you stop learning, you stop living." At Wilora Lake, we are really living.

It is a lively atmosphere and when describing our worship environment to others, I inform them, "Forget any notions that we have a bunch of people falling asleep during the services. Our folks are excited to be there, and it shows." Though we never stress denominational ties, my Baptist background does occasionally reveal itself when I ask a leading, "A-men?" at the end of a statement I want them to grasp. "If you're not Baptist, say, 'Ah-men.' If you're Pentecostal, say, "Yee-haa!" We always enjoy a good laugh and are reminded that in spite of our various backgrounds, loyalty to a denominational affiliation is not as important or satisfying as is unity in Christ and His Word.

I do recall after pulling this stunt on a few occasions that one of our Catholic ladies took me aside and spoke to me plainly but gently. "I need to tell you something, Pastor," she said in her New York accent. "It just so happens that many of us Catholics say, 'A-men' just like you Baptists do, not 'Ah-men.' So you need to stop picking on us about that." I stood corrected, but I didn't mind. She is a good buddy, like so many at the Lodge.

As I mentioned earlier, Wilora Lake Lodge, Wilora Lake Fellowship, is much more than a "sweet little ministry lovin' on old folks." It has become what you might call the focal point of our entire ministry. It is our local church, where people can do little more than faithfully pray for all our endeavors. Though we never mention money, it is a place where many have faithfully given to the work of the Lord, a few quite generously and most quite modestly. It is a people who joyfully send their pastor off to Africa and other parts of the world, while tolerating his prerecorded video sermons during his absence. It is a place where they excitedly welcome him home and eagerly wait to hear the report of what God has done. It is quite a place. An irreplaceable place.

After more than twelve years, I suppose it was to be expected that countless experiences with the residents have permanently impacted us. Observing the lives of the seniors has further compelled me to record our history, before I may reach the point when I am physically or mentally unable to do so.

In the chapter that follows, I share a few specific stories, but first I want to close my introduction to the Wilora Lake Lodge with an exhortation to you.

As I consider the beginning of our Sunday ministry there, I am reminded it was the result of *my* observation of a need and not that of another, as had generally been the case until that point. However, the same criteria for making a decision about becoming involved was applied. Was my Sunday morning calendar open? Yes. Did I and other members I could recruit have the gifts and abilities to meet the need? Yes. Were necessary finances available? Yes. Do we begin this ministry? Yes.

Are you up for some encouragement to all of us as believers? Folks, it's just not that hard to determine how, when, and where we should serve. So often in our Christian circles, we spend time needlessly trying to determine what we should be doing for the Lord, when He has placed a clear road map *before* us, *in* us, and *around* us. We miss the obvious while looking for some magical sign or listening for some magical sound. I have found that knowing and doing God's will is quite practical, not magical. I am furthermore convinced those who do not learn and practice this principle will spend much more of their lives *looking* for His will rather than *doing* it.

As discussed in chapter 2, the road map that is *before* us is His Word. I won't rehash that admonition… well, not extensively. It clearly tells us what is important to God, from the principles set forth in His Old Testament Law to the Words of the One who came to fulfill that Law (Matthew 5:17).

The road map *in* us is twofold. First is our ability to look within and see our strengths that can give help and strength to others. That may be any number of things and is usually something we enjoy or that comes naturally. Then is our ability to look *without* and simply *see.* See what?

That involves the third road map that is *around* us. People. Neighbors on both sides of our homes. Coworkers in the cubicles that surround us. If we don't know about their situations, we should find out. Most of us can say our eyes meet those of a set of semi-strangers on a regular basis, whether in our neighborhoods, workplaces, or grocery stores. It's time to do more than wave, nod, or say, "Good morning." We're accustomed to seeing each other, and my experience has been that most will not mind the overdue introduction and will respond congenially. If they do not, the fact remains the right action was taken, and God will credit us accordingly.

Simple and friendly introductions may lead to relationships that will almost always reveal needs in others—needs that may give opportunities to share faith, spiritual insight, advice, prayer support, and even material assistance.

It Gets Even Better

We need to stop excusing ourselves or procrastinating due to time, personality, or perceived financial limitations. We need to put ourselves out there. It is God who has commanded us to do so, and it will be amazing to see how He will work things out in and around us to bring joy and fulfillment. We can find what we see as our limitations do not limit His ability to use us to fulfill His will in our world.

We spend—no, we waste—too much time looking and praying for open doors. The truth is the doors are all around us, and most are already open. It may not be a door we expect, and it may not seem like a door we prefer. But it is likely a door we should enter. Reckless? Maybe to some, but what I'm referring to is faithfulness, not recklessness. Compassion, not carelessness.

We have found God blesses that motive and has, as a result, opened further doors to unimaginable opportunities. We must simply take the first obedient step, and we will likely find He is already holding our hands to guide in the steps that follow. Guide us, not pull us, push us, or force us.

And then hold on because it gets even better.

Wilora Lake worship service

CHAPTER 6

LIVE AT THE LODGE

"Be nice to seniors," I often encourage folks, "because you're gonna *be* one!" I have come to verbalize this truth everywhere I go since becoming so involved with this age group over the last dozen years. I have also become increasingly aware of this fact as I see my sixtieth birthday approaching and as I hear the server at McDonald's offer a senior discount on my coffee! Our initial activities at the Little Flower and Wilora Lake Lodge have expanded to additional facilities. Some of these involve a regular schedule, while others receive less frequent visits.

There are so many interesting stories among the seniors we have encountered. The difficulty in sharing them is not which ones to include but which to omit. We have seen many seniors grow in faith as God's Word has been shared. We have seen others find growing comfort and confirmation as they hear truths that have been a part of their lives for almost a century. Best of all, we have seen many come to saving faith in Christ as they have discovered the need for a relationship over religion. As we contemplate this, we are again reminded that God has given us the true privilege of being involved in the crucial time of their lives. Every unique experience has been precious and invaluable, but since the preponderance of our senior adult ministry has been at Wilora Lake Lodge, I will share some meaningful moments from that environment alone.

I hope I was successful in the previous chapter in conveying the impact the Lodge has had in our lives. When I say Lodge, I am now using the term to refer to a group of people, not a structure.

To this day, I cannot bring myself to address those who are nearer to my parents' generation by their first names, so I commonly add "Miss" or

"Mr." beforehand. That is how I recall people like Miss Opal, so gentle and faithful; Miss Mildred, whose smile still rivaled that of the beauty of her youth; Miss Jean, who I knew was praying for our specific needs, because she would name them without reminder. Miss Virginia, who was suffering with Alzheimer's but snapped to life and sang every word from memory when the hymns began; Mr. Ralph, who made his way without assistance to the service each week and sat in the front row, despite his blindness; Mr. Orville, who even after being relocated to another facility would have his family bring him back to "his" church every Sunday morning possible; Miss Ruth, who has to be one of the most genuine and saintly women I have ever met and encourages everyone at the mere sight of her silent and slow approach; Mr. Fred, who endured over one hundred years before leaving us, and who never lost his booming voice that met all with a positive greeting every week; Miss Elsie, ninety eight years old but still as mentally sharp as us whippersnappers.

On and on I could go, naming those who have gone before and those who remain. But I must stop at some point in order to progress with my purpose. If possible, I would ask forgiveness from any past dear ones omitted and ask understanding of those whose eyes may have opportunity to fall upon these pages. You are not left out by any means. You never could be.

Memories of Eloise

There is ample opportunity for lightheartedness in our senior adult environment, which is part of the reason I choose to include this story. Eloise was a petite lady with personality plus. She was so bright and bubbly and usually arrived almost an hour before our Sunday service every week, dressed to a T. Most of our folks dress for church in the tradition of their generation. We admire them for it and follow their example.

She was talkative but not imposingly so, and would sit and watch as we were getting things set up for the service. When finished, we would engage in conversation, and she was responsive and energetic. I might add she was just as cute as could be. She liked to laugh and expressed herself in a way that usually caused smiles or laughter inside and out.

In fact, there was an occasion when I had to be away for two Sundays on a mission to Romania, and most of our Wilora Lake team accompanied me. A friend and his wife agreed to handle the services in our absence. In speaking to me on our return, he immediately began to tell me of the "little red-haired lady," who was waiting in her chair near the front when he arrived both weeks. "She told me over and over just how the service goes every week," he said. "She was the cutest thing!" I guessed who she was in one try. "That was Miss Eloise," I said. "She's a hoot."

I often tell funny stories at the opening of our services, and I'll always remember Miss Eloise exploding into laughter at the punch line to each one, whether impressively funny or not. Her cheerful face is as vivid in my memory as it was in reality, and it still brings a smile. As my substitute noted, her hair was still a distinct red, or maybe that generation called it strawberry blond. In any case, at her stage in life, she had help keeping it that way at the Lodge beauty salon. As time passed, we noticed the periods of gray between her restored red hair grew longer, until gray became her permanent color.

When we first began our ministry there, she walked to the service with the use of a walking stick. In time we saw her graduate to a walker, as do many of the residents.

I'll always remember as I prepared to go on my first of many mission projects in Africa, she asked one Sunday morning if I would come by her apartment. It was just a few months after we had begun our ministry at the Lodge. "I have some things for your trip," she said. She shared some items she thought might be practical, especially in the area of sustaining digestive health. Then she shared a quite generous financial gift to help with expenses.

As with many of our senior friends, we noticed her mind was slipping a bit, but she never lost her ability to engage in conversation or bring a smile, as her cute and carefree personality remained. For example, we noticed one Sunday morning she was not in the service. Afterward, when Lynne was escorting other residents to their apartments, she noticed Miss Eloise in one of the sitting areas, chatting with a neighbor. "We missed you in church this morning, Miss Eloise," my wife said. Looking almost surprised and a little puzzled, Miss Eloise replied, "Was I not there?"

Miss Eloise's family relocated her, and we lost contact for a few years. In early October 2012, just a few days before I was to return from Africa, Lynne contacted me to let me know Miss Eloise had passed away. Her membership was at a nearby Presbyterian church, but the family informed us she still spoke of our Wilora Lake Fellowship as being her church and referred to me as her pastor.

"They want to know if there's any way you can handle the funeral service when you return," Lynne said. I arrived in Charlotte on Tuesday and led the service on Wednesday. It was not hard to think of appropriate comments as we paid final respects to the cute little red head and her wonderful Savior.

You Are a Special Person!

One of the residents who greeted us in our initial days at Wilora Lake Lodge and still remains is Miss Evelyn. She is noticeably attractive to this day and causes one to wonder what she looked like as a young lady. Not long after we became involved at the Lodge, I met an older man familiar with our ministry there but was not a resident. "I think there is a lady who lives there I knew as a teenager," he said. He called her name, and I told him she was indeed a resident, a real sweatheart. "We knew each other fairly well as kids," he went on. "She was about the prettiest black-haired girl I'd ever seen."

Though her hair is no longer black, I have no doubt he was right. I must also add her beauty is definitely more than skin deep. She is consistently generous in sharing her beautiful smile and is always welcoming and positive, even on days when she admits to feeling less than the best. I have never once known her to be negative in word or attitude and look forward to any opportunity for us to share in conversation. In fact, when we meet each month for the Soup, Salad, and Scripture, she is usually there with a group of friends. I have to be careful not to consistently park myself at her table and appear to neglect the other residents.

I avoid playing favorites, but her supportive response to everything one says makes her hard to resist. She's one of those who make you feel like you're the most important person in the room—if not the entire planet. I've always admired that ability in others and view it as a true gift. I must admit I'm probably not so fortunately endowed, but Miss Evelyn definitely is. Within moments after meeting her, anyone will feel like they are of value and appreciated by this new friend.

You and I have been around people who can be polite, hospitable, and accommodating but may not necessarily bestow upon us a crown of worth and importance. They are kind and courteous but do not necessarily make us feel drawn back into their company at the earliest convenience. Miss Evelyn does. She consistently reinforces this obvious quality to people with the phrase, "You sure are a special person!" Almost every Sunday when she exits the worship service, we exchange a hug and I hear her say, "We are so thankful to have you here every week. You sure are a special person!" If we are engaged in a conversation and the name of my wife or one of our team members is mentioned, I hear, "She sure is a special person!" "He sure is a special person!" "They sure are a special couple!"

Though she no longer attends worship at the Lodge, our daughter Lyndsey seems to have drawn the particular affection of Miss Evelyn. Their interaction is obviously limited. Nevertheless, not a week passes that Miss Evelyn does not ask me or Lynne, "How is my favorite girl? You tell her I love her. She sure is a special person!"

When we convey the message, Lyndsey smiles and asks, "What did I do that makes her say that?"

"I guess you were just you," I tell her. "That's who Miss Evelyn is."

So why *does* she say that to everyone? Many might ask, "She doesn't really think *everyone* is special, does she?" Is it a phrase caught in the groove of an aging mind, much like the broken record of a day gone by? I don't think so because her mind seems to be anything but weak.

I recall one Sunday as she bestowed my specialness upon me after our service, her friend Betty was behind her. Miss Betty is quite humorous and even a little outspoken, but not at all offensive. Picking on Miss Evelyn a bit, Miss Betty looked at me and said with a mischievous smile, "You know she says that to everybody, don't you?" She was absolutely right; Miss Evelyn does say that to everybody. Her comment did not at all cause me to question Miss Evelyn's sincerity, but for some reason, it did make me begin to contemplate just what could develop such a positive outlook in a person.

It didn't take long to realize everyone is special to Miss Evelyn because *Miss Evelyn* is special. *She* is special because somehow over her life, she did not miss the opportunity to learn and practice something so many of us miss: people need to feel like they matter. And it takes a small yet invaluable effort on our part to grant that need. *She* is special because she somehow perfected the ability to engage in conversation while yielding the sense of worth and importance to the other party as she does. *She* is special because she is able to make someone, anyone, feel special, whether the person deserves it or not.

Did wise parents skillfully instill this quality in her? Did God graciously implant this gift in her, to the envy of people like me? These questions I cannot answer, but I do know that she exemplifies the biblical admonitions, "give preference to one another in honor" (Romans 12:10), and, "Do nothing from selfishness or empty conceit, but with humility of mind let each of you regard one another as more important than himself" (Philippians 2:3).

I don't know if I'm actually all that special, but when I'm around Miss Evelyn, I'm convinced I am. I hope I do not have to face the time, but if I ever have the responsibility to stand and assist in saying farewell to this beautiful, black-haired girl, I know at least one thing I will say if I say nothing else: "You sure are a special person!"

I Like You!

That's how Miss Martha greeted me every Sunday morning after walking the long hallway from the Cove to our worship area in the Lodge living room. We had been involved there for several years when she became a resident, and the progression of dementia had moved her to the Cove not long after her arrival. She would point at me and repeat, "I like you," after the service ended each week as well. Truth is, she greeted everyone that way. Before long, a hug and a kiss on the cheek were included, always accompanied by her huge grin. Was it genuine? Was it part of the progressing dementia? I decided it didn't matter because I grew to look forward to that greeting and always replied with my own smile and, "I like you too!"

After a time, her daughter, Sally, came every Sunday and accompanied Miss Martha to our service. Though it grew more apparent her condition was worsening, Miss Martha never lost her positive effect on all of us. Sally would let us know week by week that Martha's condition was becoming more of a difficulty, and we could see the changes occurring. Yet, whatever else may have been transpiring with Miss Martha, "I like you!" was indelibly fixed in her mind because she never lost the habit of sharing this uplifting greeting.

Finally, her daughter took her home to care for her, and we all missed her smiling reminder that someone liked us. On January 10, 2012, I received a call from Sally, informing me Miss Martha had left this life. She asked if I would conduct the memorial service. "Her favorite Bible verse was John 3:16," Sally told me, so it was not difficult to plan my comments.

I mistakenly assumed it would likely be a small family gathering for the ninety-one-year-old saint who had been retired for almost twenty-five years. But when I arrived at the chapel, I immediately saw this thirty-year employee of the Charlotte Police Department had touched more lives than I could count. There were as many or more people standing as there were seated. There was a great mood of positive remembrance as I stood and shared the truth of the gospel as presented in John 3:16.

At the close of my comments, I offered people the opportunity to respond to the gospel. I asked those who prayed to receive Christ to indicate so by a raised hand. To avoid delaying the service, I stopped counting at twelve. Martha's life was still touching others, and our little-known ministry at a retirement center had reached into the world.

The following Sunday, I shared with our service what had happened, and we all laughed gently at the words we remembered—"I like you." In fact, when dismissed, almost all of us said our good-byes with the same words. It seems to have caught on because although Miss Martha has been away from us for a while, you can still hear, "I like you!" quite frequently. I suppose she is not so far away from us after all.

Max and the Messiah

This may be my favorite!

When we began our weekly service at Wilora Lake Lodge in August 2002, I felt impressed that a study of the Psalms would be a good direction to take. As you know, I had already been holding a monthly music and Bible devotional session at the Cove since April. Since most of the Cove residents did not make the trip down the long hallway to the Lodge on Sundays, I decided it was logical to share abbreviated versions of the Sunday Psalm messages during my visits with them.

It is commonly known most of the psalms were written by David, the most successful king of Israel and an icon in the minds of devout Jews. I found a study of this book of poetry afforded the opportunity to delve into the lives of David and other Jewish authors, which frequently included details of the historical events and customs of their times. This made for very interesting studies because the background information greatly contributed to the understanding and application of the Scripture.

I noticed a gentleman who began attending our Cove sessions. We seem to especially notice when men show up, I guess, because they are so outnumbered by the ladies at this stage of life. "His name is Max," Trish told me. "He is from Brooklyn, New York, and he is Jewish." We realized he likely joined in our monthly times together to pass the time as much as for any other reason. I was glad to have someone under the influence of God's Word, regardless of the motive.

I made sure we were introduced and made a point to welcome him warmly when he appeared. He let me know he enjoyed coming because he loved to hear the history of King David and Israel. Though we were studying the Old Testament Psalms, you might imagine our words usually turned toward Jesus at some point. Max and I had become very comfortable with each other, so he did not mind cheerfully reminding me, "I like to come and listen, but I'm Jewish. I'm not Christian."

"That's fine, Mr. Max," I would always say. "We're just glad to have you with us."

Our Wednesday meetings never pass that I do not invite the Cove residents to our Sunday service at the Lodge. Along with the invitation is the offer of physical assistance in getting them to and from the service. Mr. Max was not so inclined to attend due the distance and our emphasis on the Christian faith. However, I recall one occasion where he appeared at the Sunday worship, much to the surprise of us all. He reminded me again that morning, "I'm Jewish. I'm not Christian." I assured him Jews were indeed welcome, especially Jews from Brooklyn, as we were there to honor the King of the Jews.

Months passed, and Mr. Max continued to join us every month at our Wednesday Cove get-together. But he did not attend the Sunday service again during that time.

Then came the 2003 Christmas season. I absolutely love Christmastime. I generally share a series of four messages on the Sundays that fall between Thanksgiving and Christmas. The Sunday after Christmas, I normally resume the book study where it ended prior to the holiday season. That particular year it was still in the Psalms. However, on the Monday morning after what I thought was to be my final Christmas sermon, I arose as usual to have my daily Bible study and prayer.

When I began to look over my notes for the next Sunday's message, I was quickly impressed to take another direction. Though it was the week between Christmas and the New Year, I sensed the Lord telling me, "Stay with the Christmas theme one more Sunday." He led me to Luke chapter 2, where we find Joseph and Mary taking the Christ child to be dedicated in the temple. As I planned the sermon, I included very interesting principles of the Old Testament Law that dictated the steps a young Jewish couple were to follow in the early days of a child's life.

Like most sermon preparation, it was a great learning experience for me, and my excitement grew at the prospect of sharing with our folks. I told you that my mother had said, "You're never too old to learn," and these dear people loved hearing the background facts that made the Scriptures have more meaning.

Amid all this anticipation, I never gave a thought to Mr. Max because as I indicated, he had attended the Sunday service only once in almost two years. However, as we gathered on that Sunday, who came walking that long hallway to the worship area but Mr. Max! Our team welcomed him enthusiastically. He walked to the front row and took a seat beneath my lectern. *I know he is going to enjoy this message today,* I thought. *It is filled with information about the Jewish laws and customs that he loves.*

Though Christmas Day had passed, our service still included some seasonal songs due to the sermon content. I then shared the message from Luke chapter 2, which the Holy Spirit guided into a distinctly evangelistic conclusion. Max listened intently throughout. We do not do this at every service, but at the end of this message, I felt impressed to lead in the prayer of salvation and invite those uncertain about their standing before God to pray with me. I then asked for any who trusted Christ to share with me by an upraised hand. Without hesitation and within my arm's reach, the lone hand of Mr. Max ascended above his chair for all to see.

Following the service, as many of us offered encouragement and congratulations, he bordered on giddy, openly confirming he had accepted Christ as Savior. Grinning widely and speaking quite loudly, he repeated, "I've asked Jesus into my heart! I've asked Jesus into my heart!" For the next several weeks, he never missed a service, often saying to me, "I can't miss hearing you talk about the Bible. I must be here to hear about Jesus, the Messiah."

Not long afterward, Mr. Max took a fall, and his family chose to move him to a facility nearer to them, away from Charlotte. We lost contact, but it was obvious to us that God had brought our lives together at just the right time, in just the right place. For months he heard the message of God's Word and how it pointed to Jesus Christ. On that final Sunday of 2003, however, the Spirit somehow helped a ninety-two-year-old Jewish man from Brooklyn make the connection from his Jewish religion to his Jewish Messiah.

It's been over a decade since Mr. Max left us. In all probability, he has departed this earth. But we'll join him and all those who have received the Messiah one day in his home and ours, the New Jerusalem.

The many lives at the Lodge will continue to have great impact on those of us involved there; those who have gone before and others who have yet to arrive. These precious friends never fail to express their gratitude for our relationship with them. "You have no idea what you all mean to us," they commonly say. We are careful to assure them it is *they* who are the greater blessings in our lives, though I'm not sure they are so convinced.

After twelve years, our entire team cannot imagine a Sunday morning without sharing worship, study, and fellowship with the finest local church we know. It is quite common to be approached with the request, "Pastor Jeff, will you please conduct my funeral service when the time comes?" My answer is always the same, "I will be honored, but what do you say we don't mark the calendar!"

We love our time with these friends, so we also look forward to sharing eternity with them. Both those who were long time believers *and* those we saw come to know Christ during our ministry there. There are no more good-byes in that place, where we will all be forever young.

CHAPTER 7

DRESSED TO KILL!

Not that we're fans of Hollywood or its priorities, but my wife and I are movie buffs. We do not find broadcast television greatly appealing, so on the evenings when we have no other obligations, you'll find us settling in to enjoy a selection from our video closet. We both like a variety of genres, but truth be told, just relaxing and being together is what we like best. Regardless of the category, by the time we are finished with our day, we are generally not interested in being challenged by a complex plot. You know, the kind when someone has told you, "Now when you watch this, listen to every word, or you'll be lost." Listen to every word? Lynne and I know that one or both of us will sleep through part of the movie at some point, so a mental obstacle course is not what we need. In fact, we're hoping video manufacturers will soon include periodic subtitles that will review what has happened while we were sleeping.

We're all familiar with the motion pictures that move back and forth in time but attempt to keep the viewer on track with subtitles like "ten years later" or "one year earlier." I don't mind that, but if it is overdone, I can start to sweat.

As I continue sharing, I admit I'm trying to be careful about doing the same to you. In the previous chapters, we began to move along in time a little, but I now need to apply the brakes and once again move back to our beginning. We'll probably need to do this again before this story is told. At any rate, let's return to the late spring of 2002, when I was beginning to recover from difficulty and discover God's new direction for our lives.

You'll recall God took me to the twenty-fifth chapter of Matthew where Jesus said: "I was in prison and you came to me" (v. 35). Since He specifically placed that concern on my mind, I felt the need to investigate the possibility of ministry in prisons or jails. With multiple retirement facilities within close proximity of our home, it was not difficult to quickly become involved in that area. Correctional facilities were not nearly as accessible. Even if they were, I seriously doubt I could have walked up to the door and announced my availability, as I had at the Little Flower. How would I pursue the fulfillment of this scriptural directive? Once again it did not take long before an answer came to mind.

In our former church there was a man who had been involved in prison ministry for many years. He was under the ministry of the late Chuck Colson while in prison himself and developed his own ministry when he was released. His office was located in our area. His name is Al, and I had taken time on one or two occasions while at that church to join him in a service at a nearby facility. *I'll call Al,* I thought, almost adding a "duh" to myself.

We met for lunch a few days later. He did not know details about my situation, but he did know I was in a rebuilding mode. As with the sweet sister at the Little Flower, I asked if there were any areas in his ministry where I was needed. He answered instantly. "We sponsor prison crusades several times each year in the Columbia, South Carolina, area. We could use you to speak, do music, or both."

"Prison crusades?" I asked.

"Yes. There are many correctional facilities around Columbia—men's, women's, and youth. We have many volunteers who hold services in the prisons on Friday and Saturday evenings and Sunday mornings."

My mind instantly began to run with the information. Because of my background in music ministry, I inquired, "Could I bring a small group of voices and instruments to provide music? I could sing with them and then speak."

"Absolutely," he said. "This being your first time, you and your team would have to come early on Saturday and attend orientation that is required by the state. But it is good for three years."

"I don't know at this point who we will recruit," I said, "but I'll include that information in our promotion. I believe we can do this."

He gave me the dates of the next crusade weekend. I began inviting singers and instrumentalists to participate, and the response was positive and quick. Our son would play drums and our daughter and I would be two of the singers. My friend Harold was fully recovered from surgery and eagerly agreed to play guitar and to recruit both a keyboardist and bass player. He also volunteered to prepare the band while I prepared the singers. The band included an unexpected harmonica player!

Other friends also joined in, including Jackie, Joyce (the Voice), Jim and Kathy, and our future daughter-in-law, Holly. Through the years, I had kept an inventory of favorite songs from past music ministries. I selected several tunes and ordered music for the team.

Weeks flew, and excitement grew as we all looked toward this new experience. The combined team joined for rehearsal the week before the crusades, and if I say so myself, we were not bad. We even ordered special team shirts with our ministry logo displayed, and I made arrangements for someone to handle our service at Wilora Lake Lodge.

The Saturday in late August arrived for us to travel south from Charlotte to Columbia. We attended the required orientation, checked into our hotel, and met team members from other areas. We expected the first service to be that evening, but Al told us of an unexpected opportunity to bring a team into a youth facility earlier in the afternoon. Arrangements had been made to have a cookout and softball game with the boys following the service in their chapel. "We'd love for your group to do this," he said. "They will love your band and singers."

After getting ourselves in place, the young men entered in a very orderly and quiet manner under the supervision of their officers. Our team did a wonderful job and we watched the boys change from distant and cool to warm and attentive. I shared a message, and many responded to the gospel with an open commitment to Christ. Team members were allowed to spend some personal time with those who had done so, a privilege not often afforded in a prison environment. We then moved outside to a pavilion, where hamburgers and hot dogs were already being prepared.

I lived in Florida for years. It was hot. North Carolina can be just as hot. But folks, South Carolina, at least Columbia, is *hot!* I would not offend any South Carolinian for the world, but we have learned to expect a blast furnace when we arrive in Columbia in August. That afternoon at the boys' facility was our first prison ministry experience, and the actual outside temperature was 103 degrees. I don't know if it's possible, but the humidity felt higher. To our delight, it had been decided beforehand that a softball game was not wise. Even remaining under the pavilion was stifling, but it was obvious that the boys were enjoying this unusual privilege.

We were told a small number from our team was needed to take food to a group of young men who had not been allowed to participate in the service or the cookout due to their consistent misbehavior. They were considered less controllable and were housed in a high-security building separate from the other resident blocks. I and three other team members volunteered (maybe to get a break from the heat as much as for any other reason). The boys would be brought individually to an area where we would serve each a hamburger, a hot dog, chips, a cookie, a cold drink and a napkin.

I have been around people all my life. I have met strangers all my life. I feel comfortable with people. I feel comfortable with strangers. But the first prolonged visit to a prison is different. When you're taken into a cell block, where each inmate is behind a heavy iron door with a small opening, and you're told it is because he is considered difficult at best and dangerous at worst, it's different. When you stop and remember these hard cases are teenagers, it's different. Nevertheless, I thought I was fine. I thought I could handle myself okay. At first I did, but later I did not.

When we began serving, I was putting food items on the plate. Someone else completed the process with the drink and the napkin. I did not watch how they did that. I should have. I do not remember what caused the change, but I somehow came to be at the end of our short serving line when the next inmate arrived. He received his plate and then came to me, one of his hands holding his plate, right? Stay with me. I then handed him his cold drink, in a cup—no cans or bottles allowed. The other hand now holds a drink, so both hands are occupied. Are you with me? Then I went to hand him a napkin. No hand was available to receive it. This shouldn't be that hard, right? Maybe not, but attempting to be quick and cool, I spotted the pocket in the chest of his prison-issue uniform. I quickly folded the napkin neatly and deliberately, more like a handkerchief, and inserted it in the pocket, as you would into that of a tuxedo jacket. I looked at him, smiled and nodded proudly, gave him a farewell pat on the shoulder, and said—are you ready for this?—"There you go, *dressed to kill!*" Let that sink in.

Have you ever said something and realized you messed up even before the sound of your voice died from the room? The young man gave no indication he had heard what I said, but I could see the inaudible "O-o-o-o-o" on the faces of our three team members and both guards. I couldn't think straight after that, and I'm pretty sure I immediately demoted myself to counting chips and cookies and left the more mentally challenging task of drink and napkin distribution to someone more qualified.

Those who were with me graciously restrained their comments on the matter, at least until we exited the facility. Then they gladly shared their thoughts with me and anyone else who would listen. I've often wondered if it ever dawned on that young inmate what I said and what he must have thought if it did. I also learned that just because Jesus said, "I was in prison and you came to Me," we will not likely be an instant professional when we do… state orientation notwithstanding.

Need more proof? Oh yes, there's more. Our ministry has been participating in the Columbia crusades since 2002, but this next example took place on that same weekend, later that same evening. I figure if you're going to learn from your mistakes, you might as well make as many as possible all at once.

After leaving the youth facility, we had just enough time to run by the hotel to clean the heat off ourselves before heading to our evening service. It was at a women's work-release facility where the security was not as tight, and the women could move about more freely.

Accompanied by our ministry hostess, Terry, we arrived about an hour before the service was to begin in order to get everything set up and tested. Our presence must have aroused curiosity because some of the women began wandering in to watch us prepare. About twenty minutes ahead of starting time we were ready to test the audio system. We began a typical warm up on the first song, thinking we would sing only long enough to get a satisfactory audio balance, pray together, and then wait for the official beginning.

We were wrong. When the band began playing the lively introduction to our first piece, the women present immediately stood and joined in clapping and moving together in rhythm with the music. The door opened, and others filed in by the dozens, joining in the celebration before ever reaching their chairs. I may have thought we were just getting a sound check, but I found the service had begun. After all, I wasn't about to try to settle almost two hundred female inmates and tell them to wait a few minutes more. Our unexpected afternoon service earlier that day turned out to be a valuable rehearsal. I was having an experience I'd never had before, seeing a church service start early.

In getting to the point of my next embarrassment, I need to tell you one small piece of information we were given in our orientation. We were encouraged to be personable in the services and introduce our group members, but we were to share only first names. No last names or any other personal information were to be given to help ensure our future privacy and protection.

As our service continued, the place became alive and electric. Women in general are more emotional and expressive than men, and they were that night. Everything we sang or said was met with an enthusiastic response that made us feel like rock stars. In case you do not know it, ministers love a congregation that is engaged in the service. At least *this* minister does. Whether sung or spoken, I like to see the message is getting through. Many times in our local church services, we have to take that on faith, if you get my meaning.

That night, those women were with us. And when I'm standing before a crowd that is plugged in, my fire is fueled! But while this kind of stimulation can be good, one must be careful. That afternoon the awkwardness of a high-security situation made me lose the ability to think clearly. On this occasion, sheer excitement and enjoyment would be my demise. After we sang a couple of songs and the women calmed down enough for me to be heard, I said, "Let me introduce our team." They even responded to that comment with applause and cheers. I began—and no last names, remember? Well, you remember because I told you. That night I did not. The energy in the room had given me short-term amnesia.

I decided to start with our band. The last name of our guitarist Harold is also the name of a precious stone. He also manages a well-known jewelry dealership in our city. Off I went, giving his first *and* last names, *and* the interesting connection to his occupation. How clever of me. I continued down the line with our team members, carelessly making sure the population of this South Carolina women's correctional facility was getting sufficiently acquainted with each.

By the time I reached the third or fourth person, I noticed Terry at the back of the room, waving her hands wildly and shaking her head back and forth. I knew Terry was from a Pentecostal background, but I could not for the life of me understand why she was getting so happy in Jesus over the introduction of our team. Finally, I heard a discreet whisper from the singer standing directly behind me. "No last names."

You know the feeling of sudden embarrassment, right? When it seems like your blood (or something) begins draining from the top of your head, your mouth goes dry, your pulse increases, and sweat beads begin to form on your forehead. The enthusiastic glow on your face is also instantly transformed into a pale blank. And maybe the worst part is when you sooner or later say to yourself, *I hope it didn't show.* My memory of our orientation was mercilessly jerked back into place, and I immediately altered my introductory style. But not before giving team members more experiences to share with just about everyone—which they did.

The women in the prison were not aware of the policies we were to follow, so their energy was not diminished by the incident. The service continued with the same enthusiasm but with more self-awareness on my part. I shared a Bible message, which concentrated on the need for salvation and a Savior. I recall almost thirty ladies making a commitment to Christ that night, which helped me to learn from my blunders and to remember God works through us in spite of our weaknesses and even unintentional carelessness.

Before I share more about our prison ministry journey, allow me to pause and offer some encouragement and insight. You have already seen that although we may respond to Christ's biblical mandates with willingness, obedience, and even enthusiasm, it doesn't necessarily mean we are instantly equipped, experienced, or even comfortable with the job. I hope you are amused by my inaugural prison ministry mishaps, but perhaps you are thinking, *See, I just don't think I could do that,* or, *I'd be embarrassed to death,* or, *I'm just not ready.*

These confessions of inadequacy are often applied to many new opportunities before us, but they can serve as a deceptive hindrance to the greater blessings of God that are waiting. His blessings will not chase us down where we are, but they are there for us when we go where they are. If I wait until I feel adequate, I will always be inadequate. If I wait until I am experienced, I will remain inexperienced. If I wait until I am ready, I will never be ready. If I wait until I have faith, I will be faithless. If I wait until I have courage, courage will elude me. If I wait to be obedient to the Word of God, I remain disobedient to His Word.

As believers, we are given the freedom to determine the level of blessing in which we will live. I fear many settle into that which we can achieve rather than what only He can bestow.

What opportunities are before you? As I said, it's not a puzzle. The biblical mandates are there. They are not suggestions. They are not optional. Daunting? Maybe. Intimidating? Sure. Frightening? Sometimes. We need to remember those feelings primarily reflect us and not who goes before us. They reflect me and not who is *in* me.

Christ is not a supernatural bully who gives us commands He knows cannot be followed, so He can watch us remain in a state of frustration and failure. We should be involved in the work that is plainly important to Him, knowing He will enable, provide, and protect when we are. Our faith will grow only when we go, whatever direction that going may take.

As we do, we must again recognize and remember the words of Scripture: "And He has said to me, 'My grace is sufficient for you, for power is perfected in weakness.' Most gladly, therefore, I will rather boast about my weaknesses, so that the power of Christ may dwell in me. Therefore I am well content with weaknesses, with insults, with distresses, with persecutions, with difficulties, for Christ's sake; for when I am weak, then I am strong" (2 Corinthians 12:9–10). And, "it is no longer I who live, but Christ lives in me" (Galatians 2:20).

At that same initial lunch meeting with Al, he told me of another need. "We have a program at the jail where my office is located," he said. "We call it Lifeskills." He explained it was a seven-week program that taught inmates skills that would help them take a different life path when they reentered society. It covered topics such as relationships, financial responsibility, job interviewing, self-awareness and more. All the curriculum had a biblical perspective and was centered on Christian principles.

"Is the class open to the entire jail?" I asked. "Does everyone attend?"

"No," he answered. "Those desiring to participate apply to do so, and we can only accept a maximum of fifteen men every seven weeks. We operate the class under the authority of the county sheriff's office."

He went on. "The men who are admitted to the class spend the seven weeks together in a special area we are allowed to use. It is an open room with bunk beds and a separate area with toilets and showers. There is also an area where they have meals, and the class is held around those tables. When a seven-week cycle is ended, we hold a graduation ceremony for them and then start over with a new group."

"What do they do after they graduate?"

"Well, they return to the general population in the other cell blocks, some to await a prison sentence and others to complete their time at the jail. If all the spaces in the next class are not filled, some of them apply to repeat it. If they are so inclined, we do not discourage that."

"Do you provide the materials to be taught?"

"Not exactly. You can look at the topics we cover each week and choose one. You may develop your own study as God leads. Then you teach the class one day of that week." He kindly added, "I've known you for many years now, and I know I can trust whatever you develop. And Jeff, we need godly men to influence these inmates."

That's all it took. Remember, my schedule was still not full. The biblical mandate was clear: "I was in prison and you came to me" (Matthew 25:36) The calendar was clear, especially once every seven weeks. My abilities could meet the need. So as with the Little Flower and Wilora Lake Lodge, my decision was yes.

On the first Tuesday of October 2002, I made my way to the Union County Jail on the other side of Monroe, North Carolina. I was not particularly nervous during the forty-five minute drive from our home, but

I did pray that God would use me and help me be comfortable in this new venture. I can't be sure, but I probably also prayed I would not embarrass myself, as I had a few weeks earlier in Columbia.

As I arrived and walked toward the visitor entrance, I knew once again that I was embarking into foreign territory. Entering the building, I quickly found it was designed (or it seemed so to me) to be a bit confusing to navigate. I've never specifically discussed this with anyone there, but after a few visits, I decided it was logical to build a jail this way. The architects likely knew a visitor coming in would be given assistance, but an inmate trying to get out would need to be hindered. If that was their goal, in my mind they succeeded.

An officer took me a few steps to the first door and got clearance from "master control" to have us buzzed in. After moving through the labyrinth I have described, we were finally facing a counter, where more officers were stationed. My guide disappeared into a side room, and I stood waiting for further instructions from his colleagues.

My eyes naturally explored my surroundings. I immediately discovered a holding area behind me. It was small, enclosed by concrete and heavy bars, and had a bench built into the wall. Seated there were three young men, who I surmised were being processed for entrance into their new home. All were handcuffed to the steel bench.

As my eyes continued to wander, I again noticed the confusing angles of corridors and doorways. *If I'm ever turned loose on my own in here,* I thought, *I'll not see home again.* Finally, one of the officers behind the counter took some personal information, confiscated my driver's license, and gave me a visitor badge to wear during my stay.

I didn't realize it, of course, but the location of the Lifeskills class was through another heavy door just opposite the officers' station. I was led through that door into yet another small hallway and was immediately standing before the final door.

"They're in here," the officer said as he had the final door buzzed open. I took a deep breath.

We entered the room, and it was as Al had described. Each bunk bed was all steel, including the sleeping surface, which was covered by a very thin mat and an equally thin pillow. *That cannot be comfortable,* I thought as I made my way toward the tables, where a dozen or so inmates were seated. All wore one-piece orange prison uniforms and orange rubber sandals. Some greeted me with warm smiles, while others were more distant and lifeless.

Rising to greet me was Dom, a representative of the prison ministry, who had already spent much of the morning with the men. We introduced ourselves, and he introduced me to the class as I took my seat. No last names. Dom remained in the room with us during that entire first visit, and I was grateful. I was glad to have the added sense of security and familiarity Dom provided my first time out. It would not be the last time we joined together in prison ministry. I came to admire this big man with a big heart. He is with the Lord now, and I remember him fondly.

I did not deliberately plan to do so, but I began my time with the men that morning with a practice I have continued ever since. I give the Lord the credit for leading me to first give my name and then listen to theirs. This is an obvious practice of courtesy, but I also wanted to be able to repeat each of their names and address them personally throughout the class. In past church ministries, I had always allowed myself to gradually learn names as I spent time with people. The Lord knew, of course, my time with these men would be limited, and the gradual acquaintance I was accustomed to would not be possible. If I expected to make a more helpful impression on them in the time we had together, I would have to expect a little something of myself.

Throughout our time together, that day and in every class since, I occasionally call the name of a class member at random as I make an important point. I definitely respond to a question or comment by addressing the individual by name. This practice has helped establish an initial rapport with at least some of the guys, which paves the way for openness as we continue the class.

Through our prison ministry experiences, I have learned that almost anything I teach or preach in a correctional environment is applicable to many people in *any* environment. In fact, more than once a team member has approached me after a Sunday sermon to say, "Pastor Jeff, that message would be so appropriate in one of our prison services." I usually heed that input, and it always proves to be true.

So you see, much of what I have shared in prison environments was first shared on the outside. Whether behind bars or freely moving about society, whether wearing orange prison issue or dressed in the latest vogue, whether sharing a cell with a stranger or a home with family, we all have common life experiences that would qualify us to join together in a Lifeskills class.

In the next chapter I share the class content I have used with hundreds of jail inmates since 2002. Before doing that I must say my consistent involvement in Lifeskills continues to yield blessings and rewards, though most of these are taken in faith. With rare exception, I do not see these men again after our one-time encounter in the class. There have been a few occasions when I have returned at the end of the seven weeks to join them in their graduation ceremony. At those times, our ministry has usually provided pizza, soft drinks, and sweets, treats they normally do not get to enjoy.

We are not permitted to discuss their crimes or the penalties they face. But those who are simply serving a jail term will often tell me when they will be released. You might imagine the enthusiasm with which they share that information. However, there are many who are awaiting sentence for their offenses, and I try to especially encourage them to continue in the principles learned in Lifeskills. "God is most concerned about *what* we are," I tell them, "which has little to do with *where* we are."

Sadly, I have occasionally learned of some class members who will spend the rest of their lives incarcerated, though these often had the kindest, gentlest, and most helpful attitudes in our class. They made disastrous choices that carried disastrous consequences. My prayer for each of them is they will pursue being reshaped, though a hopeless future seems to await them.

On the other hand, there have been occasions when I have come upon former class members on the outside, which has always been rewarding. One Thanksgiving morning, a local fast-food restaurant that was closed for the holiday allowed the prison ministry to use its facility to share meals with those in need. Our ministry, including my family and other team members, joined them. Working right beside me was a young man who had been in my Lifeskills class. He told me of his new job and how his life was doing very well. He also mentioned how much Lifeskills helped him and even quoted some of the material shared during my time there.

On another occasion, I and several members of our ministry team were returning from an event, when we stopped at an intersection in the town where the jail is located. In the lane next to us was a pickup with two or three men in the back. When I recognized one as being a former Lifeskills pupil, I rolled down my window and spoke to him. He recognized me immediately, and we chatted enthusiastically until the traffic light urged us on. Life was going well for him too, and it showed in his face and rang in his voice.

In the spring of 2008, I was invited to bring our singing team to provide music at the annual prison ministry banquet held by the organization with whom we serve. Before the meal, I had stepped down the long hallway to wash my hands. I was alone until a neatly dressed but rather world-worn-looking fellow entered. We greeted each other politely and then he spontaneously announced, "I still remember what you taught us in our Lifeskills class. It has helped me a lot." I was blessed to say the least. We shook hands and returned together to the banquet area.

I was in for another blessing that evening, when the host prison ministry presented its annual awards. Our ministry was honored with the People Who Make a Difference award, which was a humbling surprise. It is still displayed in our office to remind us to "not lose heart in doing good, for in due time we will reap if we do not grow weary" (Galatians 6:9).

Being recognized by others is satisfying, but this is not our ultimate motivation for service. The majority of the good done in the lives of the Lifeskills participants is never seen by those of us who sit before them. But we can know that much has been accomplished because we have been promised, "So will My word be which goes forth from My mouth; It will not return to Me empty, without accomplishing what I desire, and without succeeding in the matter for which I sent it" (Isaiah 55:11).

It is *God* who is at work in these men, and He is not obligated to reveal to us everything He has done. At the same time, He does seem to let us see just enough results to keep us motivated, and few enough to keep us humble. That formula has become a prayer for our ministry and one God has graciously granted.

Prison Ministry music and preaching team

CHAPTER 8

BUSTING THE CONCRETE

As I share the content of our Lifeskills class, I do so as an exhortation rather than a mere explanation. The name I have given to the three-session study is "Let's Bust Some Concrete." Why this title? It is my hope to quickly gain class attention as I remind us that while forming and shaping wet concrete is fairly easy, reworking dry concrete is another story. I am applying the same idea to people.

Session 1: Explaining the Problem

The goal is to help us understand that like concrete, we were all formed and shaped at an early age in ways we did not influence but that have influenced us ever since. I call it **conditioning**, which is the result of repeated input. We were brought home from the maternity ward and immediately subjected to personalities and environments that began to mold our "wet concrete." All our infant minds were concerned about may have been a bottle and a clean diaper. But we can be assured others were giving us much more, unbeknown to us, and probably to them.

The first and foremost source of this conditioning was our families, particularly our parents or whoever may have had the responsibility of parental guardianship. The people and personalities into which we were born determined the environment in which we would learn to cope. That initial formation required no effort from us and, therefore, was not hard for us. But later in life, it may be hard on us and possibly others. Before we were old enough to be aware, personality traits were being developed in us that would linger for the rest of our lives. Some, maybe most, serve us well. Some do not. Some of the latter may even contribute to behaviors that result in prison confinement at the worst, or conflicts at home, work, and life in general at best.

The reason for this is our exposure to the consistent conditioning and input of our environment led to the development of **attitude**. Not *an* attitude but attitude or disposition. A disposition may be defined as our general mood, feeling, or state of mind, which greatly determines our outlook on life. Our attitude or disposition impacts how we view and respond to every area of our lives, including self, society, relationships (family, friends, spouse, etc.), and responsibilities (jobs and employers, debt and expenses, many relationships, and so on). We all know people who have a good disposition or a bad disposition, and it can give an idea of their prior conditioning and environment.

When we see how people deal with life, including ourselves, we see how our attitudes lead to the development of **habits**, or a general behavior. Specifically, a habit is a recurrent, often unconscious pattern of behavior resulting from frequent repetition. It is a customary manner or practice. Do you see? My attitude, my disposition, my state of mind, my general mood will shape my general behavior, my habits. And again, all of this happens for the most part before I am consciously involved in the process.

During our childhood and adolescent years, only hints of these may be seen or may not be obvious at all. However, with the onset of adult relationships, responsibilities, and realities, they become more apparent and intense. Clearer reflections of years gone by emerge, and they are obvious to others even if not to ourselves.

So what is the process we have seen so far?

>Conditioning stimulates the mind.

>Attitude (disposition) is the resulting state of mind.

>Habits (behavior, conduct) are the natural displays of the unconscious mind.

Did you notice one word that was common to each of the three statements? "Mind." That is crucial because the mind is where we live. It is where our conditioning takes place, it is where our attitude dwells, and, therefore, it is where our behavioral habits find their source.

I am not saying we are all totally messed up and had horrible childhoods that wrecked our minds. I am *not* saying we all have reasons to question the quality of parental input that did so much to shape who we are. In fact, most of us probably have more pleasant than unpleasant memories. But the fact remains that since "all have sinned" (Romans 3:23), including our parents, none of us was brought up in a perfect environment, though we may like to claim so.

Therefore, whether we land in a jail cell or enjoy freedom, we all have a piece of personality that has probably been a source of difficulty on some level and could use some reshaping. In other words, we all have some "concrete" that needs to be busted and re-formed. The need of some will be more than others, while some will be less.

If this reformation is going to happen, it will take place in the mind. As I have considered these principles over the years, it becomes increasingly obvious to me why Paul said, "And do not be conformed to this world, but be transformed by the renewing of your—mind" (Romans 12:2a).

Since the entire Bible is for all of humanity, Paul's words undeniably tell us every mind needs some transforming. I alone can determine and accept for myself where my defective "concrete" lies. Only you can do the same for you. Once determined, we can decide if we will take on the challenge of transformation or carry on as is and hope for the best, tolerating the problem areas. We will not be alone in this challenge, but it will still be easier said than done.

Session 2: Exchanging the Patterns

In session one I attempted to explain the problem. Now let's talk about changing patterns.

If you and I are to identify areas that need attention, we must take the time needed to see in ourselves what so many others have likely seen for some time. The men in our Lifeskills class have been given all the time they need to pursue this challenge, compliments of the state. I, for one, prefer not to come to the same situation in order to address myself; I assume you share that view. We will have to do what most of us say we just can't do: make the time and take the time. We know it is needed, and if we deny that fact, then it is *really* needed.

We must be willing to honestly see and confess our own weaknesses to ourselves and possibly to others, if relationships are affected. I am honest with the men of Lifeskills in telling them I was raised in a home where everyone was quite verbal. When I say verbal, I not only mean we talked a lot, but we could also be outspoken and often critical. My mother and father both had strong personalities and strong wills. My mom could spot and point out faults from a record distance. My dad, though gentle on one hand, had a short fuse and sharp tongue when tested. Combine those qualities, and we often had the opportunity to watch the "fur fly," as my mom used to say.

I thought you lived in a Christian home, you may be thinking. Christian, yes, perfect, no. My mother's practical and spiritual wisdom and insight will always be an influence in my life, as will the humorous street smarts of my father, who grew up in a northern city. Yet, my sister, brothers, and I also learned some negative ways to communicate, especially if angered or stressed. It was not that our parents were wrong in what they believed or said, but they could be destructive in the *way* they expressed it. And we learned to be the same, before we knew it was happening.

But that does not describe all of my background. As I hinted previously, our parents had a keen and quick sense of humor. I do recall the unpleasant moments in our home, but I recall more instances when our family laughed uncontrollably for hours. It was usually due to our father being on a roll of witty remarks in response to our mother's instigation. There were countless times when we children would secretly try to get our mom to "get Dad going," and she was almost always willing. It may have been around the supper table, on a long road trip, or sitting around the living room at night, with time on our hands. It was a good time in any case, and their senses of humor can be clearly seen in all their children.

So you see, there is good, and there is bad. There is positive, and there is negative. The positive we want to treasure, keep, and practice. The negative needs to be reshaped. The concrete needs to be busted and re-formed. The negative patterns need to be exchanged for positive ones.

How are we to go about this? I want to quickly point out that we will not accomplish this task on our own strength of will, so I will deal with that need in the next session. For now, let me introduce the three steps to remember and then we'll move on with the procedure of dealing with them.

First, if I hope to succeed in altering undesired patterns in my life, I must accept the **responsibility** for myself. I can spend my life blaming my parents and others for my weaknesses. If I choose that path, I will always be weak. When confronted with my shortcomings, I may choose to say, "This is the way I am, and if you don't like it, you'll just have to get over it!" If I take that approach, others will likely choose to get over it *and* to get over me.

We must all be willing to look at our problem areas and realize that while they are not totally our fault, they are now totally our problem. We can understand the influences that contributed to our current "issues," but we must also understand that neither Mom, Dad, nor anyone else is coming back to fix us. We may have unconsciously learned certain sins from them, but they are now *our* sins, of which *we* are guilty, and for which we will be held accountable. I once heard in a Minerth and Myer video series that the true definition of adulthood is "When I stop blaming my parents, family background, or others for my faults and failures and assume responsibility for myself." This initial realization will not instantly bust and reshape our concrete, but without it, we have no hope of doing so.

After we've made the mature decision to accept responsibility, we then realize some of our life patterns must be **reversed**. Do you remember the process that took place when we explained the problem? Conditioning, attitude, habits. Since that process left us with some problem areas, we need to reverse the process in those areas.

We remember our habits (behaviors) developed due to attitude (disposition). Therefore, if I desire to change my habits in certain areas, then I need an adjustment of attitude. How do I do that? Remember what brought about attitude? It was conditioning. If I desire a changed attitude, I need different conditioning. Finally, you remember our conditioning was a result of repeated input and influence. If I want to be reconditioned, I need different input and influence. This is a brief description of what will be a lifelong challenge.

Perhaps it has brought to your mind my final thought for this session. We may accept responsibility, we may recognize the steps of reversing some patterns, but we will find success to be a difficult **reality**. Remember the influence and conditioning in our young lives required no effort on our part. This challenge in our adult lives will require great effort on our part. We will likely spend the remaining years of our lives trying to conquer part of the first few years of our lives. But it will be worth it. We will see successes along the way that will encourage us to remain steadfast. We will also see setbacks that will discourage us. But with the help that is available, we can become God's finished product, which Mom, Dad and others started.

Session 3: Example to Practice

I have tried to explain the problem. We have seen the necessary steps in exchanging the patterns. Talking about this is the easy part. Doing it is another matter. As with most difficult tasks, we will not succeed alone. We need a consistent and patient Helper. We need an example to practice, which is the third and most important session of our Lifeskills study.

Perhaps you noticed the first two sessions did not include much discussion in regard to biblical and spiritual information. Perhaps you were tempted to get the idea I had developed another self-help plan to offer the men of Lifeskills. Nothing could be further from the truth, as this final step will show. The old saying, "God helps those who help themselves," is often applied to those who find themselves trapped in patterns of behavior that have yielded negative results. It sounds logical, and I've even heard well-meaning Christians quote it as being from the Bible. I frequently say that this and other adages must be found in the book of Second Opinions.

The fact is that when it comes to dealing with our sinfulness and its results, the Bible is clear that humankind is incapable of helping itself. People will never solve our problems because people *are* the problem! Speaking of himself, Paul emphasized this truth when he wrote, "Wretched man that I am! Who will set me free from the body of this death?" (Romans 7:24).

People are hopeless sinners in need of a Savior. The only One who can save us from our sin is the only One who can help us forsake our sin and maintain new behavior. His name is Jesus Christ. He died to remove the penalty of sin, which is eternal separation from God. When we believe and receive Him, we are promised eternal life in heaven. But between now and then, there is a life to be lived. That is the difficult issue for most of us.

Jesus promised there is "life more abundant" (quality of life) to be found in Him. The secret to this life is found in the apostle Peter's reminder to us, "Christ also suffered for you, leaving you an example for you to follow in His steps." Without the inspiration and motivation of His example, we face perpetual frustration in the quest to reshape the concrete that is ourselves.

In almost any of life's endeavors, we have a greater chance for success when we have an example to follow and imitate. As a voice major in college, I was fortunate to have instructors who took me to vocal workshops, where I was exposed to the finest voice coaches and students in the country. My attention was immediately drawn to those singers who had developed incredible technique and style. I watched them, listened to them, and found myself incorporating their techniques into my own singing. I never sounded exactly like any of them, but following their examples served me well, and I later earned honors and rewards of my own.

As a music minister, I took an interest in composing and arranging tunes for our choirs and orchestras. I knew my abilities in this area were limited, so I listened to the work of respected composers and arrangers, especially those who were effective in producing music for the church environment. When possible, I examined their printed scores while listening and watching how they used various combinations of instruments to achieve a desired emotion in the music. As I looked to their examples, it was exciting to develop my abilities over the years as I produced many original compositions and arrangements, both choral and instrumental.

The same has been true in the area of speaking and preaching. I consistently try to read, listen to, and learn from messages and sermons of effective spiritual communicators. Again, though I am not an exact duplicate of any of them, their examples have been invaluable.

The point has been made. In dealing with my need to reform, I need an example. To get right to the point, that example is Jesus Christ.

Many resist the idea of looking to Jesus as an example because His perfect nature sets too high a standard. However, His perfection is exactly the reason He is the only One qualified to be an example to us. Anyone less lowers the standard to the same imperfect human level where we all struggle.

In an attempt to rationalize, justify, and tolerate faults, it is common to hear, "I'm as good as the next fellow," and that would be true. You and I *are* as good as the next person because that individual has the same sin nature we do. He or she is dealing with malformed concrete, just as we are. As long as I look to an imperfect model, I can allow myself to excuse my own imperfections. I must look to a model who is higher than myself and higher than the human race.

There is only One. Jesus Himself said in Matthew 5:48, "Therefore you are to be perfect, as your heavenly Father is perfect" (complete, mature, adult). If we hope to ever leave behind incompleteness and immaturity, we will have to follow the example of Christ, the only One who is completely perfect.

As we begin to apply the example of Jesus to our lives, we must remember to begin where we *are* and not where we *were*. We must remember that if we are in Christ, our sins are forgiven. We cannot go back and clean them or correct them, and He does not expect us to. We must, "forget what lies behind and reach for what lies ahead" (Philippians 3:13). In other words, we must not dwell on the past but on what the future can hold.

You can imagine how important this principle is to men who are serving a jail term or possibly facing an extended prison sentence. They are in a state of mind where they can be overcome with crippling guilt and regret. The same can happen to all of us if we are not careful to consistently "forget" and "reach." By following His example, Christ can make us *what* we should be in spite of *where* we might be or *what* we have done.

That being said, let's look at our Example as presented in Philippians 2:5–11. I often call this portion of the study "It's Not Too Late to Finish." It has been used as a separate sermon in other prison services and elsewhere.

Since we are trying to leave our past and look to the future, we look first at how Jesus finished. Let's **see the end first**. We cannot change the past, but we all want to finish well, right? Did Jesus finish well? I say yes. Scripture agrees. Paul says in verse 9, "Therefore God also highly exalted Him, and bestowed on Him the name which is above every name." He goes on in verse 10, "that at the name of Jesus every knee should bow, of those who are in heaven, and on earth, and under the earth." He came to the earth, sent by the Father. He lived, died, and rose again, all perfectly according to His Father's will. He ascended into heaven and, "sat down at the right hand of the Majesty on high" (Hebrews 1:3), His work being finished.

Paul gives three indications of Jesus finishing well. First, **God** exalted Him (Philippians 2:9). How did God exalt Jesus? He gave Him "the name that is above every name." The word "name" in this case refers to more than just an identifying title. In the original Greek text, it has to do with character, dignity, and reputation. Therefore, Paul is saying that when Jesus completed His earthly mission and returned to heaven, so pleased was God that He declared the name of Jesus to carry a dignity and reputation that is eternally above any other that came before or after.

No one can deny the name Jesus is known to an extent beyond that of any human who has ever lived. Many are warmed, and many may bristle at the mere mention of it. But the name of Jesus cannot be ignored. His name declares who He is and what He has done, and it has been unsurpassed since He entered time and space over two thousand years ago—and blessed this world with His physical presence and a public ministry that lasted a mere three and one half years. To receive an honor of this magnitude tells us He finished well. God approved of Jesus, and God exalted Jesus.

By following His example, we too may finish well. Jesus said we have the possibility of hearing the approval we all seek from God Himself when He says, "Well done, good and faithful slave… enter into the joy of your master" (Matthew 25:21). Do we want to finish well? Do we want to hear God's blessing when we cross the finish line? We will never achieve the character and reputation that was given to Christ alone, but we can share in His glory, reshaped by following His example.

As we continue to consider the glowing finish of Jesus, we see that not only did God exalt Him, **heaven** exalts Him. The first part of verse 10 in Philippians 2 tells us, "at the name of Jesus every knee will bow, of those in heaven…" In the original Greek, the word translated "heaven" in this verse means anything that pertains to heaven or anything that is in heaven. Let's think about that for a moment.

We already know Jesus was given the highest character and reputation. And while there may be sinful people on earth who do not respond fondly to that, there is no such problem in heaven. In trying to get some picture of just what it means for all of heaven to exalt Jesus, I look at the book of Revelation's fifth chapter.

God allows the apostle John to see the throne room of heaven, where Jesus the Lamb is receiving the praise of "many angels around the throne, and the living creatures and the elders" (Revelation 5:11). John goes on to say that "the number of them was myriads of myriads and thousands of thousands." You and I know what a thousand is. We can imagine that number of beings gathered at one time. Our difficulty in understanding increases when John does not say, "thousands and thousands," but, "thousands of thousands." How many is that? Millions. How many millions? We do not know. Then the picture grows when he speaks of the "myriads." A myriad is defined as a countless number, indefinite, innumerable. Notice that he speaks similarly when he does not say, "myriads and myriads," but, "myriads of myriads." In describing the heavenly exaltation of Jesus Christ, John says there are countless numbers of countless numbers of beings, all harmoniously declaring the praise of the Son of God.

Did Jesus finish well? Absolutely. God exalted Him, and heaven exalts Him. But there is one more piece of evidence given by Paul in the last part of Philippians 2:10.

Earth will exalt Him, "on earth and under the earth." "Earth," in this case, refers to the people of the earth rather than the physical planet. Though God in His mercy presently allows foolish men to disparage the name of Jesus, the day is coming when God in His judgment will have everyone declare His lordship. Like it or not, all humankind will confess that Jesus is the sinless Son of God, the Savior of the world, and everything else He claimed to be. This further confirms He finished well.

Many who are confined to a cell and many who are not may be considered by some as lost causes, with no hope of reformation or lasting change. But by following the example of Christ, the naysayers may well have the opportunity to one day admit that our finish will be better than our beginning. Jesus indeed finished well, and so may we.

Why did He finish so well, and how may we? We looked at the end first. Now let's look at **the means to the end**.

To understand how Jesus finished so well, let's see how He lived beforehand. I suppose it would be understandable for us to say, "Of course Jesus finished well. He was perfect." While that is true, we must also remember His perfect nature did not prevent Him from experiencing difficulty, mistreatment, and extreme hatred. In fact, it was His very perfection that often invited abuse from sinful men. We must never forget that "He was tempted in all things as we are, yet without sin" (Hebrews 4:15). In spite of this, He lived in a way that made Him an example to the world ever since. What do we see in His life that will help us reshape our areas of weakness and finish our lives successfully?

First, let us back up to verse 5 of Philippians chapter 2, where we are told *Jesus had the right attitude*, which we are to reflect. "Have this attitude in yourselves," Paul writes, "which was also in Christ Jesus." The King James translation of the Scripture says, "Let this mind be in you." There it is again. Do you remember? My attitude is my state of mind, my disposition. Being of a perfect nature, living in a sinful, fallen world must have been more difficult for Jesus than for us. In spite of this, He kept the right attitude, He maintained the right state of mind, He guarded the right disposition. We may rightfully claim difficulty in keeping a Christ like attitude in this life, but we are told to do so because *He* did so. Jesus finished well because He lived in the right attitude. We can and should finish well for the same reason. We must bust the concrete of our attitude and reshape it according to His.

Having the right attitude caused Jesus to finish well, but we also learn in verse 6 that *He was self-aware*. When the verse says, "Who, although He existed in the form of God," the word "form" also has special meaning. Translated from the original Greek it means "existing even if alone or unseen," and also, "being the same as." Did you catch that? This verse is clearly telling us Jesus was the same as God. Jesus was God. Jesus *is* God.

This should not be news to those who are familiar with the New Testament because Jesus made it clear more than once that He was aware of this fact. "I and the Father are one," He said in John 10:30. He later added, "If you have seen Me, you have seen the Father" (John 14:9). Being aware He was one with the Father guided Jesus in everything He did and said during His earthly ministry. It kept Him on the right track and in the right *attitude,* in spite of the difficult circumstances He faced.

"How in the world does this apply to me?" we may ask. "Jesus may be God, but I'm not!" And that would be absolutely correct. So what exactly are we to be so aware of that would help remold our attitude and re-form some habits? My answer is simply this. Though we are not God, we are important to God, and, therefore, we may receive the help of God. Living in the constant awareness that we are so important to the One who is *all* important should definitely guide the way we live.

I remember what it felt like when I was a boy in school to notice a cute girl across the room and develop a hopeless crush on her. I especially remember what it was like if she returned the affection, rare as that was. I would always try to look my best, do my best in school, and be on my best behavior, even when she was not around. The most wonderful girl in the world liked *me,* and I wanted to look and live in a way that deserved her favor.

Most of us know what it is like to be invited to a special event, perhaps a wedding, or to be in the company of some important personality. We clean up and make sure our hair is just right, fingernails are cleaned and trimmed, and that nothing of our last meal remains lodged between our teeth. We have received an honor, and in response, we want to conduct ourselves appropriately.

Most of us will never be invited to the White House, be a guest of the royal family, or receive an Academy Award for a motion picture performance. However, *all* of us are of indescribable value to God, the Creator of the universe, the King of all Kings, the CEO of everything. Not a wealthy billionaire, not a popular celebrity, not a powerful politician, but the most wonderful being of all time and in all of creation loves *me* and all mankind. He places equal value on the one who may be enduring the penalty for the wrong he or she has done, *and* the one who may be sitting in the self-righteousness of what he hasn't done.

How important are we to Him? We are important enough for Him to come to earth in the human form of Jesus, His Son; important enough to die horribly to restore the fellowship with man that sin destroyed; important enough for Him to fully pay our debt to sin, which we could never pay; important enough to do what was necessary to satisfy His righteous demand against sin, so that sinful humanity might receive what was needed and not what was deserved.

Knowing we are important to someone of reputation can motivate and change us. Knowing we are important to the One whose name, character, and reputation are above all others *will* change us! Jesus was self-aware. He knew who he was. We need to be self-aware, to know who we are to *Him*. We need to know who we are *in* Him. His awareness guided His life and caused Him to finish well. Our awareness can do the same.

Jesus had the right attitude. He was also self-aware. Another quality of His life that guided His conduct and caused Him to finish well was this. *He avoided self-assertion.*

In Philippians 2:6-7, 11, we may see three examples of this truth. In the first part of verse 6, we learned Jesus is God. The last part of the same verse tells us He, "did not regard equality with God a thing to be grasped." In other words, He did not assert *His position.*

Jesus existed with God since before the world was made (John 1:1–2). He took part in creation (John 1:3). Through the centuries of the Old Testament, His presence was indicated on various occasions, a striking example being in Daniel 3:24–25. Then, "when the fullness of time came" (Galatians 4:4), it was time for the Savior to leave the pure and pristine environment of heaven. He entered our sin-beleaguered world, where He did not assert and demand His rights as God and refuse His dreadful mission. He did not assert His position in the heavenly realm. This attitude continued as He did not assert His position while in the earthly realm. Yes, Jesus told people on occasion that He was God, but they usually condemned Him for it. Nevertheless, He did not assert Himself in an effort to convince them with tirades and defensive speeches. He spoke the truth, and let people accept or reject the Truth.

His miracles also served the purpose of confirming His deity (John 5:36; 10:25), but when scoffers requested miracles for their own amusement under the guise of appeasing unbelief, He refused (Matthew 12:38–39). He never asserted, misused, or abused His position to prove who He was to skeptical and unbelieving men. Why? Quite simply, Jesus did not have to *prove* who He was because He *knew* who He was. He was God. He knew He was God. Therefore, He acted and spoke like God but never forced His position as God on anyone. He still doesn't.

Our world encourages individuals to seek position. Many do so with disregard for anyone around them. All too often, when people achieve that goal, they use and misuse their positions selfishly, spending much of life trying to prove who they are to everyone. The truth is that when I am trying to prove who I am to someone, the one I am actually trying to prove it to the most is probably me. You see, if I know who I am, I do not have to prove who I am. I can just be who I am and let others accept or reject me. We have already learned we are important to God, which helps us know who we are. He knows us through and through, so we certainly do not have anything to prove to Him.

In this life, we should work hard and strive to be our best in all things. But we never need to assert our position, real or imagined. Jesus practiced this principle, and He finished well. His influence remains to this day. If we follow His example, we will finish well also. Who knows what lasting influence we will leave?

Similarly, we learn in verse 7 that Jesus did not assert *His power*. Paul tells us that instead of "grasping" and demanding the rights of His position as God, He, "emptied Himself, taking the form of a bond-servant, and being made in the likeness of men."

Any Jewish readers who were familiar with the Old Testament law would understand the concept of a "bond-servant." The law of Moses stated that every seven years, slaves were to be set free. However, a slave could declare his love for his master and choose to remain with him. In that case, the slave was making the choice to remain with his master permanently as a "bond-slave" (Exodus 21:2–6). He loved his master more than he loved the idea of freedom and did not want to be separated from him.

As our Savior, Jesus loved sinful mankind more than His power and made the astonishing choice to accept the role of a bond-servant rather than be separated from His creation forever. To reach and redeem man, He would *become* a man.

> To bring me heaven, Jesus came to the earth
> To bring me eternal life, Jesus had human birth
> Wonder of wonders, the greatest miracle is this
> Jesus became what I am so I can be what He is.[1]

As we consider His choice, we must ask, did Jesus have power? Being the God of creation, He said, "Let there be," and a universe sprang into existence that still functions today. That is power. As the God of Israel, He brought plagues down upon her Egyptian captors until they were humiliated and forced to release the Hebrew nation. He parted the waters of a sea to help them on their way. That is power.

Much later, in the garden of Gethsemane, He said before His captors in Matthew 26:53, "Do you think that I cannot appeal to My Father, and He will at once put at My disposal more than twelve legions of angels?" The Roman soldiers present knew a legion was six thousand soldiers. "I can call seventy two thousand angels," is what Jesus said. Power!

When we consider that 2 Kings 19:35 tells us that "the angel of the Lord [one angel] went out and struck 185,000 in the camp of the Assyrians; and when the men rose early in the morning, behold all of them were dead," we see undoubtedly Jesus had power. He had personal power, and He had power at His disposal.

Instead of the role of the powerful, He chose the role of a servant in order to accomplish a greater plan, the salvation of a lost human race. As always, He set the example of His own words in Matthew's gospel, "whoever wishes to become great among you shall be your servant" (20:26). Jesus did not assert His power, and He is now the greatest influence in our world. He finished well.

As with position, we must not seek to assert some imagined power. Contrary to the world's way, we should follow His example of service. We may not achieve the temporary notoriety and status of this earth, but we will be considered eternally great in heaven's eyes. We will be reshaped, and we will finish well.

Third, as we learn from Paul about Christ's avoidance of self-assertion, Philippians 2:11 reminds us that by not asserting His position and power, He also did not assert *His prize*. What prize? "And that every tongue should confess that Jesus Christ is Lord, to the glory of God the Father."

This verse reminds us that everything in Jesus' earthly life was about glorifying God, not Himself. Before condescending to the earth, He had shared equally the prize of God's glory long before the world was made (John 17:5). Being equally God, glory was rightfully His. While fulfilling His mission on earth, however, He did not demand or assert His glory, just as He did not assert His position or power.

His lifelong priority of glorifying God was made clear to His disciples on the night before His death, when He told them, "Now is the Son of Man glorified, and God is glorified in Him" (John 13:31). In prayer to His Father that same night He said, "I have glorified Thee on the earth, having accomplished the work which Thou hast given Me to do" (John 17:4). His sole focus was to provide sinful mankind the way back to God, and He was that Way (John 14:6; Acts 4:12).

There are two reasons I want to consider as we try to explain how Jesus was able to "empty Himself" of His glory (Philippians 2:7 may also read "lay aside His privileges") for three and one-half trying years on earth. First, there is the obvious yet incomprehensible fact of His great love (John 3:16; 15:13), mercy (Luke 6:6; Hebrews 4:16), and grace (Ephesians 2:8; Romans 3:24), none of which we deserve. While I certainly do not want to minimize the importance of this first reason, for our purposes I want to move to the second for reasons of brevity and simplicity.

Jesus was able to temporarily forfeit His glory while on earth because He knew his eternal glory was waiting for Him when His mission was complete. The prize that was His was still His. It was just not His priority and demand while on the earth. He knew He would soon, "sit down at the right hand of the Majesty on high" (Hebrews 1:3), and He assured us all that one day He would be seen, "coming in clouds with great power and glory" (Mark 13:26; Luke 21:27). When He had the courage to repeat these words to His enemies, they were infuriated and demanded His death (Matthew 26:64–66).

John further tells us what He was allowed to see in heaven's throne room, when every created being will proclaim, "To Him who sits on the throne and to the Lamb, Be blessing and honor and glory and dominion forever." Jesus was able to avoid insisting on fleeting earthly glory because He knew a greater glory was to come: "For the joy that was set before Him He endured the cross… and has sat down at the right hand of the throne of God" (Hebrews 12:2). He gladly forfeited a lesser prize in light of the greatest prize.

This must also be the attitude of our hearts if our lives are to be reshaped and we are to finish well. However, this world seems to encourage "glory grabbing." We see it in business, we see it in families, and we even see it in the church. Our sinful human nature says "assert yourself," while Jesus' life and words say, "deny yourself" (Luke 9:23).

If we follow His example, we will live our lives to be admired by Christ rather than people, including ourselves. We will conduct ourselves according to *His* pleasure, which will result in our experiencing the greatest pleasure. We can do this knowing the glory we currently disregard will be shared with us when we join our Example in *His* glory. In praying for His disciples in John 17:22, Jesus said to the Father, "And the glory which Thou hast given Me I have given to them." If we know Christ, if we follow Christ, if we share the humility of Christ, we will share in the eternal glory of Christ!

Any glory prize we might assert in this life will be fleeting and unfulfilling at best. Neglecting this world's glory and living for God's alone is forever fulfilling. This is the Example to follow. This is the way to be remade. This is the way to finish well.

Let's review a moment. How did Jesus finish so well? He had the right *attitude,* He was self-*aware* and He avoided self-*assertion*. We've already been a while with this, but there is one more point to consider, and I hope you'll find it worth the time.

Jesus always took the right *action*. Said another way, He always did the right thing. Philippians 2:8 says, "He humbled Himself by becoming obedient to the point of death, even death on a cross."

Humanity's Creator desired to have a restored relationship with His sinful creation. The relationship was not destroyed by God; it was destroyed by man (Genesis 3). God did nothing wrong. *We* did wrong. In order for the relationship to be restored, we would have to be forgiven and made right in God's eyes. To accomplish this, there had to be a blood sacrifice, just as God instructed from the beginning (Leviticus 17:11; Hebrews 9:22). That sacrifice would have to be perfect and uncorrupted. An imperfect and sin-corrupted world could never meet that requirement, not through an animal or a person. The sacrifice had to come from a perfectly righteous environment. He would have to come from the environment of God.

Only Jesus could be that sacrifice, and He did not shrink from the opportunity. He willingly and deliberately took the action needed to save lost mankind. He took the *right action;* He did the right thing. Taking the right action was not easy for Christ. It would be the only time in His eternal existence that He would suffer indescribable ridicule, humiliation, pain, and grief. The right thing was not the easiest thing, but it was the *best* thing and accomplished the greatest good. It accomplished God's desire to provide forgiveness, salvation, and eternal life to sinful humanity, who had no hope otherwise.

If our concrete is to be reshaped, and if we are to finish well, we must follow His example by taking the right action in the choices of this life. Let's be honest, most of us know the right thing to do in most circumstances. But it is a fact of life that the right thing is rarely the easiest thing, especially in the areas of morality and integrity. Perhaps the right choice will require more effort. Perhaps the right choice will be less profitable from a worldly standpoint. In a fallen world, we can be assured the right thing will often be the least popular thing. Perhaps the right thing will just be less fun. In spite of all this, we must remember that right is always right, and only right can accomplish what is right. However popular, however profitable, however acceptable, however entertaining, doing wrong can never lead to right results.

On the other hand, while doing right may bring initial difficulty, it will ultimately bring about right results in us and many others. It will also honor the One who did right for us and will be honored by Him. When faced with the difficulty of being our Savior, Jesus took the position that said, "I'll do right if it kills Me," and it did. "Even death on a cross,"(Philippians 2:8) remember? But oh, just look at the wonderful results He accomplished. He rose again and was given a reputation above all others, and humankind is given the opportunity to spend eternity in heaven with Him.

So let us all first take the right action in following our Example, which will strengthen us to do right in all areas of life—a life that will one day end for each of us. We will die. If we live right, we will die right. If we live wrong, we will die wrong. May we follow His right example and be remade, and may we continue in that example until we finish well.

"Busting up the concrete" is a tall order. At least it is for me. How in the world are we to have any hope of success? How are we to practice this Example? The truth of the matter is that we have no hope of doing so unless His example leads us from the inside out. We will never be like Jesus by watching Jesus, reading about Jesus, or hearing about Jesus. He will never become the driving force *of* our lives until He is *in* our lives.

All of us have seen a doctor at some point and found we had some kind of infection. We were likely given a round of antibiotics with specific instructions as to how to ingest them. I am confident none of us took that medicine home, crushed it into a powder, and rubbed it on the outside of our body. That would accomplish no lasting good. It had to get inside of us if it was to deal with our problem.

If Jesus is to deal with our problems and help us reshape our lives, He will have to get inside of us. That's where our problem lies. He will come into us when invited, and then He will help remold the malformed concrete that haunts and hinders our lives.

Does He live in you? If not, invite Him in. Speak to Him right now, confessing your sinfulness and your need for His forgiveness. Give your life to Him that He may give His life to you. And then get ready. Much of your life is likely going to get much better!

CHAPTER 9

INVITATION TO THE WORLD

"Beep... beep... beep... beep." Did you hear that? You know what it is. It has become a telltale sound in recent years. You can identify its monotonous repetition even from inside your home. It might be the trash pickup, a school bus turning around, or a utility crew doing maintenance. Whatever the case, that sound is telling everyone to be aware that a vehicle of some size is backing up.

I have installed a similar device on this page. Do you hear it? There it is—"beep... beep... beep." Come on, work with me. That's right, we're backing up again. You've seen how our story began, and you are seeing how it has branched into many directions. As I share each of those, I need to return close to our beginning. But just as with that neighborhood vehicle, if you're attentive and careful, you'll have no problem.

You recall the man and his wife who invited me to accompany their mission team to Romania. When I eagerly accepted that invitation, there was obviously no way I could have foreseen the opportunities that would follow. The next morning, I immediately began developing a fund-raising letter to be sent to a few friends and family members. Before I had them ready to mail, my phone rang, and I recognized a familiar voice when I answered. It was Dr. Joe, a retired dentist I had known in our former church. I knew he had been organizing medical mission projects for several years. "I hear you are going to Romania with us," he said.

"Are you the one coordinating the trip?" I asked.

"Yes I am."

"I did not know that. This is a nice surprise. God willing, I am going. It will be nice to have a couple of familiar faces with us."

"Oh, there will be many familiar faces. Several people you know will be with us. Many of them go every year."

"Since you are the coordinator, I assume this is a medical mission."

"That's right," he said, "which brings me to one reason I called. I know Lynne is a dental hygienist. Is she still working?"

"Yes, but just two days a week. With my current situation, she has been looking to add more days so we can keep up with expenses."

"I know things may seem uncertain for you right now, but we want to invite Lynne to join you if there's any possibility you can manage it. We could use her skills in our dental clinics."

"I have no doubt that she would love it. But she is our only source of income at the moment, which is an obvious concern. Due to being part time, if she does not work, she does not get paid. Let us talk about it, and I will get back to you."

"Fair enough," Dr. Joe said. "Let me know as soon as you can, so we can include her in our travel arrangements."

Lynne happened to be working that day, so I delayed the completion of my fund-raising letter until we could make a decision. When she arrived home that afternoon, I immediately told her of the opportunity. "You know I'd love to do this," she said. "My dental experience is something I can contribute. The only problem right now is that you do not have an income, and I'm only working two days a week. I've asked for more days at the office, but that's not possible right now. I've posted my name on a network database to be called for fill-in hygiene jobs, but there are no guarantees with that." She then repeated the concern I had verbalized to Dr. Joe. "If I do not work, I do not get paid. Do you think it will be wise for me to be gone?"

"Would you *like* to go?"

"Absolutely."

"I know I'd love to have you with me," I assured her. "Why don't we tell Dr. Joe to plan on both of us. I'll include your costs in our letter, and we'll pray and see what God will do. If He is in this, it will work out. And it will be exciting to watch."

Lynne consented, and I adjusted the fund-raising letter accordingly. Within eight days of mailing the letters, we received the funds needed to cover the remaining half of my costs and all of Lynne's expenses. Most of the assistance arrived in the mail, but some donors actually came to our home to share their gifts personally and wish us well.

"Looks like you're supposed to go with us," I said to Lynne.

"I think so," she agreed. "But I still need some fill-in days. Our boss told us today that she is taking one week off during each month of the summer to be with her children. The office will also be closed another week in June for her vacation. If I miss two weeks to go to Romania, we basically will not have income in June."

"Not good," I admitted. "But your trip is covered. The Lord took care of that. Let's stay the course and see what happens."

Over the next few weeks, Lynne told me of the calls to do fill-in hygiene work on her off days. As our trip approached, we saw the Lord continue to meet our needs. Finally, one evening about ten days before our departure, Lynne and I were sitting in our den. She had her calendar on her lap, coordinating her work schedule, a sight that had become pretty common. After several minutes she looked up at me and said, "This is amazing. I have just calculated that with all the fill-in work I have done recently, I have *already* made more money than I could have if I had decided not to go to Romania!"

God had shared from His abundance to make it clear He wanted us both to have that experience. And as is often the case with our Lord, He would have more than just one reason for doing so.

As Lynne and I looked excitedly toward this new opportunity, we were not alone. Of course, there were the eighty or so team members we had been told about. But events had transpired that brought about the inclusion of some other special friends.

You recall Ted and Joyce (the Voice). Some months earlier, they had hosted in their home a young lady from Moldolva named Stela. She was in our city attending training courses that had to do with her occupation at home. Stela was not a believer, but she attended services with Ted and Joyce every Sunday. She was fluent in five languages, including English, and was as pleasant as she was attractive. Unfortunately, during her visit, she witnessed our difficulty, and I was concerned how the negative experience might impact an unbeliever. However, Ted and Joyce are mature and steadfast witnesses for Christ, and it became obvious their loving example before Stela would win the day. Before returning to Moldova, she expressed her desire to trust Christ as Savior. After the close of her final worship service with us, and being aware of the trial we were experiencing, she shook my hand, smiled sweetly, and said her good-bye. I'll always remember that she added with a smile, "You will be all right."

Ted and Joyce learned of our invitation to Romania, and they were also familiar with the project coordinator, Dr. Joe. In a casual conversation one day, Ted curiously asked, "I wonder where Romania is in proximity to Moldova?" He and Joyce reviewed their geography and found Moldova actually borders Romania on the northeast. Are you getting an idea where this is going? They began to investigate the possibility of accompanying us on our trip to Romania while simultaneously communicating with Stela. Dr. Joe told us our project would be based out of the Romanian city of Iasi, which Ted and Joyce discovered was just a few miles from Stela's home, across the border in Moldova! They arranged to join our team for the mission project, and Stela agreed to spend the week with us as a translator.

Ted, Joyce and I served as evangelists, sharing the gospel with everyone as they waited to see a doctor or dentist in one of our clinics. Stela, our new Moldovan friend and sister in Christ, sat at our side each day, helping to share God's plan of salvation that she herself had so recently received. Talk about the reinforcement of God's truth in a new convert!

In addition to renewing past acquaintances, we met many new people on the project. We were from a wide variety of churches and denominations, but served harmoniously as one, like the true church always does. I was able to speak in several churches and led morning devotionals at breakfast each day. Almost all our translators were Romanian teenagers learning English in school. Being a bit of a clown, I often hung with them in the back of our bus as we traveled to our clinic site each morning, instigating harmless mischief. The folks in the front of the bus often asked what was going on, but we shrugged our shoulders and feigned ignorance and innocence.

We ate breakfast and dinner at our hotel each day but provided our own lunches. In those days, airlines allowed heavier baggage, so the menu was extensive. Lots of peanut butter, jelly, crackers, canned meats, protein bars, candy—you name it. A group of us would gather under a tree or on park benches and open our feasts. Lunch often turned into a smorgasbord, as we shared our goodies with one another. We were also instructed to provide lunch for our translators, and it was interesting to watch the young Romanians curiously approach some of our prepackaged American delicacies. We soon learned to step into a nearby market in the mornings, where we found fresh bread, cheese, meats, and fruit. So much better for us and the Romanians.

Among our new Romanian friends were pastors who assisted in the project in various ways. Most of them could speak enough English to successfully communicate. We were grateful for their presence, as they sometimes served as buffers when attempts were made to thwart our work. Oppose a nice group of Americans providing free medical care? Oh yes, and many were surprised to see the source of the opposition.

The primary religion in Romania is the Orthodox Church. This group claims to be Christian, but like so many, it has become so dedicated to distracting church traditions that true Christian principles almost seem foreign. I will not label all Orthodox leaders with the same stereotype, but many are very intolerant toward evangelicals. Fortunately, not all of them outwardly opposed us. Most remained silent toward us while discouraging their people in regard to our mission. Our coming to each area was always publicized, and we learned that if the local priest was especially threatened by our presence, he would engage in advance efforts to sabotage our success. In some cases, there might be overt threatening action after we had arrived.

For example, one day during our first visit we had traveled almost an hour to a small town where our medical ministry was to take place. All over Romania, apartment complexes can be seen that were built under communism to aid in corralling and controlling the people. This area was no different. We arrived at one of these buildings, where part of the first floor had been converted into a children's day-care facility. It was not occupied during the summer, and the owner had generously offered its use for our clinic.

We prepared for the day as always—the check-in and triage areas, evangelism stations, doctors' and dental areas, glasses, pharmacy, children's activity area—and the morning went well. We took our lunch break and returned to work. All continued to progress smoothly.

However, about mid-afternoon, a plainly dressed middle aged man grew increasingly agitated as he stood near our check-in area. He became impossible to ignore, and though we could not understand his language, we knew he was becoming unhappier by the second. The anger and volume of his voice continued to grow as he shook fist and finger in our direction. By this time, the work on the outside of the building came to a standstill. Those serving inside with the doctors and dentists continued, unaware of the commotion. The instigator soon had children gathering around him, joining in his tirade. Suddenly the man hurled something at one of our young Romanian translators. It turned out to be a New Testament we had given to a new convert. He had confiscated it and ripped it down the middle.

No physical harm was inflicted, but we knew the situation was getting more serious when one of the children was incited to throw a rock in our direction. At that point, one of our Romanian pastors began to show noticeable concern and instructed those of us outside to make our way to the bus. "He is trying to cause a riot," he said. "He is an Orthodox priest and does not want us here. The police have been called. You must go to the bus, and close yourselves in!"

"What about those inside the building?" I asked. "My wife is in there!"

"I will tell them we must stop the clinic and leave. I will help them to the bus. When the priest sees us leaving, he will probably become calmer." Please do as I say."

Though we had met every requirement to operate a clinic in the community, our pastor-friend knew the religious troublemaker could succeed in disrupting our efforts. He was right. I and many others waited on the enclosed bus as we watched our remaining Romanian friends inform those indoors it was time to leave.

By this time, more local citizens had gathered, and many joined in the threatening tone of their predecessors. At the moment, there were no more signs of physical danger, but the anger in their voices remained heated. Inside the bus was also heated from the summer sun.

Lynne appeared in the doorway and exited the building. By the look on her face and the casual way in which she walked toward the bus, I wondered if she was still unaware of the situation. There was the crowd of locals on each side, still loud and demonstrative. Then there was Lynne, my sweet wife, strolling confidently, smiling and waving like the high school Christmas ball queen and girl's marching squad captain of years past. Don't get me wrong, my wife *is* a fairly calm sort. But I recall thinking—no, I actually said, "Does she not know what is going on? Get on this bus, girl!"

As Lynne boarded the bus, we found she indeed did not know why we were leaving our assignment early. "The pastor just came in and told us to pack up to leave," she said calmly, unshaken by our explanation of the events that prompted our hasty departure. Fortunately, that was the most intense example of open opposition to our efforts that I can recall.

Though not as threatening, there was another instance when the advance efforts of an Orthodox priest to sabotage our ministry became obvious. It was our final day of clinics, again in an area that was some distance from our hotel. It was common for us to have a steady stream of people coming to the clinics each day, but we noticed on this Friday the participation was very low. At some points, it was nonexistent. By the afternoon, there were practically no patients checking in, and we questioned our Romanian hosts as to a possible cause. One translator responded, "I asked some of the people this morning why so few are coming. They said that when the local priest learned of our clinic, he went about the community, warning people not to participate. He told them if they did, he would not perform weddings for their children; he would not be involved in their burials, or conduct other priestly services that are so important to the people." The priest had been effective in his selfish intimidation of the community, while being totally unconcerned for their physical needs.

We were left with time on our hands, a situation that will eventually move me to look for productive activity. It just so happened we were holding the clinic at the site of a new church facility, but the construction was not quite complete. The future sanctuary still had a dirt floor and was filled with scrap lumber and other supplies. An adjoining wing had a finished fellowship hall and a couple of smaller rooms. It also housed a bathroom, but the fixtures were not installed, so no water was available. Behind the building was the temporary restroom, an outhouse.

These little pleasure palaces are a common site, especially in rural Romania, and I and others have been forced to use them more than we would like to remember. I especially enjoy the looks on the faces of our proper American women as they enter and exit the experience. Commenting about the disturbing fragrance is surely unnecessary, but it came as a surprise to me to learn of the insects that eagerly embraced this environment. I do not mean the flies. I expected them to show up. It was the bees. I had always thought they are drawn only to sweet surroundings, so I must have missed part of a science class along the way. This bunch was reveling in an atmosphere that was anything but sweet. But there they were, a lot of them, swarming busily and enthusiastically. Needless to say, the experience was to be approached with care, realizing that not only would the nostrils suffer a biting penetration, but there was also the potential of the sting of a zealous bee. Having used this type of facility more than once, I came to the conclusion that maybe God had sent the bees to distract me from the smell.

There was one other concern that entered my mind in regard to our winged outhouse attendants. These are the creatures that give us honey. When I picture a honeybee drawing nectar from some aromatic bloom and transforming it into honey for human consumption, it is almost always a pleasantly appealing image. But the thought of these little creatures producing honey from the by-product of human digestion is another matter.

I was relieved to learn years later from a beekeeper that honeybees are never attracted to an environment of waste, so these were either yellow jackets or another species of bee. No doubt you entomologists out there are rolling your eyes at me right now, but hey, we all have to learn. And that also does not change the fact these relatives of the honeybee could have inflicted the same unpleasant pain.

As I further describe our facility, we found it featured another common shortcoming. There was no seat. There was only a hole in the floor that opened into the gates of hell. Since this was not an unusual sight in Romania, I knew the locals must have been adept at handling the situation. But I shuddered at the thought of my fellow Americans and I having our sense of balance so tested on inexperienced leg muscles. "Wow, this place needs a seat," I told our team. "There's lumber inside the building. If we can find some tools, I'm going to build one."

"How do you know they want one?" one of the women asked.

"I don't, but maybe they don't *know* they want one," I said. "Once they have it, they might be excited over the newly discovered luxury. And besides that, wouldn't *you* like to have one, if only for today?"

"Now that you put it that way, yes. And if the people here decide they don't like it, they can always remove it."

"I like the way you think. And I'll tell you what. We'll ask our translators if the people like it. If not, we'll remove it before we leave. Besides, the indoor bathroom will be finished soon, and this will be a step toward their new life of comfort."

In the unfinished sanctuary we found the necessary lumber, all old and rough. We were also fortunate to find a greatly used hammer, some crooked rusty nails, and a very dull bow saw. If you know tools, you know a bow saw is not designed for the job I was undertaking, but it would have to do. The accuracy of the work would also be hindered by the fact we found no measuring device. So I found a square of cardboard to mark as a cutting guide and asked everyone to undergird me in prayer as I entered the odiferous realm.

Once inside, reality returned as I found I would have to be into a seated position to effectively get the measurements I needed. *What was I thinking?* I wondered as I sat on the floor, with my legs hanging into the unknown. Changing my mind would result in losing face, so I quickly made the necessary marks and emerged from the suffocating enclosure. After straightening the old nails as best we could, we installed the support rails on each side wall. I was fortunately able to make the measurements for the bench seat without sitting. Soon we were standing there, looking at what was quite possibly the most luxurious outhouse in that community.

In the next few moments, I think all our team and translators stepped by to look upon the accomplishment. There were no "o-o-o's" or "ahs" but there was ample laughter. I'm not sure if it was for pleasure or because they could not believe someone would commit to such a task merely to relieve boredom. I didn't really care which. All I knew was that I had set a goal and achieved it. And I was convinced that a small difficulty of Romanian life had been eliminated, at least for the patrons of this particular outhouse. And yes, it did get used before we left, and no, there was no request to remove it. The roughness of the lumber seat was a concern, but when we considered the equal roughness of their Romanian tissue paper, we figured it to be a toss-up as to which would cause the most discomfort.

Despite the occasional opposition, much good was achieved during this project. My wife and I and other friends were exposed to new and valuable opportunities that began ministry involvement that continues to this day. In just five days of medical clinics, hundreds of people were seen and treated by doctors and dentists. In this setting, medical treatment is limited to short-term needs that can be addressed with antibiotics, pain relievers, vitamins, topical applications, and bandages.

Dental service is restricted to the extraction of teeth, since a full-care clinic is not realistic. There has been more than one occasion when watching the dentists hover over patients all day, wrestling with stubborn extractions, I have thought, *Oh my aching back!* Nevertheless, I have noticed through the years that once these medical professionals become involved in this type of ministry, most return year after year to serve again.

During the week many responded to our evangelists by indicating a desire to trust Christ. To be sure, one must wonder about the sincerity of such a response in the face of free medical care, but our responsibility was to present the message of salvation as best we could and allow God to deal in their hearts.

We made new friends, both American and Romanian. There was Pastor Viorel, who is known as Vio. He was the one who took charge of the threatening situation created by the angry priest. I have not seen him in several years, but Vio was a physically large man, full of energy and enthusiasm for all he does.

We enjoyed sitting with him at mealtime and hearing of his work in the area of beginning new churches. He told us of a new church being developed in a town called Rupea, and invited us to return in the future and join in ministry with him there. Since our ministry was still very early in the development stage, we were always alert to new opportunities that would grow out of existing experiences. Ted, Joyce, Lynne, and I began to converse about the possibility. We knew the medical project would again be available the next year, so we began to brainstorm how we might combine the two.

One of our new American friends was Kevin. Like so many of our new acquaintances of recent years, he remains a dear friend and partner in ministry. He is a career army reservist, which has taken him to tours of duty in both Iraq and Afghanistan. His primary focus in life is a faith-based ministry much like our own, and he is very enthusiastic in his service to the Lord. His personality is jovial, positive, and contagious. He and I immediately enjoyed our new relationship. For several years, Kevin had served as the "front man" for Dr. Joe, going into a country and doing advance coordination with pastors and community leaders. He treats no one like a stranger, which means he will talk to anyone about his faith in Christ not long after meeting them.

The extent of Kevin's ministry was not limited to his assistance in the medical projects, as we would soon see. We shared common priorities, and he began to share with Ted and me plans for future opportunities in which he wanted to include us.

He specifically shared that he was to return to Romania in about six months, serving with Crossfire Ministries out of nearby Asheville, North Carolina. This impressive and successful ministry uses the sport of basketball to reach people in the United States and countries around the world. "We will be bringing men's and women's teams who have had college-level experience to compete with high school, college, and community teams here in Romania. At halftime, we share the gospel with the entire audience. We'd love to have you guys with us."

"I won't speak for Ted," I said, "but I'm not sure I can be much help. I haven't touched a basketball in years, and I never played in high school or college. If you get me on the court, you'd better have a medical professional handy."

"Oh we have the basketball players. What we need you to do is sing during halftime. And both of you can help share the gospel with spectators at the games. You could also serve as a team pastor, Jeff. I've heard your morning devotions, and I think you would have some things to say to our team. Maybe we could have you start each day with a breakfast Bible study."

The interest of both Ted and me was quickly piqued. But return to Romania so soon? At this point, our ministry was literally weeks old. Though we had seen indication of God's gracious provision, we were understandably guarded in being quick to commit ourselves. His question was impossible to answer immediately, but we assured Kevin we were open to the idea and would communicate our intentions as soon as possible.

The first overseas experience of our new ministry came to an end. However, the door was wide open to future service, and we were ready to be involved in whatever God had in store. And that's a good thing because we were going to find—just as you are going to find—things were going to get even better!

Romania Medical mission team

CHAPTER 10

A VOICE FROM THE PAST

As always, the weeks and months following that first experience in Romania raced by as we responded to increasing ministry opportunities at home. Relationships were developing with Romanian believers, and we were already looking forward to serving alongside Pastor Vio at the new church start in Rupea a year later. We decided I would participate again with the medical project, and our ministry team would join me afterward.

Ted and I had also not forgotten the possibility of returning with Kevin and the Crossfire ministry in just six months. God continued to prove Himself faithfully generous toward our young ministry. So I practiced the same decision-making criteria as previously described—the calendar is clear, I have the abilities necessary to meet the need, and God has provided for the expense. By late summer, Ted and I committed ourselves to join Kevin and the Crossfire team for their mission, which would begin the day after Thanksgiving.

Weekly church services continued at Wilora Lake Lodge, activities were in full swing at the Little Flower and the Cove, and we had reorganized our prison ministry singers to prepare for the upcoming Christmas season. As you might imagine, before we knew it, the week of our return to Romania was upon us.

From the beginning of our new ministry, I made it a habit of calling my mother the night before I left on a trip. As you know, she had been in ministry for several decades. However, she was never thrilled to see her youngest getting on those "outdated airplanes and wandering all over the world." At least she never admitted being thrilled about it. I made the call as usual, but before I describe the course of our conversation, I need to share some family history that will give insight into our exchange and the events that follow.

You already know my father was in the US Air Force. From 1959 until 1962, we were stationed in Chateauroux, France. I was not quite five years of age when we moved there. However, my memories of our time there are clear and detailed. Not long after our arrival in Chateauroux, my parents joined with other Baptist air force personnel and formed the First Baptist Church. Not surprisingly, it had a modest beginning. We met in a house that had been recently vacated by the air force chaplain. I will share very exciting information later about more renewed connections with this experience, but for now, I simply point out it is the earliest memories I have of a church life.

I recall leaving our base home on Sundays and driving into town in our 1956 Pontiac. I remember the short walk from our car down the cobblestone street to the church entrance. Inside was an L-shaped room, transformed from the first-floor living area into a sanctuary for worship. It could not have held many people, but as a small child, it seemed plenty big to me. It was where I first recall learning the hymns of the faith and hearing sermons that began to impact my young life. It was also at that church where, at age seven, I realized the need for a Savior and placed my trust in Jesus Christ.

On occasion, the church hosted guest preachers. They often had a foreign accent, and to this young and inexperienced child, that meant they must have all been French. One of these was an energetic speaker who visited us about twice each year. I remembered him simply as Monsieur Hodoroaba. One Sunday evening, he spoke about Moses and the burning bush from Exodus chapter 3. I primarily recall him telling all of us to be, "a burning bush for Jesus Christ."

As is usually the case in a Baptist church, at the close of the service there was the opportunity for public decisions to be made for Christ. A friend of mine stepped forward and trusted Christ as Savior just as I had done some weeks earlier. As he expressed his joy over the boy's decision, Monsieur Hodoroaba closed the service by declaring, "We are all now burning bushes!" Though quite young, I never forgot that comment. One might wonder why.

I now return to the conversation with my mom, forty years after our return stateside. After sharing about our Thanksgiving holiday, I expected to spend a few minutes patiently listening to her comment on my new life of "dangerous" travel. Instead, she asked a question that would lead to the fascinating adventure I am about to reveal. "Son, do you remember Monsieur Hodoroaba in France?" she asked.

"I sure do. I remember him preaching about Moses and the burning bush. He told us to be burning bushes for Jesus Christ. I'm not sure why I've remembered that all these years, but I have."

"Well he was not from France. He was actually from Romania. He would get Bibles and Christian literature to smuggle back into Romania, which was still under communist rule at that time."

"Now that I did not know."

"When you go to Romania, ask the pastors you meet if they know Jeremiah Hodoroaba. He will be an old man by now, if he is still alive."

"I will do that. Won't it be something if I can find him!" We talked awhile longer and then said our good-byes, with my promise to pursue the assignment and bring news immediately upon my return. *Wow, I cannot wait to see what may come of this,* I thought.

Our team arrived in Bucharest on Saturday afternoon, my second time in six months. We immediately boarded vans under the leadership of Pastor Vio, who was also hosting this effort. We made the very long, late, and cold drive to our base city of Constanta, on the Black Sea. On Sunday morning, the team was divided into two groups, and each was sent to a nearby church to participate in services.

As we rode on our small bus, a Romanian pastor accompanying our group was in the seat in front of mine. His English skills were more than adequate to handle conversation. Soon into our exchange, I began my inquest. "Please tell me," I began, "are you familiar with a Jeremiah Hodoroaba?"

His eyes immediately grew large with surprise and curiosity. "Hodoroaba," he said, "yes, we all know Hodoroaba. How do you know of him?"

I shared the history you now know and how I was hoping to possibly have contact with the preacher from my past. "Is he still alive?" I asked.

"No, he died two years ago."

I was understandably disappointed at the news but not at all discouraged. I would continue my quest to discover any information possible to satisfy my own curiosity, and to bring home to Mom. I would not be frustrated. During the course of our stay, whenever we visited another church, whenever we played a school basketball team, or during any event when a new pastor was with us, I repeated my question, "Do you know of Jeremiah Hodoroaba?"

The reaction was also repeated. With common excitement and enthusiasm that almost bordered on adoration, I would hear, "Hodoroaba! Yes, I know Hodoroaba!" Additional comments were added, such as, "We owe everything to Hodoroaba. He helped to keep true Christianity alive in our country during the years of communist dictatorship. He saw that many received copies of the Word of God. He wrote Christian articles, which were printed in his basement and then distributed. He also had a radio station in his basement from which he would teach the Bible and share the gospel. All of these things he did at the risk of terrible persecution at the hands of the communists."

I further learned this Romanian hero of the faith often had his door kicked open by the authorities and was taken to jail. I learned communist laws would not allow someone of his practice to be executed, but apparently they tolerated just about any other treatment. For instance, there were occasions when his captors tormented him by placing a bed of gravel on the floor of his cell, then forcing him to kneel as if praying. He was typically coerced to remain there until his bare knees were bleeding and bruised. Somehow, he survived it all, and his resolve was not diminished in the slightest.

The more I learned of this man, the more I realized the unknown privilege that had been mine to sit as a child under his enthusiastic yet gentle exhortation. I also began to realize God caused me to remember his words for over forty years. He had truly been a "burning bush" under the harshest of circumstances, so he was qualified to encourage us all to do the same on that night so long ago. And while all of this was exciting and revealing, it was not all there would be to the Hodoroaba experience. There is more. Boy, is there more!

Though Pastor Vio was our host on the current project, and though we had plans to return to work with him the following summer, we had not spent much time together. Consequently, I also had not yet questioned him about Jeremiah Hodoroaba. In fact, it was the day before we were to return home when the subject was finally broached. We were making our way back to Bucharest, and Vio had invited me to ride with him so we could discuss the plans for our next mission project. Somewhere along the snowy and icy drive, I revealed I had known the iconic Romanian Christian. Vio's shocked reaction was so abrupt it seemed he would take the car into a skid. After quickly regaining composure, he began to inquire of the circumstances behind my knowledge. I gladly shared the details for the umpteenth time and added, "I was hoping to possibly make contact with him, but I understand he died."

I ask you now to read carefully.

"Yes, he died not long ago," Vio agreed, "but he has a nephew. His name is Cristian Hodoroaba. He is known as Cristi. He and his wife run a children's camp each week during the summer outside the town of Fagaras. It is less than an hour from where we will be next summer. When you come, if you wish, I will take you to meet him!"

"I absolutely wish," I assured him, as my anticipation of the opportunity immediately took flight. Though I had no idea at the time what form it would take, I began to sense the Hodoroaba adventure was just beginning.

Six months came and went, and we found ourselves in Romania once again, this time with a team of musicians, children's leaders, and a small construction crew. As expected, we traveled to the very quaint community of Rupea, in the Transylvanian hill country. It was one of those places that make you feel like you've stepped into a simpler past. There were even the ruins of a centuries-old castle keeping silent vigil on a hill above the town.

We led children's Bible school activities in the morning, while the construction crew began adding a second-floor apartment for the new young pastor and his wife. After lunch, others of our team joined in the construction work, while some visited homes, sharing the gospel and inviting people to attend the nightly services that featured our music team and my Bible messages.

Just a few days into the week, Pastor Vio informed me he had contacted Cristi Hodoroaba and told him of the American visitor who knew his uncle and wanted to meet him. "He is to call me tomorrow to let me know when we may visit," Vio said. Cristi did call the next day, but it was to tell Vio that he preferred to drive to Rupea that evening, visit briefly after our service, and then return home. I eagerly awaited his arrival as our day progressed until he finally appeared at the rear of the small sanctuary at the close of our service.

He was a young thirty-something with thick, dark hair and an equally thick mustache. He had dark, sometimes piercing eyes that explored the room until they ultimately fell on me. His expression revealed he had discovered the one who had such intrusive interest in him. I recall he did not seem to share the same level of curiosity in return.

Following the service, we were introduced. I began to tell the story that resulted in my desire to meet the nephew of a great man who made an impact on a seven-year-old boy. Cristi was acceptably polite but not at all enthusiastic. He spoke fluent English but had little to say about his uncle. I began to feel his visit was little more than a courtesy and probably a bit of an inconvenience. I don't remember the full content of our abbreviated conversation, but I do recall it was not the mutually exciting encounter I anticipated. After little more than courteous platitudes, we bade each other a mannerly farewell.

As he drove away, I remember thinking, *Is that it? That is the extent of a meeting that was over forty years in the making?* It seemed as if that was the end of that, and I admit being disappointedly baffled. But as you will see, it was not the end of that. Unbeknown to me, God had more to prepare before the fulfillment of a plan. Without regard toward any further Hodoroaba experiences, we decided at the close of our Rupea project that we needed to return again the next year to continue the work we had begun. It was the summer of 2003.

Fast-forward one year, summer 2004.

Good progress had been made on the apartment over the year, and we went to work toward its completion. We also resumed morning activities with the children and the evening services of music and preaching. I had not pressed Pastor Vio to pursue further contact with Cristi Hodoroaba, so I assumed we would be singularly focused on the ministry in Rupea. However, early in our week, I was surprised when Vio told me we had been invited to bring the entire team to Fagaras the next afternoon. Cristi and his wife, Daniela, wanted us to stop at their home and then make the twenty-minute drive to the site of their camp, which they called Camp Bit of Heaven.

Our team arrived the next day as scheduled. We were welcomed with cold drinks and ice cream. Cristi and Daniela had three lovely children who were understandably timid but very polite and accommodating. After introductions and some small talk, we boarded our vehicles for the ride to the camp. Cristi invited me to join him in his van, which I gladly did. I was pleased to find our conversation was much more engaging than the year before. I encouraged him to tell me of the camp and their ministry there. He did so cheerfully as we passed by abandoned factories and through several villages.

The town of Fagaras seemed decades behind our American environment, and each village we entered took us even farther back in Romanian time. I could see the foothills of the Carpathian Mountains drawing closer. After passing through one last village, the roughly paved road turned to gravel.

We finally turned off of the road and approached the edge of a wooded area. *Where are we going?* I wondered but soon saw we were approaching a beautiful mountain stream and the narrowest bridge I had ever seen. Cristi brought the van to a crawl. *There is no way we can fit on this bridge,* I worried, but I kept my thoughts to myself. He slowly proceeded onto the structure as I quietly held my breath. There was barely an inch of space between the outside rearview mirrors and the guardrails, but I could tell Cristi was adequately experienced to deliver us safely across. He informed me he and his colleagues built the bridge out of the flatbed trailer of a large cargo truck and homemade concrete pylons. I would soon learn of further examples of their simplistic and resourceful ingenuity.

We stopped at the gate that guarded Camp Bit of Heaven. Tudor the caretaker was waiting to welcome our caravan of three vehicles. It was a simple place and not at all what I would have expected in a children's camp that was actually in use. Almost nothing about the facility was finished. The rough structure we saw in one direction was the cooking and meal area, and separate boys' and girls' outhouses were nearby (complete with flies and some kind of bees). Between those were two one-room cabins, one for Tudor and the other for Cristi and his family while camps were in session.

Opposite these structures was the main camp building. It had a basement and three floors, and was glaringly incomplete. Though the roof was finished and offered some protection from the elements, most windows were covered with old canvas or shredding plastic. Gesturing toward the main building, Cristi explained, "One day this will be where we will hold all activities. We have been working on it for several years, as we have had the money to do so. But as you can see, it is far from finished."

He went on to inform us that until this summer, children slept in tents, using the outhouses and having meals in the temporary kitchen area. However, the second floor of the main building had been prepared enough to allow the children to sleep in bunk beds. As you might imagine, the guidelines regarding the legal occupancy of a building must have been different in Romania than in the United States.

We left our vehicles and made initial glances around the very plain and unequipped campground. We followed Cristi as he motioned for us to enter the building. Rough concrete steps ascended to the main doorway, which was covered by a worn piece of canvas. Inside was the large main room that was to be used for dining and activities. The concrete floor was also rough and unfinished, as we would find to be the case wherever concrete was used.

We continued across the room into a hallway that accessed the rest of the building. On both sides were bare and unfinished rooms. These included a future food preparation area, dishwashing area, food storage and refrigeration, storage closets, and a room that would sleep two. Across from this room, which was just inside the rear entrance to the building, were the future bath facilities for boys. No room had flooring, fixtures, or tile—nothing.

We descended a set of rough concrete steps to the basement. There were several rooms that would each have a future use, but like the area above, nothing was near completion, and the floor was dirt. There were some construction materials stored there, as well as some items that were used in camp recreation. In one corner of the basement was a large hole in the ground. Cristi told us it would house the pump that would eventually supply the building with water from a well that had already been dug.

We returned to the first floor and the unfinished concrete staircase to the second story. Without guardrail or banister, we carefully made our way to the next floor, where we found the future girls' bath facilities, a smaller unfinished room for sleeping, and finally the two larger sleeping areas. The latter were the areas used when camps were in session. They featured rough wooden floors, crude bunk beds, and wires hanging from the ceilings with light bulbs on the end. As I recall, these were the only areas furnished with electricity.

At the opposite end of this floor was an opening to a covered porch, which had a very wobbly and—we were happy to find—temporary staircase leading to another large outdoor terrace on the first level. We passed on the opportunity to walk on those steps, as we still had the third and final floor to visit.

We returned to the staircase area and proceeded up the unguarded wooden steps to the top floor. Except for the hallway, there were no completed floors in the rooms on each side, so we could see into the sleeping areas below that we had just visited. At the top of the steps was a room that would be a single bath, and the rooms on each side of the hallway would be future sleeping areas, primarily for camp staff. At the far end of this floor was an A-framed meeting room, which was illuminated by full windows that revealed a view of the mountains.

We asked questions throughout our tour, and Cristi answered as best he could. He and Daniela had a great vision to influence children for Jesus Christ, as well as a great plan for the use of the Camp facility. "We dream of the day the building is complete," Cristi said, "but we know that this will take a very long time. That is why we have not waited to hold the summer camps. One day we will use this building, but we want to teach children now."

We made our way back to the lower porch, where cold drinks were waiting. Cristi accompanied me as I walked around the building to get some pictures. As we stood looking at the monumental task remaining, I told him, "Cristi, over forty years ago, in a little church in Chateauroux, France, I heard your uncle Jeremiah say, 'Be a burning bush for Jesus Christ.' I have never forgotten his words, and now I understand why. You and I are not here by accident. I believe God has brought us together. I want to ask you a question. How much do you think it will cost to complete the construction of this building?"

"We estimate that it will take fifty thousand US dollars," he said.

"I'm not a builder or a contractor," I said, "but I think it will take every bit of that. Cristi, we are a very small ministry, only two years old. We have never had fifty thousand dollars. But God does. I cannot definitely say what He wants to do, but I am going to pray for His guidance and provision. If He will give us the money and if you will agree, I would like to organize a project for next summer to help you finish Camp Bit of Heaven. There are four floors. I would like to bring four teams, one team a week, and do as much work as we can. I will stay the entire month of the project. I know this would require a lot of effort from you and Daniela, and I do not want to presume upon you. Is this something you would be willing to do?"

"Yes, of course," Cristi answered.

His answer lacked the enthusiasm I would have expected. It was almost as if he was just being polite, and I was reminded of our first meeting a year earlier. "All right then," I said. "I'll pray, and I'll stay in touch with you about it. Okay?"

"That is fine."

We gathered our group and returned to our mission in Rupea. Though still a bit mystified at Cristi's emotionless reaction, I was already motivated toward our possible return to Romania in 2005. I began to pray each morning and sensed in my spirit that it was going to be a reality. It was more than just a sensation. Somehow I knew.

Less than a week later, we returned to our Charlotte home on Monday night. Our daughter had left my phone messages on my desk. I decided to unpack, get a good night's sleep, and spend the next morning catching up on ministry issues. After lunch I would return calls.

As I worked my way through the stack, I came upon a message from a friend in Florida, who was working in real estate development. To protect his anonymity, I will call him Wade. We had been longtime friends when he and his family were a part of our church in Charlotte. About a month before our Romania trip he asked me to pray for success in the upcoming opening of a land development.

More than ten years prior, he came to me with concerns about his family's financial situation. As I normally do when discussing such matters, I asked him about his stewardship habits in regard to direction we are given in the Scriptures. He confessed that due to his financial circumstances, he was not doing anything. Not tithing, not giving in any way.

I recall admonishing him, "Wade, God has promised that if we'll give, it will be given to us. God told His people in the Old Testament that if they would obey Him in the practice of the tithe, He would 'open the windows of heaven and pour out blessings that they would not be able to receive.' He also promised to 'rebuke' that which drains and destroys our resources (Malachi 3:10–11). Sure, some Christians try to say that tithing is not a New Testament principle and, thereby, justify a lack of generosity. But nowhere does Christ or the apostles dismiss the practice. In fact, the first believers did not stop at 10 percent. They 'sold all they had and laid the proceeds at the apostles' feet to be distributed as everyone had need'" (Acts 4:34–35).

I continued. "I want to challenge you to do something. When you get your next paycheck, inadequate as it may seem, I want you to immediately, without thinking, take 10 percent off the top and give it to the Lord."

"That will be tough," he answered. "I already know it is spoken for in monthly expenses."

"I'm sure it is. But taking care of things yourself is not working. You have to give God's way a chance to work for you, or your situation is not going to improve. Do this, take that 10 percent, put it in an envelope for your church or some ministry, and as you do, tell the Lord, 'I want to obey and please You more than I want to make a house payment, more than I want electricity, more than I want to drive a car, more than I want to eat.' Then see what God will do. I believe God responds to that kind of genuine faith and love toward Him. In fact, it is interesting that while the Bible says we are not to 'test' God (Deuteronomy 6:16; Matthew 4:7), He tells us in Malachi to 'test Me now in this.' God knows money is such a sensitive issue for all of us, yet it is the only area where He says for us to test Him and prove Him to be true or false. What you have here is an opportunity to let God show you what He will do in the area of your finances. His Word is clear. The next step is your obedience and faith."

"Okay, I'll try it—with my very next paycheck. And by the way, my wife will be glad to hear this. She's been trying to tell me this all along."

"Great. Then she won't be a hindrance. Let's get together again in a few weeks to see how things are going."

Things did improve for Wade and his family. Until I returned this phone call over ten years later, little did I know just how much. Wade answered, and we exchanged our hellos. Then he asked, "Do you remember the opening I asked you to pray about with me?"

"I do. I prayed for you every morning while I was in Romania."

"Well, we had it one Saturday while you were gone. We sold every lot we had in the first six hours, and our company made over 41 million dollars! I had to call and tell you."

"I'm glad you did, Wade. Congratulations. I'm happy for your success."

"There is another reason I called," he said. "I remember the advice you gave me that morning years ago about obeying God in my giving. Ever since that day I have done what we discussed. I have given to God first, and He has faithfully taken care of us. I want to let you know that those of us involved in the company will be paid our commissions over the next year, and I want to give to your ministry out of mine. So during the next year, I plan to send you between fifty and seventy thousand dollars!"

Though I was confident God would do something since our visit to Camp Bit of Heaven, I was taken aback. Here I was, just a week after my conversation with Cristi Hodoroaba and less than twenty four hours after returning home, and the provision was apparently being dropped in my lap. As I hung up the phone, Lynne could tell my conversation was unusual. She asked, "What was that all about?"

"That was the money for Cristi's camp." I told her the details of the conversation with Wade. Over the next year, he was better than his word, as he sent our ministry seventy-five thousand dollars. After we received the first portion two months later, I contacted Cristi. We put our four-week project on the calendar for late May and most of June 2005.

Since the finances so expeditiously appeared, I boyishly considered it a foregone conclusion that the necessary laborers would as well, and I was not disappointed. By late fall, we had full teams for each week from the nearby towns of Mint Hill and Weddington, the First Baptist Church of Charlotte, and Conway, Arkansas. There were also a handful of team members who joined us from other locations.

Fast-forward once more to 2005.

On the Friday before Memorial Day, I made my way to the Charlotte airport with the first of four construction teams. The previous ten months were spent communicating with Cristi, planning for tools and supplies, sending weekly e-mails, holding team orientation meetings, and coordinating travel for over forty people. We made the overnight flight to Germany and then on to Bucharest. Cristi met our noon arrival, and we loaded our belongings in a small bus for the four-hour drive to his home in Fagaras. Since there were still no functional bath facilities at the camp, the teams would have meals and lodging in the Hodoroaba home and travel each day to work.

Any women reading this must agree Daniela Hodoroaba has to be some kind of saint to be willing to host ten or more people in her home each week for four weeks! A saint she is, and so much more. Her meals were incomparable in quality and bounty. She and her sweet mother were untiring in retrieving fresh fruits and vegetables from their own garden. We watched as the evidence of each feast was cleaned away, only to see them begin the preparation for the next. We packed lunches to take to our worksite and quickly learned to anticipate the repast that awaited us at the close of each day.

There was the expected variety of work to be done at the camp. Due to the lack of tools, quality of the supplies, or simply the Romanian culture, progress would not be characterized by the blinding pace to which Americans are accustomed. Much of the paint did not come ready mixed, there was no premixed joint compound for the drywall, and most of the lumber was from the local sawmill and needed to be planed. When we discovered a crucial need, we contacted the captain of the next scheduled team from America and ask him to fill our order, if at all possible.

You'll recall there was no water supply inside the building, so we made constant trips to the temporary set of faucets located near the outhouses. These were fed by a large tank on the first-level terrace that collected rainwater. All in all, our team members worked well together and chose to enjoy the required adaptations to a different way of life. We were even lighthearted in our reluctant approach to the outhouses, grateful we would at least end each day with indoor bath facilities on our return to the Hodoroaba home.

I was relieved to see the four-week project was going quite smoothly. Each week the team would arrive on Saturday, sleep in a bit on Sunday morning, and hold a team worship service in the Hodoroaba home. On Sunday afternoon, we visited the camp facility to acquaint the new team with the work to be done. On Sunday evening, we attended the worship service at Betani (Bethany) Baptist Church, where the Hodoroabas are members. We were always invited to have team members share testimonies and sing, and I usually gave a Bible message. The people of this church and their pastor, Petru Groza, have become very dear to us.

Each team then worked Monday through Friday morning, and then spent Friday afternoon shopping and preparing for the late-night drive back to the Bucharest airport. The return flight was at 7:00 a.m. on Saturday, which required a 4:00 check-in. So every Friday of our project, we departed Fagaras at midnight and drove the grueling four hours. Most of the team would drift in and out of sleep, but I sat in the front to keep the driver awake. After delivering the team to the airport, Cristi and I would go to a friend's or relative's home in Bucharest, where we would get several hours' sleep before returning to meet the next team at noon. This pattern continued for the four weeks, until I departed Romania with the final group.

During this time, it was our privilege to develop relationships with many of God's choice believers, which we still enjoy today. American and Romanian pastors, youth leaders, Sunday school teachers, teenagers, carpenters, handymen, and more united to help Cristi Hodoroaba, nephew of the late Jeremiah Hodoroaba, to see the most concentrated progress on his Camp Bit of Heaven facility to that point. Because of the extreme amount of work to be done and the obstacles described, we knew a finished product would not be realized by four teams in four weeks. We also knew our commitment to Cristi and his dream had just begun. We now shared his vision to see the camp completed and used as intended, which resulted in our return over the next five summers.

Our ministry contributed a total of fifty thousand dollars during that time, and though a few unfinished details remain, the facility is now being used for all activities. The temporary outdoor kitchen and outhouses are no more, and one of the cabins has been enlarged to accommodate a family when needed. Since 2009, the facility has been used to house medical evangelism teams that have been organized by our ministry and the church in Conway, Arkansas. We have also sent teams to assist Cristi in conducting camps for the Romanian children.

During my initial month-long stay in 2005, exhausted team members would find the shower and wander off to bed not long after dinner. Cristi and I would usually be the last to retire, which afforded us time to get more acquainted. I think it was about the middle of our third week together that Cristi shared something with me in the dim quietness of his living room that will remain with me always. It would also forever alter my perspective on the workings of the Lord in our lives and in our world.

"Jeff," he began, "you recall when we first met in Rupea two years ago."

"I do."

"And you remember when you visited Camp Bit of Heaven last year."

"Of course. How could I forget?"

"Perhaps you noticed I did not act very excited at either of those times."

"Yes, I did notice. I wondered why, but I did not plan to say anything to you about it. We are here, that is what matters."

"I want to explain the reasons I acted that way. Through the years many Americans have visited us, and they all say they want to help. They promise to return with money and people, but they never do. When you saw the camp last year and spoke of returning to help us, I thought you were like the others. I really did not expect to see you again. I know now that you will do what you say, and I am very thankful for all you are doing."

"Well, Cristi, we prayed, and God provided what was needed. It is more than being obligated to a human promise. It is being part of a plan that God was preparing when I was a child, and before you were born."

"There is another reason. You speak so highly of my uncle Jeremiah, and he was truly a great man of God. Our family respected him and knew that the things he did were right and admirable. However, in a communist country, when a man like my uncle worked to spread the Christian faith, the government made life difficult for his entire family. For example, I applied to college five times, and the communists saw to it I was always denied. Though we respected him, it was like a curse and never a blessing to be related to him. When you came and brought this help to us, it was the first time we feel we have been blessed as a result of our relationship with my uncle Jeremiah."

I was both touched and astounded by his revelation, but I do not recall saying much in immediate response. However, as his words took residence in my mind, I realized God had allowed me to be a part of a very special plan. A plan that was much more than building a Christian camp facility in the hill country outside of Fagaras. A plan that was more than making an amazing connection with a voice from my past. A plan that was much more than helping a once oppressed Romanian boy finally feel good about his ancestors. A plan that was more than any one of us or every one of us. It was a plan to have a glimpse of something far greater than all these combined. It was God allowing me to truly realize beyond spiritual platitudes His greatness and eternal nature. A plan that, for me, had unknowingly begun almost forty-five years earlier, a period that some would call a lifetime.

There I was, a bratty child at best, who probably had to have his ear thumped in order to sit still long enough to hear, "be a burning bush for Jesus Christ." Words that were likely forgotten by this animated young lad by the "Amen" of the closing prayer. But they were preserved in his mind by God, who was working toward the future of him and many yet unborn. I am reminded of God's words to Jeremiah the prophet that applied to me, Cristi and to us all: "Before I formed you in the womb I knew you, and before you were born I consecrated you" (Jeremiah 1:5).

Before we existed, God set in motion His plan that would use a dedicated Romanian crusader, the US Air Force, a little Baptist church in France, the youngest child of John and Vada Andler, a humble Fagaras family, and a financially struggling friend. Yes, meaningful accomplishments would come of it, but the bigger lesson was to see God's greatness and His eternal dealings. We can possibly begin to understand Peter's words, "With the Lord one day is as a thousand years, and a thousand years as one day" (2 Peter 3:8).

Our plans seem large. Our problems seem big. But our God is huge. While we can never totally understand the hugeness of God, we can by faith totally believe it, and allow that belief to transform our thinking and our living. When we face difficulties, we can remember our God has no difficulties, and ours may be seen in His perspective. When we are overwhelmed by life, we can remember our God is overwhelmed by nothing, and we may have His peace. When our faith seems to be looking into a paralyzing darkness, we can remember our God is eternal Light, who sees past, present, and future—and we can walk on.

In this "voice from the past" experience, God allowed me to see He is at work in the lives of His children when we know it and when we don't; when we see it and when we don't; before we are born, while we are here, and after we are gone. He brought to life Paul's words, "for it is God who is at work in you, both to will and to work for His good pleasure" (Philippians 2:13). I found that "His good pleasure" also becomes my good pleasure when I am submitted to Him because He truly does "work all things for our good" (Romans 8:28).

Not only is He with me in every circumstance I face, He saw it coming. Why shall I worry? Why shall I despair? My eternal Father was working His eternal plan in my life before I had life or was aware of my life. I am not that plan, you are not that plan, but we are *part* of that plan. We are privileged details in His vast picture, details that He loves, He has chosen, He is using, and that He will never overlook, omit, or abandon.

Yes, it is fair to say life was getting considerably better for me since that very low time not many years earlier. And yet, as you have surely figured out by now, we had not yet seen the extent of what better could be.

Petru and Jeremiah Hodoroaba" (Cristi's father and uncle)

Cristi Hodoroaba family

Camp Bit of Heaven progress

CHAPTER 11

WHEN LIFE WENT SOUTH

I have always had an appreciation for flowers, especially roses. I recall accompanying my mother to a local nursery one Saturday when she was on a mission to dress up our yard. Perhaps it was unusual for a teenager, but I was immediately taken with the colorful variety of roses, to the point I left my mother to pursue her mission alone. My instant favorite was a rich salmon-colored variety I still favor today. I decided I wanted roses, and my mom let me add my new love to her landscaping plan. I would learn that a display of nursery-quality roses would require constant care and attention. I had acceptable results, and my appreciation for roses has continued to this day. However, I now prefer the popular knockout roses, because they require less care and usually maintain a blanket of blooms.

Do not be concerned, I have not forsaken my purpose and assumed the role of a gardener. As we progress to the next experience I will share, it occurs to me our ministry has been much like the blooming of a rose. Just as a single rose may contain twenty to forty individual petals, each of our opportunities has been unique, though springing from a common bloom. You have seen examples of the life that emerged from our roots of difficulty, including rewarding involvement with senior adults, prisons, jails, and overseas missions. We have also found that some may combine to result in yet another unique opportunity. It is such an example that I want to pursue as we proceed.

You remember Kevin from our first excursion to Romania. As his ministry developed over the years, he became involved in additional areas. In late 2003, he invited me to accompany him to Central America. An evangelistic crusade was to be held near Leon, Nicaragua. I would simply assist in various areas as needed. It would also be a good opportunity to become acquainted with Terry and Arlene, the host missionaries who were coordinating the event.

Terry is a retired hospital administrator who is profoundly gifted in the area of administration. He and Arlene now lead their Central American mission organization called Open Eyes Ministries. On retirement, Terry (a man much younger than his years), felt drawn to ministry in Central America but was considered beyond the age accepted by denominational mission agencies. So relentless was his call that he and Arlene established their own ministry and made their way to Nicaragua. That God was leading their steps is undeniable, as they have been used to begin many new churches, form innumerable cell groups, train Christian leaders, host countless mission teams, and see thousands profess Christ. Their influence has spread across Central America, as Open Eyes has also established ministries in Honduras, Costa Rica, and El Salvador.

As expected, my first visit did not require extensive involvement in preaching, singing, or teaching. But I did begin meaningful relationships with Terry and Arlene, many Central American believers, and other believers from the United States. Before leaving, I was told of a group that was building a home the following January for a young mother and her children. My calendar was clear, and the trip was not extremely expensive. I wanted to continue the development of my relationships in the area, so I made plans to return, despite the fact construction work was not—and now definitely is not—my area of giftedness.

During that project, having a smaller team afforded me the opportunity to become better acquainted with Terry. By week's end, we made plans for our ministry to return in November to lead an area-wide crusade in Sebaco, Nicaragua. We would bring singers and instruments, and I would do the preaching. Truth be told, that is what I would have preferred to have done on my first visit. However, as I consider that process and many others in my Christian experience, I am reminded we must submit ourselves to the steps God has ordered as He brings us to His (and often our) desired place of service. Even a well-intended attempt to circumvent His process will result in a cheapened version of His plan, though in our eyes, it may appear to be successful. The fruitful relationship we have enjoyed with Open Eyes Ministries has given testimony to God's working in its birth and development.

It Gets Even Better

Since the 2004 crusade in Sebaco, almost every project in the region has been of a similar nature. In addition to Nicaragua, we have led crusades in the Honduran cities of Comoyagua and La Paz, and in Puntarenas, Costa Rica. These have featured our ministry singers (who sing in English and Spanish), and I have served as the preacher.

We arrive in the country on Saturday, worship in area churches on Sunday, and often meet with city leaders and have television or radio interviews on Monday. Monday evening features a rally sponsored by area churches to draw attention to the crusade. Usually held in a public venue, such as a street or civic arena, it is energetically infused with music, testimonies, and speakers, including myself.

The crusade is held on Tuesday through Thursday nights. We have met in soccer arenas, large covered shelters, and in a mid-city plaza, where a large Catholic cathedral hovered over us. Our ministry is responsible for covering most of the expenses, while Open Eyes Ministries does the advance preparation. This includes printing and distributing flyers, strategically placing posters, suspending banners across streets, producing television and radio ads, hiring audio equipment and technicians, and reserving buses and drivers to transport those from outlying areas. In addition, there is the obvious need to hire security for the crusade site, as well as having the utility company provide electricity.

In these crusades, we have seen nightly attendance range from hundreds to four or five thousand. At the closing invitation time, many come to the platform for special prayer. Many others recommit their lives to Christ, and still dozens more make first-time professions of faith in Christ as their Savior. We have also learned the completion of the crusade services does not necessarily mean people's responses end as well.

I will always recall the experience we had in Puntarenas, Costa Rica, in April 2008. We enjoyed a very successful campaign, which concluded as usual on Thursday evening. A ministry activity was scheduled for the next afternoon, so on Friday morning we were free to shop and have lunch in an area on the Pacific Ocean. It was a relaxing time, with our team gathering up souvenirs and enjoying lighthearted fellowship with each other and our translators.

As Lynne and I strolled through the seaside market with a team member or two, we suddenly began to hear shouts of, "el pastor, el pastor." I turned to see a local man coming toward us, obviously trying to get my attention. He was wearing one of those incandescent vests that indicated he was a city employee assigned to the area, likely for security. He was visibly agitated. I immediately caught the attention of my translator, Lucila, and motioned for her help.

He began to share with us how he had attended the crusade service the night before. Through Lucila, he said, "I heard you speak of Jesus Christ last night. I stood outside my home, which is next to the place where you were preaching. I heard the music, and I heard your words. When you asked for people to come forward to give their hearts to Jesus, I wanted to come, but I did not. Then I was not able to sleep. All night I prayed, 'God, please let me see that man again, please let me see him again!'" With tears in his eyes, he continued, "Just now in this place I have been praying, 'Let me see that man again,' and I looked up, and you were here!"

"*Quiero que Jesús en mi corazón*," he pleaded repeatedly. I am far from fluent in Spanish, but I had learned to recognize *"Jesús en mi corazón"* meant "Jesus in my heart." By that time, several of our team members had noticed what was happening and joined us with controlled enthusiasm. To ensure his understanding, I repeated a concise explanation of the gospel message. We all stood and prayed with him as he confessed his sinfulness to God and opened his heart to Christ. One of the local pastors had joined us, and he instantly began the steps in drawing the new convert into the church for spiritual development and fellowship. We all agreed our shopping spree had become the best we'd ever encountered, and our lunch at an outdoor restaurant took on a special atmosphere of fellowship.

While the scope of the evening crusades dominated our thoughts during these Central American missions, it is worth noting other activities were featured during the day. My wife, Lynne, and the other ladies often led women's ministry conferences in local churches, while the men visited hospitals and jails. It was common for me to be invited to satisfy the curiosity of the local media with radio and television interviews. These sometimes evolved into extended call-in broadcasts that presented the challenge of unrehearsed questions

Favorite daytime activities were the fiestas. These were impromptu gatherings in parks or street corners that featured our combined American and local teams doing skits and music, sharing the story of Jesus, and distributing gospel tracts, candy, and small gifts. As He always does, God sufficiently enabled each us to fill each task. It was always humbling to see people in these places seem to look to us as some kind of authorities in spiritual matters. That realization motivated us to more thoroughly prepare and pray as we approached our time before them.

Early 2005 was when Terry informed me that Open Eyes Ministries was expanding into Honduras. He and Arlene would be hosting their first mission team in the base city of Choluteca. "The team is made up of fairly young people," Terry explained. "If you are available, I'd love to have someone with added maturity and experience to join them ("Maturity," of course, meant I was older). They are to be with us in April." I was honored at the invitation and excited to be a part of the inaugural mission project in Open Eyes' new venture.

As I recall, the purpose of this initial project was basically to help Open Eyes become acquainted with local churches and community leaders. We held church services nightly. They featured the usual music and preaching but also exhortation from Terry about the partnership that was soon to be available in leadership training and encouragement. I wondered what the attitude of the existing Christian community might be toward this missionary "invasion," but I learned they welcomed the guidance and responded positively.

In all our experiences with Open Eyes, teams began each day with the sharing of biblical insight. Each evening also ended with group time, when the day's events were evaluated. One night early in the week, we shared a quite peculiar and sobering set of events that has lingered in my memory. Please understand that while I am keenly aware of the Evil One who is the "god of this world" (Ephesians 2:2; 2 Corinthians 4:4; John 12:31), I am not given to looking for a "demon behind every bush." Nor do I seek or advocate sensational and supernatural explanations for every unusual occurrence. However, on this particular night, it would seem our experience with the paranormal was undisputable.

Though the time of sharing had begun with the usual comments, a consensual discussion soon ensued that team members were sensing oppression in their daily service. "There seems to be a lack of spiritual freedom in what we're doing" was the observation of many. They began to describe more specific incidents, most of which had taken place during the night before.

Terry told of being awakened in his first-floor bedroom, which was located on the front side of the mission house. Just outside his window was the locked iron gate, which secured the concrete wall that enclosed the facility. "Over and over I heard the whispered call of 'David' [Dah-veed, the name of our primary driver]. I finally roused Arlene and asked if she heard the sound. She had not. I got up and investigated, but no one was there. It was very strange."

During the previous night, a commotion also occurred in the women's sleeping area due to what was thought to be a malfunction in one of their beds. Then one of the young women in our group added to the unsettling discussion by explaining the events surrounding the commotion.

"Sometime during last night," she began, "I awoke and sensed a presence in our room. It was not just the other women in the beds around me. I looked from my top bunk to see the figure of a woman standing at the foot of the bed. Somehow she didn't seem totally real, like she was there but not really there. It was very unsettling. Then this 'woman' moved as if she would climb the ladder to my bunk. No one was in the bunk below mine, and I called to the person in the next bed, on the lower level. She awoke, and I asked her if she saw anyone or anything around my bed, but she did not. About that time, my bunk suddenly collapsed onto the empty bed below! We turned on the light, but except for the problem with the bed, nothing was visibly wrong."

Had she really seen something? Was she dreaming? Was her imagination just activated by nocturnal fear? I honestly did not know what I thought at the time, but the experiences of our evening had not ended.

Terry and Open Eyes Ministries had only been in Choluteca for two weeks. He explained how our mission house had recently been vacated by a group heavily involved in drug dealing, prostitution, and worse. "I don't know what we all think in these matters," he said, "but this house has hosted all manner of evil before we rented it. Perhaps it would be well if we spent some time praying and specifically asking God to rid this place of any evil presence and to dedicate it solely to His purposes."

About that time there was suddenly an incredibly loud and explosive sound outside. Our house and the entire area were left in total darkness due to the loss of electricity. As you might imagine, our nerves were a bit rattled by this time, which was demonstrated by the multiple screams jolted from several in our group. After everyone calmed down, I reluctantly volunteered to feel my way to the next room and retrieve my flashlight. Others also found flashlights or lit candles. We agreed it was time to select a partner or two and go to various parts of the house to pray.

Terry asked me and local friend Pastor Eduardo to circle the house outside as we prayed, while he and others would pray inside, both upstairs and down. After a few prayerful laps, Eduardo and I approached the front of the house, where Terry and others were waiting for us. "Jeff," he summoned, "I want you to come to my office with me. There seems to be a specific presence there like nowhere else in the house."

We reentered and made our way by flashlight to the corner room at the rear of the first floor. I'm not sure why, but I was leading the way and reached the office first. I shall never forget that when I stepped in the doorway, I felt something against my chest, as if opposing my entrance. You will notice I did not say I *sensed* something. No, I *felt* something. There was no one or anything visible. There was nothing I could touch, but it was there. "Terry, something is resisting my entrance into this room," I said. "It's like nothing I've ever experienced before." It was a chilling experience, but I felt a calm from the Lord giving me the confidence to say, "I'm going in. *We're* going in, and we're going to pray against this."

I stepped into the office, followed by Terry and several team members. I recall the air being dense and dank, and there was an odor that was both foul and sweet. The atmosphere was distinctly darker than the rest of the house. We joined hands and began to pray for God's power over the evil stronghold that seemed to be defying us. As we prayed, the presence that undoubtedly inhabited that room faded, as did the unusual odor that had recently prevailed. The damp thickness of the air also subsided, and we all felt the peaceful presence of God make Himself known throughout the house. He was "guarding our hearts and minds in Christ Jesus" (Philippians 4:6).

We were accustomed to the absence of air-conditioning in the house, but the loss of electricity also rendered our fans useless as we retired for the night. The stagnant hot air was uncomfortable, but we still slept peacefully after experiencing firsthand the promise that "greater is He that is in you than He that is in the world" (1 John 4:4). The remainder of our initial Honduran project was free of oppressive powers, and there were no more strange occurrences to distract or hinder us.

Terry had become aware of our interest and involvement in prison ministry. As a result, he arranged for our team to lead the Sunday morning service in a local church that was actively involved in the nearby prison. Church Pastor Dubon had also arranged for us to hold an afternoon prison service later in the week. Knowing some are not comfortable with this type of ministry, we opened the opportunity to volunteers.

As our partial team arrived at the prison, the first sight was a fairly large area of unfinished construction located beside the older facility that was in use. The growth of weeds and brush informed us the construction site had remained unmolested for some time. "What's going on here?" a team member asked. "Did the government run out of money?"

"That's actually an undertaking of Pastor Dubon and his church," Terry said. "They have been trying to build a chapel for some time. The Honduran government will permit them to do so, but they must also include the required outer walls, guard towers, chain-link fence, and razor wire. As you might imagine, the cost is great, and they are building as money is available. Right now they are trying to raise additional funds." As we neared the security entrance, Terry indicated we would have a closer look at the construction project after our visit, when Pastor Dubon would tell us about their efforts.

By American standards the security procedures were inadequate, and we were easily admitted into the general population. As we moved unaccompanied through the hot and harsh environment, we noticed many inmates busily engaged in activities which required a variety of tools. *Any of these could be used as a weapon,* I thought.

The pastor explained these men were working on various crafts, which they were allowed to sell to support themselves while in prison. That his words were not all that comforting was rendered irrelevant when I noticed the strategically located guard towers overlooking the facility. Each was manned by a heavily armed officer, who we learned would swiftly respond to disruptive behavior, and questions may or may not be asked afterward.

Approximately thirty inmates joined us for a service in a vacated work area. I could tell most were accustomed to participating. Others observed from a distance, curiously catching a glimpse of the rare American visitors. Since our visit was a departure from the church's usual ministry schedule, we were allowed only thirty minutes. We shared music and a brief gospel message. We soon found ourselves outside once again, ready to hear the story behind the incomplete construction we saw on our arrival.

Pastor Dubon told of the years his church had been involved in the prison, conducting worship services and teaching the Bible. He had shown us the secondhand store his church operated to generate funds that assisted prisoners and their families, and to support the construction project. However, in spite of their steadfastness, the amount of money needed for such an undertaking was slow in coming. Given their rate of progress, it was obvious the completion of the project was likely years away.

The chapel structure had just enough walls erected to support the beginning of a roof, and the floor area was still bare ground. Foundation footers had been dug for the walls and towers, but progress had halted at that point. Summing up the site were a few stray concrete blocks and rusty rebar lying amid the weeds and an abandoned pile of gravel or two. Is this sounding familiar?

Keep in mind it was April 2005, which means we were excitedly anticipating the Camp Bit of Heaven construction project, less than two months away. As this new need was before me, and as I considered what we were seeing God do in regard to another part of the world, I had to at least investigate further. "Do you know the projected cost of completing this facility?" I asked.

"Yes," Pastor Dubon replied.

I responded with the only responsible approach when addressing financial needs we encounter around the world. "I can make no promises. Ours is a small ministry with limited resources, but we have seen God provide in wonderful ways when faced with needs. If you will provide a copy of your budget, I and others will pray that God will use us to help you. We do not know what He will do, but we know what He *can* do. If He will bless us with the resources needed, we will bless you."

By the end of our week, Pastor Dubon did provide me with a copy of their needs, which totaled $24,101.00 (US dollars). I wondered if God would once again provide for a great need so soon. I began to pray He would do just that.

Unlike the Romanian experience of less than a year earlier, there was no phone call or e-mail message to return when I reached home. Nor was there miraculous financial provision promised within the first twenty-four hours of my return. No, it took a little longer. I continued to pray God would help us to meet the need, and in about three weeks, that's exactly what He did.

One evening Lynne and I were relaxing when the phone rang. It was a local friend I had not heard from in a few months, and who was not aware of our visit to Honduras. After some friendly catch-up, he began to explain the primary reason for his call. "I've been hearing good things about your ministry," he said. "It sounds exciting."

"It is indeed," I told him. "We are enjoying ministry now more than we ever have."

"Well that's the reason I called. We've seen some good profits in our business recently. God has blessed tremendously, and I want to share part of this with your ministry. Within the next month, you will be receiving a check from me in the amount of…"—Are you ready for this? "… $25,000!"

I giddily told him of the need we had discovered in Honduras and of our prayers in the days that followed. He was excited as well. Following our conversation, I immediately e-mailed Terry and told him the news. We agreed to withhold the information from Pastor Dubon until the money was in hand, and we were both anxious for that time to come.

The $25,000.00 check never came in the mail. Instead, our friend and his wife invited Lynne and me to come to their home for a brief visit and then out to an early dinner. He gave me his offering at that time, but there was an added surprise. With him that evening was a business partner who had become aware of our ministry. He added his unexpected gift of $8,000.

I contacted Terry, who eagerly passed the word to Pastor Dubon. I was told the news was met with joyful tears, followed by a church wide celebration. We began sending funds later that summer, which were handled through Open Eyes Ministries. They maintained accountability and provided us with progress reports.

Completion of the project would take the better part of a year, but Terry, Pastor Dubon, and I agreed we wanted to reunite sooner for a full crusade in the prison. It was obvious God's favor was upon that place, and we wanted to strike while the iron was hot.

And why would His favor *not* be upon it? "I was in prison, and you came to Me," (Matthew 25:36) remember? God is *always* active wherever and whenever His Word is active. The crusade date was set for November 2005. Our prison ministry here at home was evolving into prison ministry overseas, and we were expectantly elated at the opportunity that was waiting.

Life was indeed becoming filled with one rewarding experience that would lead to another. Busy activity continued to energize and motivate us. Our rose was in full bloom. *This just keeps getting better,* I thought. *How long can this continue?* All I know to say is I'll just tell the story. You decide!

Crusade crowd, Sebaco, Nicaragua

Comoyagua, Honduras crusade

CHAPTER 12

PRISON BREAK

After developing the relationship with Pastor Dubon and the prison ministry in April, we passed through the summer of 2005 and the Romanian children's camp project as previously described. Amid our continuing ministries at home, we were soon facing the fall and our return to Choluteca. A prison environment is intimidating to many, so we were not surprised to recruit only four people, including myself. Ted and Joyce would accompany me once again, as would Joe, a dear Georgia fellow I met on my first visit to Nicaragua two years earlier. He had already accompanied us on other mission journeys, which included serving as crew foreman during one of our recent weeks in Romania.

The small number did not discourage us. We knew members of the Choluteca church would assist with music and in other ways. Their presence would also assimilate us into the environment more comfortably. Furthermore, we were told prison officials would be happier about a smaller number of foreign faces converging on the facility at one time.

We arrived on Saturday as usual, worshipped with Pastor Dubon's church on Sunday, and had various activities on Monday, including a trip to the prison. While there, we met with those in authority, mainly to allow them to become familiar with their visitors. It was exciting to see the laborers' great progress on the outer walls of the new construction area. They made good use of the initial funds we sent two months earlier.

We arrived in the early afternoon on Tuesday to begin the three-day crusade. As before, we passed unaccompanied from the security checkpoint into the main compound. Our Honduran ministry partners led us to a large area between what appeared to be two main cell blocks. Given the intense heat of the equatorial sun, we were grateful the entire area was shaded by a metal roof.

Using a small audio system, our hosts gave a brief greeting and began singing before the crowd of about a hundred. They were seated in those stackable plastic chairs that seem to have found their way to every remote corner of the planet. Many others were standing, sitting, or moving about at a distance, trying not to appear too interested. The doors to the cell blocks were unlocked to allow the inmates the freedom to participate. Many stayed just inside and peered through the doorway or a barred window, as if in an effort to remain anonymous.

The success of the Cholutecan church's ministry was evidenced by the participation of many inmates in the singing, as well as their supportive response to the testimonies of the Americans. Each day Joyce shared her lovely voice. She even prepared a couple of songs in Spanish, for which the crowd expressed enthusiastic gratitude.

I followed the music in each service with an evangelistic Bible message and extended the invitation for the listeners to respond with decisions for Christ. We were not informed of specific guidelines, but wisdom dictated I follow our American prison protocol and not suggest the traditional altar call. It might encourage an unpredictable number of inmates to step forward and congregate too closely around us.

I recall the response in that first service as not particularly overwhelming. But our three-day experience was not to continue that pattern. We remained for a while after the close of the Tuesday meeting, mingling with inmates who responded. That was apparently time well spent because when we arrived on Wednesday, many of them were waiting on the other side of the security checkpoint, greeting us with waves and smiles. As we reentered their domain, many stepped forward to carry whatever we had in our hands, even if it was just a Bible or bottle of water.

One young man greeted me with perfect English, and I learned he was from the United States. As I contemplated the concrete sleeping bunks, open drainage, holes in the roof, and stifling heat, I was sure he wished he had chosen to misbehave in America rather than Honduras.

Though there were those who still chose to lurk behind corners and remain aloof, the crowd in the worship area had grown considerably. We sensed an atmosphere of enthusiasm and anticipation as we began. They were even more responsive to the music, and the compound came alive with spiritual energy. You have already learned about this preacher, so you understand I was increasingly motivated as I impatiently awaited my turn to address the congregation.

The response to the gospel also grew from the day before. Dozens indicated with an uplifted hand that they wanted to commit whatever life they had left to the Lord Jesus Christ. There were tears of repentance and joy, hands raised in praise and surrender, and hugs and handshakes between hardened criminals and free individuals. Both now shared the true freedom found only in Jesus Christ.

As on the previous day, we once again remained afterward for a more extended time of fellowship with our growing group of Christian friends and brothers. More inmates relaxed and joined in the festivity, and we discerned their growing acceptance and trust. Some even requested our autographs on the inside cover of their Bibles or on stray pieces of paper they managed to find. Our four American team members concurred that this prison was the only place any of us had ever been, or ever would be, considered a celebrity.

Each time we left the facility, we noticed additional areas that obviously housed other inmates that were not exposed to our ministry. Not wanting to omit anyone from the opportunity to hear the gospel, we asked about the mysterious prison wings. We were told the smaller area nearest the security entrance was inhabited by female offenders, while the larger area beyond them housed the facility's most dangerous criminals, known as the "gangsters." "May we invite them to attend our service tomorrow?" I asked.

"The men and women are not permitted to be in the same area," our translator explained. "And the gangsters are under the highest security. They are never allowed to leave their area for any reason and have no contact with anyone but each other. They are considered too dangerous. Many are violent drug dealers, and others are guilty of murder, rape, and more. Even the guards rarely enter their area. Their food is passed to them through an opening in their gate, and they are watched constantly from a guard tower."

At the risk of appearing reckless, I asked, "May we be permitted to visit these areas before our ministry is finished tomorrow?" Our translator posed the question to the officer in command, who said he would investigate the possibility and give an answer later that day.

I assured our small team that if allowed, only those who were of a mind to participate would be expected to do so. To their credit, each one enthusiastically agreed to be included, and we all were eager to hear the decision of the authorities. Though we expected to be allowed entrance to the women's area, we felt the chance of a visit with the gangsters was slim, given the description of their character and environment.

Later that evening, we received word as promised that we would be permitted to visit both areas the next day. A morning visit was required, before returning to lead the final afternoon service. We happily complied with these conditions, as our prayer to cover the entire facility with a gospel witness would be realized.

Our first stop on Thursday morning was the women's area. The team of four Americans and our Honduran partners were admitted and the door locked behind us. The guards remained on the other side as usual. A row of open cells allowed the women to move in and out of a small outdoor area, partially covered by the familiar metal roof. One or two were hanging articles of clothing to dry in the sun, while most were just sitting on a concrete step or one of the plastic chairs that were insufficient to accommodate all of them. Without television or other entertainment to occupy them, most of the women sat idly lifeless, enduring the challenge of the sluggishly passing time.

Others, however, were busy tending to a need we did not expect to see—their children. It was explained to us that the women who had children who were too young to attend school, and who had no source of care on the outside, had to care for them in the prison. We were obviously touched by the plight of these pitiful-looking innocents, who were either sitting lifelessly beside their mothers, playing with some object imagined to be a toy, or even feeding at a maternal breast.

Our time was limited, so we immediately began meeting the women, shaking hands, sharing smiles, and talking with them through our translators. We also shared Spanish Bibles and literature provided by the missionaries. Like so many people we meet in the realms of the outcast, they were grateful to have whatever attention we offered. They listened intently to our witness, displaying an openness that far exceeded our initial encounter with their male counterparts. At the close of our time together, twelve of sixteen women indicated a decision to trust Christ as their Savior. As we moved to our next visit, there were again the tearfully joyful embraces of those who were once total strangers physically, spiritually, geographically, and culturally—but who had instantly been joined as family through a common faith in Jesus Christ.

As always, without human discussion or contemplation, the Word of God again proved itself true before our eyes. "There is neither Jew nor Greek, there is neither slave nor free man, there is neither male nor female; for you are all one in Christ Jesus" (Galatians 3:2). In only a few short moments, we would see further confirmation of this truth.

As we were led to the gangster area, we experienced a moment of truly mixed emotions. Our hearts and minds were overjoyed at the experience just shared with the women. But we were simultaneously overcome by sober caution as we approached this group of potentially menacing men. We reached a heavy iron door that was surrounded by towering concrete walls. These were topped with layers of both razor and barbed wire. The walls had no windows or bars through which to get an advance glimpse of the environment, and the iron door had only one small opening with a sliding cover.

Our escort then did something that gave our group insight into the actual level of dark respect commanded by the dangerous men inside. His clanging tap on the door was answered by a tattooed face peering through the small opening, followed by the guard's *request* that we be permitted to enter.

Most of my prison experiences had taught me the officials "rule the roost," and inmates do as they're told, when they're told, and how they're told. But on this day, it was obvious that although the gangsters were in captivity, care was taken not to antagonize them. It became equally obvious that we would not be admitted if the boys inside were not agreeable, and I quickly decided I was fine with that. Our experience during the first two days had also let us know we were likely to be on our own—if we were permitted to enter at all. *Oh boy,* I thought, *what have we gotten ourselves into?* Notice I said "we," though it was I who requested this opportunity. Looking around at our team, I asked, "Anyone want to back out?"

"We're committed," they agreed, as we saw the guard unlocking the door in response to our entrance being granted.

We were ushered past the guard through the narrowly opened door, which was then locked behind us, just as I had suspected it would be. We descended a few steps into a concrete courtyard bordered on each side by covered areas that seemed only useful for gathering and shelter from the elements. There was an opening in one of these that led into the living quarters, and our team agreed we had no interest in seeing what was inside. On the far end of the courtyard, the wall continued to tower above us, completely obstructing any outside view. Where the walls met in a corner was a single guard tower, manned by one guard armed with a deadly assault rifle. These particular inmates may have been considered dangerous, but it became very apparent that any unruly behavior on their part would be no match for the firepower that was well out of their reach.

My translator informed the gatekeeper who admitted us that a group of Americans had come to visit, and were requesting to see everyone who was willing. By this time, several of the gangsters had emerged from their living area or an inconspicuous corner. We were soon approached by two quite foreboding characters, who we somehow immediately concluded were "in charge." They received us politely enough and permitted us to speak with the men who were clearly under their influence. As we began to gather under the shaded area nearest the door, I quietly advised our group to arrange ourselves between the inmates and the exit.

I could tell this environment was not going to lend itself to icebreaking and warm introductions. Without much delay, we got right to the business at hand. I explained who we were and why we were at this prison so far from our homes. I further explained that although they were likely able to hear our daily services from our audio system, our desire was to visit them personally. Not all of the twenty-nine gangsters chose to join us, but those who did by now were listening intently to their fair-skinned guest.

I shared with them the unconditional love and grace of God offered through Jesus Christ, and how He desires a relationship with everyone, regardless of position in life (John 1:12).

I warned of the coming physical death of all people and the unavoidable encounter with God's judgment (Hebrews 9:27).

I spoke of the inevitability of eternal punishment for sin but also the possibility of forgiveness and eternal life, again offered through Jesus Christ (Revelation 20:15; Ephesians 1:7).

I explained how the sin nature with which we are all born is what separates us from God, and how our sinful deeds, however mild or heinous, are simply the inevitable symptoms of that nature (Psalm 51:5; Romans 3:23).

I told them that because of this, the reality of eternal judgment was something they faced *before* they had dealt in drugs, *before* they had murdered, *before* they had raped, extorted, or worse (John 3:18).

I assured them they were not in bondage because they were in prison, but they were in prison because they were in bondage (Proverbs 5:22).

Like all men without God, they had been enslaved by sin, which had first deceived, then destroyed, and now mercilessly reappeared to demand its damning due (Numbers 32:23).

I called on them to understand their only hope of losing sin's dominance over them was to accept the One who destroyed that dominance on the cross (1 John 3:8).

I called on them to understand that while receiving God's forgiveness and eternal life in Christ would not free them from the temporal bondage and penalty of prison, it would free them from the eternal bondage and penalty of sin.

I called on them to believe that they could, "know the Truth, and the Truth would make them free" (John 8:32).

Thirteen of those men responded by indicating a desire to follow Christ. Just as with those in the general population two days before and the women moments earlier, we again stood amazed at how a newly shared faith in Jesus changed apprehension to acceptance and hardened criminals to gentle converts. We remained with the men for as long as we were allowed. We were joined by others who had observed from a distance but were now drawn into our comfortable company.

The two leaders continued to serve as spokesmen for the group, and they began to tell us of life in the gangster lockup and the needs they faced. Simple things like light bulbs to replace those that were broken or burned out, paint to spruce up the gathering areas, and a soccer ball.

Unlike our American prisons, we learned that in Honduras, family or friends of the inmates are responsible for providing them with basic needs and occasional wants. These included clothes, personal hygiene items, medicine—just about everything but the small servings of rice and beans they were fed twice each day.

We knew not to promise our new friends we would help, but we did promise to ask if our help would be permitted. We also promised to get word to them as to the answer. On our way out of the prison that morning, we were pleased to have the officers give their approval, and were told we could reenter the gangster facility when we returned that afternoon for our final crusade service.

Before returning to the mission house for lunch, we drove immediately to some small shops, where we purchased light bulbs and two soccer balls. We decided we would work through our missionaries and Pastor Dubon's church to have the painting done, since it was a task that would require more personnel, supervision, and time.

We returned for the closing service early enough to visit the gangster area beforehand, excited about our gift-giving encounter. They were waiting for us, and we were all noticeably more comfortable in approaching each other than just hours earlier. Due to our schedule, we quickly made our presentations. These previously intimidating ruffians smiled gratefully, and quickly started tossing and kicking the balls around the courtyard like the young boys still present within them.

It Gets Even Better

As we prepared to leave, we gathered to exchange good-byes and gratitude. The two leaders stepped forward, and we could tell they desired to speak. Their group became still and quiet, giving continued indication these two young men were in command.

"We thank you for taking time with us," they said through Lucila. "You have shown us kindness that others do not show. You have done what you promised to do, while many others do not. We will not forget you, and you are welcome to visit whenever you wish. And when you do, you will be respected, and you will be protected."

As I contemplated his words, I realized our team had come to be the safest in the very environment that had been described as the most dangerous. I was reminded of the times when Jesus exercised caution when faced with potentially ominous situations (John 10:39–40). His sensitivity to the Father's plan sometimes took Him into gaping maw, knowing that He was under divine care (John 11:7–10).

Said another way, while we should "not tempt the Lord our God" with careless spiritual heroics, a genuinely humble desire to obey His directives, coupled with prayerful sensitivity to His circumstances and impressions, can yield a valuable result. We will learn that regardless of what our eyes may see and our ears may hear, the safest place in the world is walking in the footsteps of Jesus. Footsteps that are always in the center of the Father's perfect and, therefore, protected will.

During lunch prior to our return that afternoon, our team had discussed the fact there was still one group at the prison with which we had not had the opportunity to share the gospel. The guards. So productive had been our experience that we considered our task incomplete unless we at least attempted to present the message of Christ to every group associated with the prison. Terry and Lucila agreed to approach the officiating officer with the proposal while the rest of our team was clearing the security checkpoint. As they followed us into the main prison area for our final service, we were given the exciting news that we would return at eight o'clock the next morning, when we would be allowed twenty minutes with the guards on duty. We had one crusade service remaining, but we were already anticipating the added privilege.

The excitement at our final afternoon service increased even more, both on the part of our team and the general population. The number of those actively participating in the service had also increased; the main worship area almost could not contain them. And there was an unexpected surprise. The women we visited that morning had been allowed to attend. The singing was energetic and enthusiastic, and many who were unfamiliar with the songs participated as best they could through smiles, clapping, and upraised hands.

I recall one moment in that service when, during the music, I noticed an inmate near the front of the crowd who seemed to be embroiled in a private emotional struggle. The restrictions learned in American prisons fought against my desire to go to him and offer support. But after several moments of observing his difficulty, I decided against better judgment. This prison did not have the constraints to which I was accustomed, so as the music continued, I left my place with the pastors and missionaries and made my way to his side.

Due to the language barrier, any attempt to offer verbal encouragement was futile, so I simply placed my arm around his shoulder and continued to sing. He wrapped his arms around my waist and leaned his head on my shoulder as his struggle erupted into sobs. Finally, his grip loosened, his tears eased, and he turned his face toward the musicians. We remained arm in arm until the singing ended. The time came for me to speak to the crowd, so we exchanged smiles and handshakes. I could tell a mere silent gesture of compassion was all that was needed to help him traverse that particular moment of trial. The environment warned of the risk involved, but it seemed the Spirit impressed me that sometimes, even when precarious, need must override risk, and compassion must overrule apprehension (1 John 4:18).

At the close of that final worship experience, many more inmates expressed a desire to follow Christ. Our last post-service fellowship and farewell time felt much more like a warm and loving church atmosphere than that of a prison. It was clear God had been at work in that Central American lockup long before we arrived, and He kindly graced our quartet of Americans with the blessing of joining Him.

While statistical reports are not our primary concern, the number of those responding to the gospel was significant. I will absolutely share that information, but not before I share our final encounter with the prison guards.

My limited prison ministry experience had taught me that the staff of most prisons are either unavailable or uninterested in our activities. In their defense, they obviously have to be preoccupied with security and safety, so a joint ministry effort that would require their attention and that of the inmates would not be wise. At any rate, as I considered our meeting with the guards at Choluteca, I was a bit surprised they had agreed to the idea. That is until I learned the commanding officer who had accepted the proposal was a believer.

When we arrived the next morning, he had twenty guards in double formation, waiting for us just outside the prison entrance. We were introduced, reminded of the time limitation, and asked to immediately proceed. I shared the gospel concisely, aware of the need to allow time for a meaningful response on their part. Sixteen guards indicated a decision to receive Christ. One of the four remaining was the Christian commander.

Once again, our instant fellowship in Christ removed prior barriers and awkwardness as we bade farewell to our new brothers. In this encounter, our listeners were wearing uniforms, badges, and bearing arms, but they were in no less need of Christ than their incarcerated counterparts.

This did not bring our involvement with this prison to an end, but a pause for an exciting progress report is in order. During our three-day campaign, over half of the prison population of four hundred came to know Christ; including almost two hundred in the general population, twelve of the sixteen women, thirteen of the twenty-nine gangsters, and sixteen of the twenty guards. The prospect of our ministry assisting in the completion of the prison chapel was even more exciting than ever, as the need for the facility had quickly become intense.

I was fairly certain our relationship with Terry, Arlene, and Open Eyes Ministries would be permanent. But I could not foresee if the same would be true of the Cholutecan church and prison. However, when we were invited to return and participate in the dedication of the completed chapel, I knew our response was to be a resounding yes.

Terry and Pastor Dubon promised to inform me as soon as progress would allow them to set a date, which they did early in 2006. We were to return in late August and early September. Although there was ministry to experience at home, in Africa and Romania beforehand, I was already anticipating the event as being a highlight of the year.

Get ready, we're fast-forwarding again.

With a calendar filled with ministry opportunities, the months did not pass slowly. Not surprisingly, our return team was the same as before—Ted, Joyce, Joe, and myself. After all, who in that previous experience was not eager to witness the potential spiritual progress made since the last incredible encounter?

We joined once again with an exuberant Pastor Dubon and his congregation on Sunday morning. Afterward, we took a ride to see the completed chapel structure, along with the required walls, towers, and fences, though the dedication service was not until Thursday.

There is typically nothing attractive about unpainted concrete blocks, plain cement floors, or even glistening new razor wire, but this place was breathtaking. Possibly the most gorgeous worship facility I had ever seen. We all shared smiles, hugs, and reactive comments. And I'm pretty sure Joyce released a tear or two; okay, maybe not just Joyce. We joined in a prayer of thanks and asked God's blessing on all that would happen in that place. It was all undeniably exciting, but I must insert at this point that my main reason for including this story concerns more than the dedication of an edifice.

We led church services in the evenings. Local newspapers and television and radio stations had requested interviews, all curious about the "wealthy" Americans and why they were willing to finance a Honduran prison construction. Each was an opportunity to testify to the love and gospel of Christ, and we were careful to take advantage.

The week became especially interesting when Pastor Dubon told us his church had received permission to provide hot meals and cold drinks for everyone in the prison on dedication day. The only catch was the funds needed to cover the cost would have to be raised in the two days remaining before the service. Of course, the visiting "celebrity" benefactors from the United States would figure prominently in the fund-raising effort.

The primary activity was taking to the streets during very busy times of the day with a public address system, sharing the gospel and telling of our need. Joyce sang, and I preached. Though not known for their material abundance, the Cholutecan citizens were enthusiastic and beyond sufficient in their response. Pastor Dubon gleefully informed us a feast would be provided. There would be roasted chicken, beans, rice, vegetables, and an ice-cold soft drink, all of which would be an unknown luxury to the prison population.

The morning of the chapel dedication arrived. Though the facility was complete, a plan for transferring the prisoners into it was not. They were only allowed to participate remotely by means of our audio system. The chapel was bustling with attendees, including local pastors, church members, political and prison system officials, and the media. Several dignitaries gave greetings and brief addresses, Joyce sang, and I preached the dedication sermon.

On behalf of his sponsoring church, Pastor Dubon presented our ministry with a beautiful plaque that commemorated the occasion and thanked us for our benevolence. Needless to say, it is in a cherished place of prominence in our ministry library where, God willing, it will remain until I no longer have a say in the matter.

After the closing prayer of dedication, we proceeded to serve lunch to over four hundred inmates. I suppose it could have been a potentially dangerous situation, when our team, the church members, and other volunteers carried a meal in each hand, trip after trip, to the eager prisoners. To the contrary, it was a wonderful reunion with friends and Christian brothers gained less than a year before. Not even the extra-oppressive Honduran heat could drain the atmosphere of enthusiasm. But it did make the ice-cold drinks a special hit—to all of us!

We then noticed something that had remained unchanged. The gangsters were not included. We remembered the spiritual progress in that area months earlier, but most of the men inside that complex were still unconverted. All of them were still suffering the earthly consequences of their deeds, a truth forgiveness or even conversion will rarely erase. We requested entry so that meals might be shared with them, and our wish was again granted. Guards carefully tended the door as our team and a few friends managed to get almost thirty meals and drinks inside.

For the third time in less than a year, we found ourselves securely enclosed with the gangsters. The same two men were still in authority, and we were treated with the respect they had promised. We also noticed several areas had been recently painted, and all the visible light bulbs seemed to be in working order.

We led them in a prayer of thanks for their unexpected feast. As they ate contentedly, we again shared the message of salvation. As the gospel presentation and the consumption of their meals ended almost simultaneously, I called for a response to Christ, as I had before. Many more men responded to the invitation, and we were again moved as we heard them pray, confessing sin and their need for a Savior.

When we moved to leave their compound for the last time, we were approached again by the two men in charge. What I was told through our translator is the principal reason I have taken you on this return trip to the harsh Honduran prison. After thanking us for the meal and our visit, the preeminent leader added, "Because of your visits last year and today, everyone in this area is now a Christian. We all believe in Jesus Christ."

I remembered, and you remember, how in the early days of our journey God reminded me of His words, "I was hungry and you gave Me something to eat, I was thirsty and you gave Me something to drink... I was in prison and you came to Me" (Matthew 25:35-36). We had done all three that day, and as it always does, Christian action validated the Christian message. Once again, those who experienced the love of the gospel gladly received the Lord of the gospel. We concluded our ministry in that prison with a peaceful and grateful satisfaction, knowing God had graciously included us in one of His unique opportunities.

Terry and Arlene relocated Open Eyes Ministries to another part of Honduras. Our partnership with them has not yet taken us back to Choluteca. However, we have continued to have wonderful prison ministry experiences in areas of the country nearer their headquarters.

There's the small prison in La Paz, where our ministry provided concrete and roofing materials to complete an addition to the existing chapel. There is a larger prison in Comayagua, where we first ministered in 2007. A fire in February 2012 killed over 350 inmates in the same facility. We returned nine months after, with toiletry kits for everyone in the repopulated prison. We also saw many come to Christ during our two-day evangelistic emphasis.

Finally, we held another two-day campaign in the national prison, a mammoth three thousand inmate facility located just outside the capital city of Tegucigalpa. There was a murder on the day before we arrived and on the day after we left, and we were told these were fairly common. As for our two days in-between, we were informed the inmates had a level of respect that restrained them from violence while ministers were present. At the close of both of our services, it was touching to see faceless hands extended through the narrow bars of second-story cells, located in such a way as to disallow eye contact. Hands extended to indicate a desire to receive Christ as Savior after hearing the gospel message echoed from our audio system. Hands that joined many others, whose faces we could see.

"The harvest is plentiful," Jesus said in Matthew 9:37. There is nothing more joyful for the believer or a church than participation in the reaping of that harvest. If we can set aside our hesitations, which are often caused by *who* or *where* that harvest may be, His joy will not escape us. And when He sees His desires are ours, He will not fail in ordering our steps in the appropriate direction (Psalm 37:23).

With the gangsters

Team member Ted Smith shares gospel with inmates

CHAPTER 13

NOT AFRAID OF THE DARK

Simon says, "Banku and fried rice is not what feeds your soul! You must feed your soul the Word of God!" Maybe I should have given advance warning, but we have just made a transatlantic leap from Central America to west Africa. You have seen how our rose has blossomed in many directions. Less than a year after our 2002 beginning, our flower would take us to the Dark Continent.

As our ministry began, I was naïvely pursuing the steps in officially establishing our nonprofit organization when Lynne and I traveled to Romania for the first time. When our project leader, Dr. Joe, learned of our plan, he shared the name and number of a friend who had recently entered a similar ministry. "All of this process will be fresh on his mind," he said, "and I'm sure he would help you. His name is Roy, and he's a lot like you—in church ministry for many years but moved into full-time evangelism and missions a year or so ago."

I gladly made the contact on our return home, and Roy and I met for lunch. This was one of those encounters that we think is going to accomplish some simple purpose and be done, but turns into much more. Roy did share very helpful information to get me started on the necessary legal process. But as we got acquainted, he also told me of his fresh involvement with ongoing evangelistic ministry in the west African nation of Ghana. I honestly do not recall if he extended the invitation or if I offered my partnership, but before long, we were making plans for a combined evangelistic effort in March 2003. The partnership continues in Ghana and has spread to many other areas of the world. I remain grateful Roy welcomed our new ministry in coming alongside his efforts, as our involvement in Ghana has been by far our most consistent, extensive, and productive overseas endeavor.

Almost a dozen years of partnership has developed a friendship with Roy like few others. I'm always reluctant to call someone a best friend, but he comes as close as anyone.

The dates of that first African experience, March 2-19, 2003, were especially significant to me. Our departure date would mark the first anniversary of our spiritual "exile." As the day approached, our friend Jackie commented, "It is amazing how far you have come in a year. This same day a year ago a familiar way of life came to a painful end, but now, just look. You have been to Romania twice, you are involved in ministries here at home, and on the very date that was so dark a year ago, you are boarding a plane for another new adventure!"

Yes, God was continuing to be what He is—good—and was continuing to work all things for good in my life. I had no idea what to expect of my first visit to the Dark Continent, but I was ready to find out.

Roy's friend James also joined us on my initial journey. A kind-hearted, bi-vocational pastor from the eastern part of our state, it was his first trip to Africa also—and his first time to be on an airplane. He has since made several trips, but we still share a laugh about his walk through the jet way to board our initial flight. When we reached the door of the aircraft, James literally stopped and nervously eyed the entire circumference of the entrance, as if entertaining the notion of changing his mind. He mustered his courage and took his seat next to Roy. By the end of our first flight, he was gaining a confidence about flying and has not given indication of hesitation since.

Considering that our ministry in Ghana has continued on a semi-annual basis for almost a dozen years, a travel log of the historical details is not a practical approach for our present purpose. I hope to paint a picture that adequately draws you into our experience, but I will likely omit as many details as I include. At any rate, you will still meet many people and visit many places that were unknown to me in 2002 but now figure prominently in my life.

Let's do it this way. Come along with me, and we'll travel to west Africa together. Keep in mind that we will be away for two weeks, sometimes three.

Depending on the airline, we may travel directly to Germany and then on to Africa. Or, we may stop in New York or Washington DC and from there travel to the Ghanaian capital of Accra.

We will be met by our host and project coordinator, the Reverend Doctor Samuel Lartey. "Sammy" is an energetic and determined pastor who is in his mid-sixties. Often called "bishop" because of his coordination of the many other pastors and personnel who serve under his authority, we can be assured he has carefully prepared for every detail. Transportation, lodging, meals, drinking water, and translators will be waiting. Not to mention the schedule of multiple schools where the gospel and Bibles will be shared daily. At least two village film crusades have also been scheduled each night, when a movie about the life of Christ is shown, followed by a presentation and explanation of the gospel to crowds who have likely just experienced their first motion picture. We Americans affectionately call Pastor Sammy "Samwell," and we remind ourselves at some point during every project of his immeasurable value.

The time of our arrival in Accra, along with the distance to our project base, will determine whether we spend the first night in the city. Additional factors also influence the decision, such as the time needed to acquire local currency and the usual stop at an American-style supermarket. We'll purchase any desired items such as snacks and soft drinks, as these will be very difficult to find wherever we settle. In the past we brought these from home, but due to packing restrictions, convenience, and increased availability in Accra, we now prefer this process.

Whether we remain in Accra or proceed to our project site, it will be best if you forget your concept of an American hotel. Though the hosts will be very accommodating and hospitable, even the nicest lodging by Ghanaian standards is probably not a place you would willingly choose in the United States. You are not prepared for the differences in the standards of quality. The cleanliness of our accommodations is not generally an issue, though the age, style, and condition of some of the furnishings may make it appear so.

Sammy usually manages to find us lodging that includes indoor plumbing with running water, a fan, and maybe even a struggling air conditioner. But be prepared. The electricity or water, or both, may shut down as often as once a day... or more. Typically the hotel is prepared, especially for the loss of water. A large plastic container in your bathroom, much like a garbage can, is filled with water and a dipper. The chilling experience of unheated water running down your back first thing every morning is fairly unavoidable. You see, even when the public utilities are functional, the water heater mounted on the wall likely doesn't work. But there is a positive side. If you are an early riser like me and are the first to enter the bath facilities, you can become a human alarm clock. Even your muffled reactions to the initial contact of the water are still sufficient to awaken your roommates.

There is another item of interest before leaving the subject of water. You may think you were dirtier than you thought when you see the brownish tint of the water running off you and down the drain. Dirt may be the reason, but when you've thoroughly cleaned yourself and notice the color is unchanged, you realize it is the water itself. Fortunately, this is not the case as a rule, but when it does happen, we take comfort in two ways. First, after encountering the African heat, humidity, and dust, you find that even discolored water is a welcome refreshment. Second, you experience an unsurpassed fulfillment of anticipation when you finally arrive back home, enter your own shower, and wash it all forever away. At least until your next visit.

Before we delve further into our adventures, you need to meet some of the personalities that are a part of our Ghanaian family. As far as the Americans are concerned, you've met Roy and James, but there are others who have accompanied us enough to be considered regulars. There is Mark, a pastor from Asheville, North Carolina; Andy, from Apex, North Carolina; and Nick, who lives north of Charlotte. There is also Craig, who recently relocated from the Washington DC area to Raleigh. Finally, our friend Dr. David brings his dental skills (and supplies, God bless him) on the occasions when we include medical clinics in our overall plan.

Most of these partners are not vocational ministers but all share an enthusiasm for the people of Ghana and their openness to the gospel. Though we in this group rarely see each other outside the Ghana trips, we have found that sharing the close proximity of our evangelistic efforts for two weeks at a time results in a level of familiarity equal to that of longtime friends.

Whether our American team is just Roy and myself or includes others, we are grateful to be joined by the indispensable host pastors who receive us in Ghana. In addition to Pastor Sammy is his right-hand man, Pastor Simon Akpolu, whom you met when I opened this chapter. Though the coordination, budgeting, and implementation is simultaneous, we actually conduct two projects while in their country. Pastor Sammy accompanies Roy each day, while Pastor Simon has served as my guide and partner since our initial campaign. Our teams are centrally located but travel to different points every morning and evening.

Also assisting us through the years with translating, Bible distribution, handling equipment, and other details are Pastors Ebenezer Agbleze, Samuel Tehteh, Jacob Jacobu, Emmanuel Ayikuma, John Amaule, and others. Amos and Delanyo Akpolu, the sons of Pastor Simon, also lend a hand.

I realize these names hold little meaning to you, but I simply cannot omit them from my story. They are prominent in the lives and work of all of us who visit their country. These gentle Ghanaians go beyond the call of duty to ensure our safety, convenience, and comfort to the extent we are seldom allowed to carry our own water, camera, or even a Bible. When you see their ingenuous environment and culture, you will understand why they and all Ghanaians seem to take such a plain and practical approach to life.

For example—picking on James again—we often recall with another chuckle his first encounter with Pastor Sammy. Early in the conversation, James noticed the dazzling whiteness of Sammy's shirt against his dark skin. He could not resist the well-intended question, "How do you keep your clothes so white?" Pastor Sammy looked at James with an almost curiously puzzled expression and answered stoically, "We wash dem!"

"These men did not come to Ghana for a summer holiday," I have heard Sammy pray. And when we set out the first morning to take the gospel presentation and Bibles into schools, we soon understand his meaning. The drive itself is eye-opening, as we jostle our way across severely deteriorated pavement, washboard dirt roads, and washed-out trails. The golden oldie "Shake, Rattle, and Roll"[1] often comes to mind. Each time we reach a school, a quick self-exam is in order to ensure all body parts are returning to their correct locations.

We will visit some schools that are located in the vicinity of the town or village where we lodge. Most will be in remote and secluded areas, where Americans are surprised to find people at all. You can imagine the adverse effects the terrain has on a vehicle, so do not be surprised if we are delayed by a flat tire, loose steering linkage, or worse. Finally, though it seems we are driving through a forsaken wilderness, it will suddenly appear—a school.

Remember when I said to forget what you know about American hotels? The same goes for schools. Some may be a grass roof supported by poles of bamboo or tree limbs with a floor of dirt. Most, however, are crude concrete structures with open rafters and a metal roof. They also feature permanently open windows and doorways. There is no concern about theft or vandalism, because nothing is left on the premises in the evenings or on weekends. Desks are made of rough lumber and usually accommodate at least two students each; three when they crowd together to hear the *obruni* or the *yavo,* the white man. That may take place in one room, or if the school is too large, students, faculty, and furniture are moved outside under the available shade.

Coming from American culture, you will be quite impressed by the level of genteel respect displayed by the uniformed students. Unless instructed to move to our meeting place in a singing march formation, it is obvious from their energetic gathering that they are indeed normal young people. However, when the headmaster or his representative calls them to attention, it becomes equally obvious they have been disciplined in mannerly etiquette.

Pastor Simon has informed us the proper behavior of the youngsters is due to the lingering British influence and the accountability to their parents— and to all adults when in public. Seeing a thin cane or rod in the hand of the headmaster or other authority is commonplace, and you can expect to see it forcefully used if a student is brave enough to challenge the rules of the occasion.

I recall one morning when we arrived at our first school. All the students were already in their classrooms, with the exception of a short line of souls outside, who were each receiving three punishing strikes to the backside. Curiously disturbed at the sight, I asked Pastor Simon if he knew the reason for the punishment. He replied, "They are guilty of excessive tardiness. They are warned that if they arrive late for school more than three times, they will be punished."

I'll leave you to yourself in debating their disciplinary practices, but I will say it is refreshing to experience the exemplary conduct of these third world children. The opening, "Hallo-o-o," of the headmaster is answered with a, "Hi-i-i-i," from the students and then repeated to be sure all have come to attention. To see them collectively rise at the entrance of an adult into their midst is pleasantly impressive. To hear them in unison as they bestow, "Good mah-ning, sehs," upon the guests who have appeared before them; to hear, "Tank you, seh," accompanied by a curtsy after receiving a Bible; to have them scurry to provide the most comfortable chair available for their guest and to be sure it is first wiped clean of dust or dirt.

If we arrive at our first school of the morning before their official time to begin—horrors! There they are with small, straw brooms, sweeping floors, outside walkways, and even the bare ground free of any paper, leaves, or debris. Grassy areas, which are sometimes quite expansive, do not remain unnoticed for long before the mowing team is dispatched. Each wields the tool of choice, a machete. No gas-powered mower, no old-time, rotary, push mower. A machete. It's quite a sight to see these primitive landscapers go after their job with such energy, and I can assure you grass is flying in every direction until the entire area is evenly manicured. Their environment is so substandard by American ideals that we may wonder why all the fuss. But they insist on beginning their day in presentable surroundings. And I say, "Good for them!"

After explanations and introductions in regard to our presence, we move into the focus of every school visit, trying to be mindful of their time. "How many desire to go to heaven when you leave this earth?" is the question asked early in our comments, to which all give a heartily positive response. We often ask for opinions on how one may obtain eternal life. Though the school may be sponsored by a Christian denomination, and though you may have heard a familiar hymn of the faith being sung on our approach, the answers are normally vague and biblically uninformed.

"We must understand three very important steps if we hope to have eternal life in heaven," we continue. What follows is a very concise summary of the message we share, and it has remained unchanged in every venue we have faced since my involvement began in 2003. While we agree Christian service has a variety of "faces," we are dedicated to the purpose of evangelism in our Ghanaian ministry, so our message is consistently simplistic.

First, we *must understand the truth about ourselves.* We all have a sinful nature (Romans 3:23), passed down to all people since Adam's failure in the garden of Eden. Our sin separates us from a perfect and holy God (Isaiah 59:2) and will keep us out of His perfect and holy heaven.

Second, *we must understand the truth about Jesus Christ.* God's Old Testament law required the blood of a perfectly clean and spotless sacrifice be shed in order to forgive sin. This centuries-long practice pictured and prepared the way for the final sacrifice that God, Himself, would provide in Jesus Christ. The New Testament marked the end of the old practice, as God sent Christ into the earth. Born of the Virgin Mary, He was fathered by God the Holy Spirit (Luke 1:35) and, therefore, inherited the perfect nature necessary to be the perfect and final sacrifice for sin. Upon His death, burial, and resurrection, God opened the door of heaven to all.

However, not everyone will go to heaven, as we see in the third step. *We must understand the truth about eternal life.* God's desire is that all people be saved, but He does not force salvation or eternal life on anyone. It is offered to us as a gift that must be willingly received or rejected (Ephesians 2:8–9). Each of us must make a choice. We may confess sinfulness, repent, and receive the gift of Jesus Christ, which is eternal life. To do nothing is to ignore and refuse His gift and to spend eternity separated from Him in torment.

So do they respond? My, do they respond! We are careful to explain to them the importance of making a genuine, independent choice. We are careful to warn against a response that is merely a polite acceptance of a visitor's offer. We are careful to warn against praying an empty prayer as a reflection of others who might be praying around them. We are careful to remind them to be truthful in their hearts and minds, which are clearly discerned by our omniscient God. Still, by the dozens—and depending on the size of the crowd, by the hundreds—they bow reverently and confess Christ as the way to eternal life and invite Him into their lives.

"Do you think they were all sincere?" I am commonly asked. There is no way I can confidently answer that question, because unlike God, I am not all-knowing. However, as soon as we see the enthusiastic response on the part of these students, we also carefully inform them of what will take place in their lives if they made a genuine decision for Christ—truth that every professed believer would do well to contemplate daily, regardless of the continent of residence.

"If you have truly received Christ, you will now have a desire to follow Him and live for Him," they are encouraged. We urge them to remember it is not those who merely say, "Lord, Lord," who will enter the kingdom of heaven, but those, "who do the will of the Father who is in heaven" (Matthew 7:21); Jesus said, "If you continue in My word, then you are truly disciples of Mine" (John 8:31).

How do we, "do the will of the Father," and, "continue in His word?" By *knowing* and *living* the Word of God. The Word of God is the *will* of God, so we must not neglect His Word in our lives. We must all be careful of assuming the correct verbal and emotional response to the gospel is the only evidence necessary to show that true repentance and salvation have occurred. While the desire to live eternally and escape God's wrath is undoubtedly sincere in everyone, the authentication of a true conversion is seen in the direction a life takes *following* that initial step. Therefore, a real experience with Christ on the part of supposed converts probably cannot be determined instantly. The real experience will be verified as time passes, as a person demonstrates a hunger for Christ, a desire to know more of Christ, and a desire to please Christ by serving Christ. Desire determines drive, and all of these will drive the genuinely converted person to pursue the knowledge of God's Word and exposure to environments that will feed and fulfill that desire.

"We are going to give you a copy of God's Word," we tell the new African disciples. "Read a portion of it every day, perhaps beginning in the gospel of John. As you know God's Word, you will come to know God. Go to a church where they teach the Word of God. The prayer you have prayed today is important, but it is not what will change you. The Word of God will change you and make you like Jesus. Will you do this?"

"Yes, please," is the polite reply.

"You also need to pray each day," we add. "Speak with God, and listen to God. Tell Him your troubles and fears. Pray for your family, friends, and school. Ask Him to help you understand His Word as you read. When you make a mistake, and we *all* will still make mistakes, ask Him to forgive you (1 John 1:9). He loves you and wants to bless you. He has no desire to harm you."

Finally, the students are admonished to be a witness of their new faith. "You are not ashamed or embarrassed about your decision today, are you?" we ask.

"No-o-o," is the unanimous answer.

"Then let your family and friends know you have received God's forgiveness and eternal life, and tell them how that has happened. You can help them receive Christ also."

We are sometimes told by a student of the difficulty ahead due to a Muslim family, and we may hear an ensuing story of how that has played out in the days following. It is inspiring to often see an undaunted attitude in the face of potential unpleasantness.

Pastor Simon takes over, and it is at this point he declares, "You must feed your soul the Word of God!" He supervises the distribution of Bibles, which includes New Testaments for the older students, gospel of John booklets for the younger, full Bibles for teachers who make a decision, and a large Bible for the school. The latter is signed and presented to the headmaster. Simon then instructs that a Bible reading club be formed at the school with the promise of an occasional pastoral visitor, who will investigate its progress.

Ever attentive to proper etiquette, Pastor Simon's request for permission to leave the school is followed by a formal word of thanks from the headmaster or other representative. We often hear something like, "We are grateful that you have come to us, and we thank you for sharing the Word of God. We will not forget the truth you have told us, and if you return, we pray you will find us living the words you have shared." Hearing their farewell, it would seem they discerned the meaning and the mandate of the gospel.

Following a half-day of school ministry, our team returns to the hotel. We wash away the heat and dust, rinse out shirts and socks, and settle in to share stories of the morning. There will be a few hours to fellowship, rest, read, or study, while hoping the electricity will remain available so we can have some comfort in the afternoon heat. As darkness approaches, it will be time for our drivers to again "collect" us (as they put it) and head out to the film crusades, where more adventure awaits.

Jeff Andler and Simon Akpolu at school

School from 2nd story steps

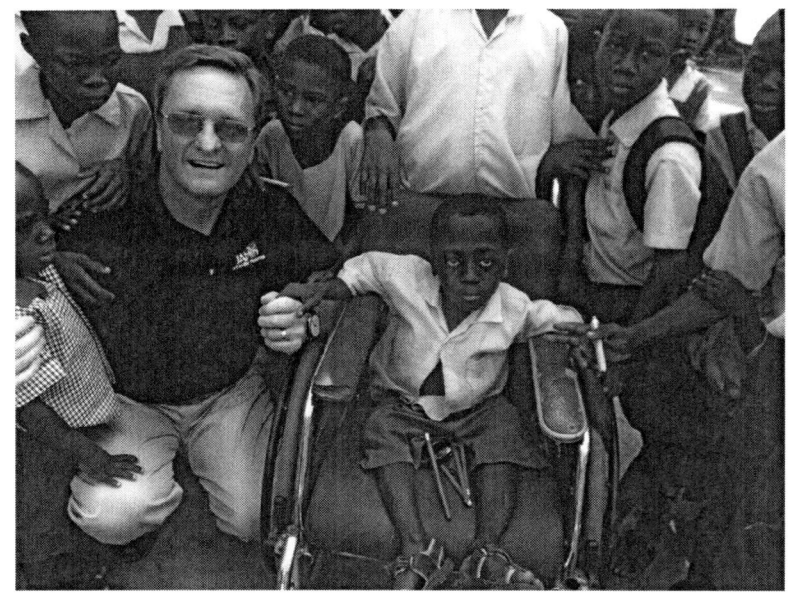

With Young Ones

CHAPTER 14

INTO THE NIGHT

"Aren't you afraid when you go to these places?" You can imagine how many times I've heard that question from friends and family. It's more than understandable when you consider someone they know is about to venture into an environment that is totally foreign. Whether an American prison or an African village, there are bound to be potential surprises and dangers lurking, right? Dangerous? Maybe. Unfamiliar? Definitely.

Every time we arrive in Accra, the swarming crowd waiting in the transportation area is a reminder that "We ain't from here!" Fortunately, the most threatening individuals we face are the desperate souls who are determined to carry a suitcase in hopes of receiving a badly needed tip.

Shortly after arriving it is usually approaching nightfall, but the lights of the Ghanaian capital ward off the darkness much like any other city. However, when the sun sets in the areas where we conduct our ministry, we experience one of the many reasons why this land may be known as the "Dark Continent."

When it comes time to venture into the villages where evening film crusades are scheduled, the distance to the particular site determines if we will leave our hotel in the afternoon with the Ghanaian setup team, or wait for the driver to return for us after they are prepared. Distance is determined as much by minutes as by miles due to the typically horrid conditions of the roads and trails that must be traveled. If the time needed to reach the village is extensive, we board the vehicle and head out for a long afternoon and evening, with water bottles, snacks, and flashlights in hand. The ride will likely be a repeat of the jarring experience that morning, so by the time we arrive at our destination, we can feel physically drained and disheveled.

The African crew goes to work immediately, unloading the audio crates and cases, speakers, mounting poles, projector, movie screen, generator, table, and chairs—all in preparation to show the life of Christ on film. I was taught as a youngster that when you see work being done, you lend a hand without being asked. Unless I absolutely insist, that philosophy doesn't work with my Ghanaian friends because they see it as inappropriate for their visitor to join in the labor, even though we are supposed to be sharing in a joint effort.

One of the first items out of the van is one of those stackable plastic chairs. I'm almost positive it followed me from Central America. It is placed in a shady spot for me to relax and wait. The audio system is quickly engaged so that a musical recording can be played, to announce our arrival to all who hear. Children usually appear first, which generally takes me from my seat to walk, take pictures, entertain, and be entertained. Very young children may be quite frightened at their first glimpse of the white man with the strange hair. Their older counterparts are curious and playful.

As the sun begins to set, the music continues to play, and the microphones are tested, all to the point of the obnoxious audio phenomenon known as feedback. The countryside will be audibly bombarded in this manner throughout the entire evening. While the Ghanaians seem to be oblivious to the annoyance, many of us Americans find it nerve-racking, usually before Jesus has performed His first miracle on film.

At the onset of darkness, teenagers and adults arrive, and attendees arrange themselves on the ground, under trees, on logs or rocks, and in the doorways and windows of nearby huts. The host pastor takes the microphone and welcomes the crowd, states our purpose, and the movie begins.

Though the American-made film is translated into a Ghanaian dialect, it may not be the one spoken at our current location. If not, one of our local team members must remain on the microphone and voice a second translation. We are sometimes amused at the dramatic license taken, as when the crucifixion scene is enhanced by "Ow, ow," and, "O-o-h, oh." After hearing this during our first few visits, I finally asked Simon, "Why does the translator need to say 'ow' and 'oh' at the point of Jesus' crucifixion?" In the usual stoic manner the answer was given: "Because it hurts." For most in the audience, if not all, it will be the first time

It Gets Even Better

to witness such a visual display, so there is no problem holding their attention.

At the risk of appearing to desire pampered treatment, we admit a measure of relief when the evening location is closer to our hotel. In this case, the Ghanaian team is able to begin the afternoon setup without us. After they are prepared and nightfall signals the beginning of the movie, a driver is sent to collect us in time to share the gospel message at the picture's end. Though this procedure shortens an otherwise lengthy and tiresome day, it has presented us with some interesting adventures just the same.

In one of our early projects, two taxis were sent to our hotel each night to transport Roy and me to our respective film sites. That meant a total stranger would appear at our door, inviting us to board a rather dilapidated vehicle and disappear into the night. We cautiously joked about how simple it would be for one of these strangers to lose us in the darkness, never to be seen again.

We made it to our destinations, but my confidence was not bolstered by the fact that on our return the first two nights, the taxis I rode both had a flat tire. The second had no spare. I was beginning to think I would be spending the night in the black Ghanaian countryside with a stranger and heaven knows what else. But something pleasantly unusual happened; in fact, unheard of. A four-door pickup approached and offered assistance. Not the usual two-door but a four-door, which meant an extra seat in need of passengers. When you consider that we usually ride "forever" at night without seeing another vehicle, the appearance of this rescue was amazing.

The taxi driver loaded his deflated tire in the back and then joined me in the rear seat, leaving his crippled vehicle behind for the night. As we closed the doors and traded introductions with our new chauffer and his wife, I was further amazed to realize we would be enjoying the rare treat of air-conditioning. The remaining ride to the hotel was filled with congenial and comfortable English conversation, which revealed our benefactors to be believers!

While my ride the next night did not feature a flat tire, it presented a new experience. After turning off the main road and driving for some time on a dark and deserted trail, the driver informed me he needed to stop and add water to his radiator. I watched him empty an old, plastic water jug, and we progressed successfully to our film crusade.

The return trip was another story. On the same stretch of road, the driver brought the car to a stop, grabbed his jug, informed me he was going for water, and quickly disappeared into the bush. In an instant, I was sitting completely alone in darkness. While trying to ignore the fact I had just been totally deserted and wondering where he expected to find water, I noticed the flickering of light through the distant bushes. I concluded there must have been some dwellings tucked away in the area, as several sets of young eyes emerged from the brush outside my window. They were curiously and harmlessly investigating the lone white man who had unintentionally invaded their territory.

"How are you?" is commonly understood by most Ghanaians, and I was answered by the usual, "We ah fine, an' you?" That was where our ability to communicate ended. But it was enough to establish an atmosphere of friendship and safety. Sure enough, the driver soon returned with enough water to satisfy the car's thirsty radiator and deliver me safely to my night's rest.

Our safe passage through many nighttime adventures reminds me of David's words, "If I say, surely the darkness will overwhelm me, and the light around me will be night, even the darkness is not dark to Thee, and the night is as bright as the day" (Psalm 139:11–12).

Whether the eyes of the head or the heart, God sees clearly when we must squint and strain. He detects every detail where we must reach for a lantern. He is no less able to provide complete protection in the dark of the jungle midnight as in the light of noonday, whatever that jungle may be. We cannot always know what our days have in store, but we *can* always know He sees the darkness coming before we do. He has our protection and rescue positioned and waiting to function according to His purposes.

As for the actual film crusade services, most are predictable. A crowd of varying size gathers, the film is shown, the gospel is presented, and many indicate a desire to trust Christ. Predictable in this case does not mean unexciting, as sharing the old story never gets old, and seeing people respond is always rewarding. But on occasion there are additional occurrences that linger vividly in the memory.

By way of examples, it's not unusual to have an intoxicated villager be disruptive, but such an instance is quickly brought under control by our Ghanaian hosts. One individual did not make himself known until after the event was completed, and our equipment was being dismantled with only flashlights to rival the darkness. I began to notice a man following my every step and lingering uncomfortably close. Finally, one of our local team members took my arm and said, "Come with me to the van. This man has been drinking and thinks you have money. If he thinks there is a chance, he may try to harm you." I went to the van and remained with my protector.

On another occasion, I stood at the appropriate time to explain the gospel message of the film. A woman began to run back and forth through the crowd, shrieking like a banshee. Her ghostly, black garment was trailing eerily behind her in the breeze created by her movement. Our team subdued her as well. An investigation revealed she had recently lost her husband and was overcome with grief.

James testifies of the night when a juju priest came to the film crusade intending to cast a spell on him. The witchdoctor was captivated by the story of Christ and confessed Him as Savior!

Andy returned one evening telling us how a commotion erupted at the edge of the crowd about the time he was to present the gospel (Maybe you've correctly discerned this is usually the time distractions arise). When the disturbance finally settled, the explanation was given that a fair-size cobra was invading audience space and had to be dealt with.

That's not the only run-in we've encountered with critters. One night I stood to share the gospel but was interrupted by a villager who rose and moved me aside, so he might stomp the four-inch scorpion crawling near my feet. Being made aware of their presence, I continued speaking while pointing to additional approaching scorpions. They seemed to be unusually curious that evening, to their demise. All were similar in size to their deceased leader, and I was comforted little by the information that the smaller versions are actually the most venomous.

Especially memorable to me was a film crusade experience to which I will dedicate more detail. Located not far from the ocean, it was a larger village, and our Ghanaian associates estimated that perhaps almost fifteen hundred people were in attendance. The event was without incident, and we saw hundreds indicate a decision for Christ. As we packed the equipment for the journey back to our hotel, one of the pastors approached me, escorting a man who was noticeably unsettled. I could see in his hand a worn paper bag, which I learned contained various lotions and fragrances. "This man uses these things in his worship of the sea spirits every night," I was told. "His life has been controlled by demonic influence, but tonight he heard the gospel from his hut and wants to receive Jesus Christ. He wants to be free of the spirits that control him."

He released the bag as I carefully reviewed the gospel with him, ensuring he understood and was ready to make a sincere commitment to Christ. Simon and two other pastors had gathered with me, and we all gently placed our hands on this desperate soul. As I led him in the prayer of faith, he began to quake and tremble. And as he repented of sin and confessed Christ, he collapsed limply and became still on the ground. Our Ghanaian friends knelt beside him, helped him to a seated position, and began to comfort and encourage him in his newfound faith and freedom.

Seeing they had the situation in hand and could more effectively communicate with him, I returned to assist those loading the van. Only moments had passed when I felt something behind me. I turned to see the new convert, quite calm, submissive, and in control, fall to his knees before me. He held my hands and repeatedly expressed his gratitude.

I was touched by this reminder of the man Jesus delivered in Mark 2:15 who, once tormented by demons, sat with Jesus "in his right mind." However, I was also reminded of the incident in Revelation 19, where the apostle John bowed to worship at the feet of an angel. Like that angel, I was immediately uncomfortable with this man kneeling before me. I kindly instructed him through translation to rise to his feet, and we thanked God together for the wonderful change in his life. He lingered as long as he could before disappearing into the darkness—without the bag that once represented his bondage.

We were all quietly peaceful as we completed our preparation for the return ride—a ride that somehow would not be nearly as uncomfortable as the one earlier that evening. For the first time, I found myself grateful to my

Ghanaian friends for driving the audio system at such uncomfortable levels. Somehow it wasn't too loud after all.

Just before boarding the van, I once again felt something behind me. This time it was much more abrupt and imposing. One of the pastors was pushing me aside as he aimed a flashlight toward my feet. Yes, a large scorpion was inching toward me. It was finally destroyed after several stomps of my rescuer's foot, which was shod by only a flimsy flip-flop. The thought of the proximity of such a creature was a bit unnerving. Yet, this faded in significance as I continued to reflect on the manner of spiritual deliverance we had just witnessed. My rest that night was peaceful, and I had a feeling that in a dark village hut a few miles away, a new brother in Christ was experiencing the same for the first time in his life.

We occasionally venture into the villages for reasons other than the nightly film crusades. While the experience is less foreboding in the light of day, it can be no less interesting.

It was a Saturday, and our host pastors had scheduled a service for dozens of new converts awaiting baptism. Having never seen a baptismal pool in any church building in Ghana, I knew this observance would be held in whatever body of water was available. Based on previous experience, I assumed it would be some extension of the Volta River, which always seems to follow us wherever we go. However, in the area of this particular project, the only water conveniently nearby was a small lake that was actually formed by the overflow of the Volta during the rainy season. That season was months past, and the distance to the cleaner and more appealing Volta was too great for our crowd to walk. The lake was owned by the village next to it, and local pastor Ebenezer had gained permission from the village elders for our service. Realizing this village practiced false religion, we were grateful for their willingness to welcome our presence and practices.

We would find again that there are reasons for all circumstances. Keep reading. I haven't said this in a while; this really gets even better!

As our group of American missionaries, local pastors, believers, and baptismal candidates made the long walk down the dry and dusty trail, the morning heat increased by the minute. Roy and I consistently noticed one of the women walking laboriously ahead of us, quite obviously great with child. "Is she all right?" we asked Ebenezer.

"She is in labor," he answered. "The baby is coming, and she needs to go to a doctor. But she has been waiting to be baptized and refuses to go until she obeys the Lord in baptism first." Roy reacted with his trademark "Oh my!" and immediately suggested she be the first to be baptized, while we returned to the village to bring the Land Rover to collect her in all of her wetness. Our hope was to at least get her back to the main road, where a public bus would soon pass and hopefully take her to the nearest clinic. "When you return," Ebenezer said, "you can cut through the brush straight to the road without going back to the village."

We left Mark and James to handle the baptisms and quickly made our way to retrieve the temporary ambulance. When we returned to the lake, she was waiting, freshly baptized, soaking wet, and in the travail of childbirth. A sheet was wrapped around her, and Roy and I helped her to lie down in the back seat. "Let's get her to the road," I insisted to Roy, "I don't know nothin' 'bout birthin' no babies!"

We had to drive slowly, as the two Ghanaians who walked outside the vehicle made sure our path was clear. Saturday morning Tarzan movies were a boyhood favorite of mine. Here we were, moving through the African bush, with our guides clearing the way. The only thing missing was the distant call of the Ape Man signaling that help was at hand. Where was Tarzan when we needed him?

Just as the road came into view, one final obstacle was draped in our path. A rare power line was sagging between two poles at the level of our headlights. Our helpers were not tall enough to raise the cable above the vehicle, so they each stepped on it, holding it on the ground long enough for us to pass over. Fortunately, no damage was done to the vehicle, the cable, or most especially, to our brave assistants.

We pulled out of the bush onto the edge of the road and immediately saw a bus approaching. One of the Ghanaians succeeded in getting the crowded transport to stop and receive the struggling mother-to-be. The driver assured us a clinic was in a small town a short distance away. Roy and I breathed a sigh of relief, both glad the story of delivering a baby would not be in our repertoire. Later that day, we were told the young lady was indeed delivered to a clinic, just in time to give birth to a healthy baby boy.

I still contemplate the amazing event we witnessed. Two people came forth from water that day, a baby boy to new life in the world and his mother to new life in Christ. A son that was *born,* a soul that was born *again.* My prayer for that little guy, and for us all, is to find it in ourselves to emulate the example of his determined young mother and convert. No, I'm not sure that insisting on baptism while in intense labor is actually required by God. But to know Him and to be determined to follow Him in a way that transcends comfort and convenience is a quality that every believer would do well to covet. Only heaven knows the extent to which the kingdom would profit.

Have you kept reading? What happens next is good… uh, even better!

By the time Roy and I had our adventure behind us, the baptismal service at the lake was coming to a close. As Mark, James, and the final candidates were drying themselves of the murky water and the residue it left on them, Ebenezer informed us we were all to pay a respectful visit to the village elders.

We were welcomed with the usual Ghanaian meekness and courtesy, and began our tour of their typical community of mud huts and grass roofs. At the back area of the village was a path that led to a structure that stood to itself. As we approached, we could see that only the charred mud walls remained. The roof and all that was in the small building had been burned away. We could see that much of the landscape surrounding the rear of the village had been affected by fire as well.

With Ebenezer serving as our mouthpiece, we asked the obvious question. "What happened here?" The village elder who was leading our tour explained. The ruins before us had been a shrine that housed the village god. It was fashioned from wood. "The brush around us caught fire and spread to the edge of our village. Our shrine was destroyed, along with our god. We need a new god," is what the village elder actually said to us. As our hearts pitied their spiritual ignorance and deception, our American team looked at each other and almost simultaneously declared, "We can help with that!"

Our prepared schedule did not include this village, but Pastors Sammy and Ebenezer seized the opportunity to obtain permission to hold a film crusade on the Sunday evening after the Americans departed for home. Permission was granted, and we later received a report that almost two hundred villagers indicated the decision to trust Christ in response to seeing His life portrayed on film. As is the usual practice in such situations, representatives from the nearest church were sent the next Sunday to conduct services with the new congregation.

Just when fire had destroyed their false hope, God graciously allowed us to be present to offer them true hope. They needed a new god, and they were mercifully afforded the opportunity to receive the *only* God they needed, the *only* God there is, the God that is impervious to fire or any destructive force of earth. The God who is reached through His Son Jesus Christ, the God who makes His shrine in the very hearts of those who receive Him (1 Corinthians 6:19; Galatians 2:20). In regard to this experience, it is truly fitting when we often hear the Ghanaian children sing,

All of de other gods, they are de works of man

You are de Most High God, there is none like You.

Jehovah, You are de Most High, Jehovah, You are de Most High God!

Jehovah, You are de Most High, Jehovah, You are de Most High God![1]

There are so many more stories to tell, which means there are so many more to be omitted. Hopefully enough has been shared to give an adequate picture of our African story and the lasting impact it has had in their lives, and ours. Whatever work God begins, He continues until completion, and we are blessed to continue the observation and the involvement in that progression.

I think of Pastor Emmanuel, who tells us of the continuing success he is having in reaching many Muslims with the gospel in the area of Atibubu, about three hours from Kumasi. This is the northernmost area we have visited, where the Muslim concentration is greater.

It was there in early 2011 we held a medical project, treating hundreds of patients and seeing thousands of decisions for Christ. Andy quite capably filled the role of the daily coordinator of the medical team. He reported one day the heartfelt comment of a Muslim observer. "There is something powerful about your God," he said. "You help everyone, not just Christians."

Again, when the love of Christ is seen *in* His people, the gospel is made more appealing to many who are *not* His people. Yes, it is the Father who draws people to Christ (John 6:44), but I wonder how often His love in believers is used as an effective magnet?

All the Americans agree our experiences in Africa have made us more aware of evangelism at home. James says, "Going to Ghana has changed my life. I am now bolder with the gospel where I live." Andy reports, "My experiences in Africa have made me more evangelistically minded. I used to be a 'regular' Christian, but now my perspective has changed. Time is short." Dr. Roy agrees: "It will result in a changed priority at home."

They are absolutely right. Seeing people saved results in a greater awareness of people who *need* to be saved. Seeing people saved results in *wanting* to see more people saved. Seeing people saved must also result in my willingness to be God's tool in seeing people saved. It will result in propelling me to do what Pastor Sammy says of our efforts, "We go where others dare not go." Down a rougher, dustier road, into a darker, blacker night, to a more remote and isolated village.

What cost can be too high? What risk can be too great? Jesus made it clear that the worth of just one soul cannot be equaled by gaining the entire world (Matthew 16:26)—not all the gold, not all the silver, not all the diamonds and precious stones, not all the oil, not all the undiscovered wealth, not all the fame and influence. He confirmed His claim by giving Himself to redeem fallen mankind who was created in His image. He came where no one else could come to do what no one else could do, and did not hesitate.

May we never hesitate to say to Christ as we echo Pastor Sammy's heart, "I will go where others will not go, I will do what others will not do, I will say what others are not saying, I will give what others are not giving." Those who receive Christ through that witness are worth it all, even if it is just one. Our lives will be blessed. Our lives will be better. And even if one day our lives are required, it will be a sacrifice yet unequal to the worth of that one soul.

Ghana President John Mahama with Roy Mason and Jeff Andler - 2012

James baptizes woman in labor

CHAPTER 15

NO BAG FOR YOUR JOURNEY

There is a question that arises almost without fail, even when I share an abbreviated version of our story with someone. It is a logical question after hearing enthusiastic tales of travels to distant lands, the construction of children's camps and prison chapels, the coordination of medical projects, local home restorations, and more. Has the question crossed your mind? If not, let me help you out because I love to respond when people ask, "So how is all of this funded?"

As I begin, let me first assure you that you are not about to endure a plea for financial partnership and support. You did not come this far with me to be pressed in regard to money; and guess what? We are not interested in talking about money. It's not what we do. Money can be a delicate subject, but talking about how God has faithfully provided is an excitedly different matter altogether. I encourage you to relax and enjoy the examples of God's consistent provision toward us—examples that will hopefully encourage your heart and build your faith as they have ours.

I trust you remember how God first reminded me of His concerns on this earth, and launched me onto the path that lay ahead. As you saw, I busied myself by pursuing that path, but had the idea it would probably be a bridge to something more akin to ministry that was familiar to me. We have seen the journey that followed. However, I was not initially aware these activities would become permanently vocational rather than just temporarily therapeutic.

In those early days of uncertainty, God's provision was seen in dramatic ways. Within three months after our separation from steady pay and position, we had ten thousand dollars more in the bank than before! He was making it more than obvious that we were not going to starve or become delinquent with ongoing expenses. And as described, increased ministry activity kept me occupied and satisfied. I was seeing like never before the truth of "Seek first the kingdom of God… and all these things will be added unto you" (Matthew 6:33). I was also enjoying the new experience of *service without stress.*

Having returned to speaking terms with God, I recall praying one morning, "Lord, I thank you for the provision and for the opportunities to lead a productive life. I still do not know what you are going to have me do permanently, but—" God hasn't often done this, but it was as if He stopped me midsentence and dead in my tracks. I'm almost sure I heard Him say, "Hello! You're doing it! Keep doing it!"

Keep doing it? My ministry life had always been more scheduled and structured, so I had not considered I was moving to a life of days that are truly ordered by the Lord rather than church plans and programs. *Okay,* I thought. *God has been providing. I see no reason why He will stop. I am enjoying ministry more than I have in a long time. Okay, keep doing it.*

After sharing this epiphany with a slightly skeptical Lynne, I continued to discuss the subject with close friends, primarily those you have met. My friend Ted responded by offering some practical advice. "If you believe this is the direction God wants you to take, you should consider establishing an official faith-based ministry. Give it a name, set up a nonprofit status, and let people give. Once they know what you are doing, I think a lot of folks will support your efforts."

Heeding his insight, I went to work on the process. I learned the first step was quite simple and mainly involved a phone call to the Internal Revenue Service. There would be periodic steps that followed over the next fifteen months that would complete the IRS recognition of our nonprofit ministry. Despite our often stereotypical attitude toward this agency, I was pleasantly surprised to find each phone conversation engaged me with some very kind and patient people.

I was first told our ministry needed to have a name. *What to call it?* I wondered. As much to speed the process as for any other reason, I decided to use my own name and called it Jeff Andler Ministries. I almost immediately noticed a combination of letters that formed a nickname by which we are known, "JAMin." This name seems to catch on quickly, and while people may not always remember Jeff Andler, they never seem to forget "JAMin."

We are often referred to as "JAMin. Ministries," which once caused our clever son to observe, "Dad, you need to tell people it is not 'JAMin Ministries.' That would actually make it Jeff Andler Ministries Ministries." He was right, of course, but if people manage to include "JAMin," I don't usually correct them.

Coinciding with the time we were establishing our ministry, I was invited to lead worship at a nearby Christian businessmen's conference. The man and his family who were leading the conference had led a faith-based ministry for many years, and I looked forward to any advice he might offer. We sat alone at dinner one evening. "Your years of involvement in churches mean you know a lot of people," he said. "You need to let them know your plan and ask them to consider giving support." It sounded like practical advice, though a degree of discomfort was sparked inside at the thought of becoming a fund-raiser.

Why? You met my mother, who had led a ministry for almost fifty years. Almost forty of these were totally faith-based. I had often heard her say how she never asked people for money, but petitioned God only. I admired that, and I witnessed her ministry receive consistent provision. I also had recently read some of the history of George Mueller, the nineteenth-century minister who operated orphanages in London. As a testimony to others, he predetermined he would pursue the Lord alone for his needs. He subsequently ministered to over ten thousand orphans and preached the gospel near and far.

Though I yearned to have a similar testimony, I justified myself for the moment and accepted the counsel I heard. I made plans to pursue a strategy the very next week.

For several weeks, I made phone calls to former church friends and acquaintances that led to enjoyable visits and occasional meals. Lynne accompanied me on some of these, and while we enjoyed renewing friendships, I never completely suppressed the discomfort of asking for money. Lynne liked it even less. We did realize some modest response but not nearly enough to support a ministry or a family.

Finally, we were to have lunch with a successful couple, who had invited us to their country club. In the days prior, I was becoming more uncomfortable with fund raising. I had been spending more time on the phone pursuing people and, therefore, less time pursuing God. I sensed the Lord saying to me, "What are you doing? I did not tell you to 'seek Me first and make appointments.' I told you to 'seek Me first,' period."

Lynne and I enjoyed our lunch with them, and though they were financially capable, they pledged no support. On the way home, I looked at my wife and declared, "That's the last one of those I am going to do. I will not spend any more time trying to raise money."

With noticeable relief in her expression, she replied, "Good, because I was ready to tell you that I am not comfortable doing it anymore." That was August of 2002, less than two months after the official beginning of our ministry.

What happened? I had my weekly phone conversation with my mom just a few days later. When I told her of our fresh determination, she reacted predictably. "Now you've got it!" She added, "Jeffery Paul, if this ministry is of the Lord, you will not have to be concerned about finances, ever."

As usual, she was right. By the end of August, our income had increased to the highest one month amount in our young history. By the end of that year, our first seven months, we were far ahead of expenses. Far enough that our board of directors decided that from that time forward, each month that ended with surplus funds would prompt our ministry to share financially with others around the world.

Now in our second decade, we consider ourselves blessed to see this practice continue unbroken. Our leadership shares the conviction that God is honoring in us the promises he makes to everyone. "Give and it will be given to you. They will pour into your lap a good measure—pressed down, shaken together, and running over. For by your standard of measure it will be measured to you in return" (Luke 6:38). And, "He who is generous shall be blessed, for he gives some of his food to the poor" (Proverbs 22:9).

Examples? They seem endless. In human terms, I suppose some would be considered small, some great, and some in between. But when I consider the fact someone has responded to the impression of God on our behalf by offering a gift of any amount, all are huge. Typically, the gifts we receive are in the form of money, but support also appears in other ways such as clothing, office equipment, supplies for mission projects, and more.

I recall when I was preparing to travel to Africa for the first time. I was on my early morning prayer-walk when I passed the home of an older couple who had been a part of the church I had previously served. I heard my name called and turned to see Judy stepping from her porch in my direction. Harmlessly outspoken and sweet, she said, "I noticed in your recent newsletter you are going to Africa soon, is that right?"

"Yes, in less than two weeks," I answered.

"Do you have good shoes?"

"Good shoes?"

"That's right, good shoes," she repeated emphatically, as if I hadn't heard.

"I suppose so."

"I imagine you will be doing a lot of walking over there, and the ground will probably be rough. You need good shoes to protect your feet. Will the shoes you have do the job?"

"I'm sure they will. They're not new, but they're not that old. I'll be okay."

"You know what? You need to have good shoes. Come inside with me, and I'll get my husband to tell you when he can take you to the store for new shoes."

I began to give a polite gesture of protest, but her insistent character took command. "Don't argue with me, Jeff. We want to do this. Now come inside!"

I had learned long before the two words in the English language that can spare one a lot of trouble, so I used them in response: "Yes, ma'am."

We visited briefly and planned the appointment. By day's end, I was the proud owner of a pair of top brand walking shoes. That was not the last time. Before returning to Africa on future trips, there were more visits to the shoe store, the clothing store, and more. I'm not sure why my feet were so important to Judy, but in those early years, they remained consistently protected. Maybe she was led to consider, "How beautiful are the feet of those who bring good news of good things" (Romans 10:15).

Prior to another Africa trip, I was in a well-known retail store, gathering items needed for the journey—snacks, candy and supplies for the children, and gifts for my host pastor and his family. When I proceeded to check out, a store employee also known to me from a former church was working in the area. We exchanged greetings, and as I unloaded my merchandise, she knew me well enough to curiously ask, "You have quite a collection of stuff. Whatcha got going on?" When I told her of my trip to Africa, she immediately said to the checkout clerk, "Apply my employee discount to his things, and use this to pay for it." She retrieved a one hundred dollar bill from the pocket of her smock. The sale totaled about eighty-five dollars, and she insisted I keep the change to buy a meal or two on my trip. She has since been a frequent donor to JAMin.

It was during that 2002 December trip to Romania when our bus driver approached me in the second half of a basketball game and gave an almost prophetic challenge. I had sung during the halftime breaks of several games, when Rahdu came and complimented my singing. "How old are you?" he asked.

"Forty-eight years," I admitted.

"Have you made recordings of your singing?"

"No, I never have."

"God has given you a powerful voice," he said soberly. "The day is coming when your voice will no longer be what it is today. You should record your singing so people may still be blessed after your voice is weak." I thanked him for his kind words and practical advice. The idea of making a recording had always appealed to me, but I never pursued the effort, primarily due to time and financial limitations. Even after Rahdu's admonition, I gave it little thought.

It Gets Even Better

A year later, I was at my desk in early December when the phone rang at 11:30 in the morning. An unfamiliar voice greeted me. "Jeff Andler, you do not know me, but my wife and I saw you sing on the televised service of your church over ten years ago. Her health prevented her from attending regularly, so we would watch your church on television. One day after you sang, my wife looked at me and said, 'If I die before you do, will you ask that man to sing at my funeral?' Jeff, my wife passed away this morning about 8:30, and I'm trying to keep a promise."

I asked him the day and time of the funeral service. When he told me, I explained our ministry policy to him. "If I have the abilities to meet the need and if the calendar is clear, the answer is yes. I'll be glad to help you."

I met this seventy-five-year-old gentleman for the first time on the morning of his wife's memorial service. I was grateful God helped my voice to be strong and clear as I sang the requested songs. Following the service, I pledged my prayer support to him. He thanked me and said, "I will be in touch with you."

One evening the next week, he kept his promise. "Your singing was everything I remembered, Jeff. Our family loved it, and we thank you for helping us." I acknowledged his kindness and then he asked a question that echoed my Romanian friend of the year before. "Jeff, do you have recordings of your singing?"

"No, sir, I do not."

"Why not?"

"Well, sir, I've thought about it, but there are reasons why it was never a priority. Raising children, busy in my church, you know. Also, making a recording the right way is expensive, and I just never felt like I could justify the cost."

"Jeff, you don't know much about me, but God has blessed me through the years. I've been very successful in business. I'd like to see you make a recording, and I believe others would enjoy it also. You've been such a help to me. If you would consider doing this, I'll be glad to pay for it."

Obviously not expecting this kind of offer, I tried to manage an appropriate response but probably did not succeed. I did express concern over his open-ended generosity and informed him I had no idea exactly what to anticipate by way of cost.

"Let's do this," he offered. "The Christmas holidays are upon us, so we're not likely to accomplish anything until afterward. Why don't you look into the details, and get back to me after the first of the year. Can you do that?" I agreed though I had no idea where or how to pursue the assignment.

The next day I had a call from a friend, who was scheduled to provide special music for the next Sunday's service at our Wilora Lake Lodge church. I told him of my conversation the previous evening, and he instantly responded, "I have a friend who has a lot of experience in producing Christian records. He's a great guy, and I know he will be glad to talk to you." He even had a phone number handy. Before the day was through, the producer promised to have three production budgets ready for the first of January. Three, because I wanted to present my benefactor with fair choices in the expenditure of his money.

I suppose I'll always remember what he said when we sat at his business conference table on that first Thursday of the new year. He looked at the most expensive budget figures and said, "Why do we need to look at the other two? You want to do this right, don't you?"

"Yes, sir, but to be fair, I wanted to let you see that there are choices. This is your money, and you should have every say in how you spend it."

He thanked me for my honesty but persisted in his choice. He then sent his assistant to retrieve a checkbook. He and I remained at the table, and I listened as he talked fondly about the wife who had so recently departed. It sounded as if they had never gotten past the stage of youthful sweethearts, and I remember hoping the opportunity to speak from his grieving heart eased his burden.

After three months of calendar planning, musical arranging, securing copyright licenses, and contracting necessary musicians, we went into a studio and produced a recording of ten selections. These included many original compositions. It was a special experience to have our daughter, Lyndsey, provide vocals on some tunes and our son, Jeremy, play drums.

When the project was complete, I let my generous friend know there was money remaining from his initial investment, but he kindly instructed me to "Hold onto it for use in your ministry."

It was during the above process that I received word a dear friend from our former church had passed away. Both he and his wife had been faithful members of our choir and were especially helpful during demanding seasonal productions. I was on my way to the recording studio for a planning session when I stopped by their home to visit the grieving widow. She informed me it was their desire to have me sing at his funeral, and I agreed. It was held on a cold, gray day in February. After the service, I accompanied the funeral party to the burial site, where I offered my final condolences and farewell.

A month passed, and I found myself in the same store I mentioned earlier. Turning into a long aisle, I noticed my recently bereft friend approaching. Our eyes met, we greeted with a hug, and I asked of her progress. We talked for a while and laughed over common memories of her husband and my friend. Suddenly she interrupted and said, "While I'm thinking about it, I have something I need to give you."

"Do you need me to come by for something?" I asked.

"No, I have it right here, something for your ministry." She reached into her purse and retrieved what was obviously her checkbook.

Feeling a bit on display, I quickly suggested, "You can take care of that another time. Why don't you just drop it in the mail?"

"No," she insisted. "I've needed to do this, and if I don't do it now, I'll continue to forget. My husband and I talked about this before he died. He wanted you to have this."

I stood silently as she wrote, and then handed me a check in the amount of $5000.00. I was understandably overwhelmed and was totally inadequate in my bungling attempt to express proper gratitude. "He loved you," she said with a slight quiver in her lip and a growing mist in her eye. "We both love you, and we both wanted to help you in your new ministry." We visited a little longer and parted fondly. After gathering my needed items and my composure, I thought while walking to my car, *I really love this store!*

Since making the decision to remain uninvolved in fund-raising and allow God alone to care for our needs, He has proven Himself dependable. We continue to stand upon the words of Jesus as He commissioned His disciples in Matthew 10:9–10, "Do not acquire gold, or silver, or copper for your money belts, or a bag for your journey." Any time, attention, and effort we might spend acquiring would be lost to ministry.

I am not condemning those who feel it necessary to engage in raising funds, in fact I have helped some do so. But while we at JAMin know we can approach those who have *some,* we have chosen to only approach the One who has it *all* (Psalm 24:1). While we thank the Lord for those who have a *measure* of concern to see God's work done, we know He is *immeasurably* concerned to see His work done. He has committed Himself to underwriting that work in those who share His priorities (Matthew 6:33).

Our experiences with God's sufficiency do not end with the above examples. You know about the tremendous provisions for the Romanian children's camp and the Honduran prison chapel. You might also be interested to know about the Christmas gifts provided for one hundred children associated with the inmates and guards of that prison. There is land that was purchased in Africa and church buildings constructed; a kitchen and dining facility for the purpose of feeding street children in Costa Rica; food, medical supplies, and sewing machines for oppressed Christians in Pakistan; and financial support shared with young missionaries in China, Romania, American college campuses, and more.

There have been sweet and unassuming elderly women who have amazed us with unexpected and sometimes overwhelming inheritances on their passing. I can tell you of unexpected phone calls requesting a visit, when very generous checks have been delivered. I can tell you of precious souls who have faithfully shared gifts of varying amounts each month through the years. There are also those who are unable to contribute monthly, but do so as regularly as possible.

I will tell you that both our children graduated from college with no debt. That the ministry that began paying a very modest salary in the early days has gradually added benefits and a retirement plan. And that the expenses of the Andler household have been consistently met and exceeded. Perhaps you recall when I told the Lord early on, "If I starve, I starve." Apparently that is not going to be a problem, as we have consistently worked much harder at losing weight than gaining it.

We have never once faced an upcoming ministry opportunity wondering if necessary finances would appear at the last minute. We have never had to delay or cancel a scheduled ministry due to a lack of funds. We are not underwritten by any church or mission organization. Our Provider has never had and never will have an emergency. Therefore, neither have we, and neither will we. We have been made completely confident that "my God will supply all your needs according to His riches in glory in Christ Jesus" (Philippians 4:19), and that He, "is able to do far more abundantly beyond all that we ask or think, according to the power that works within us" (Ephesians 3:20).

Amid all this delight, I must not fail to point out that just as God occasionally allowed Paul to use his own abilities to support his ministry (Acts 18:1–3; 20:33–35), I have had the privilege of doing the same. To those who may have the idea that this is a contradiction of the principle I have stressed, I respond with a confident, "Not so." Willingly neglecting the opportunity for my talents and gifts to be used in contributing to the support of our ministry should give reason to question my motives and conscientiousness.

A few years into our ministry, I was approached by a local pastor who needed my help temporarily filling a vacancy soon to be created by his departing minister of music. After developing a plan that would mutually accommodate my existing ministry responsibilities and the new commitment, I agreed to the part-time obligation. The process involved in my decision was the same one with which you have become familiar. There was a need, my abilities could fill that need, and the calendar could be arranged to attend that need.

When financial compensation was offered, I immediately made the decision to treat the opportunity as an extension of our ministry, and therefore I would not benefit personally. Anything the church desired to do in return for my services would be directed into our ministry budget and used alongside other contributions.

The arrangement that we expected to last possibly a few months has turned into almost ten years, and has included leadership in both music and senior adult ministries. Just as Paul used personal skills to show good faith in sharing responsibility for the provision of his ministry, I have been pleased to serve in the same way.

There is another valuable dimension associated with this service. Pastor Steve and the loving believers at this fellowship have become our dear friends and regular partners in ministry. We now share relationships that did not previously exist but are now personally and spiritually vital to us. It has kept me properly associated with a local church, and they have been wonderful in their encouragement to JAMin.

Have there been occasions when our ministry was exposed to a need but was not used to meet that need? Absolutely. But as we gratefully enjoy the opportunities when God chooses us to be His tool of choice, we also realize there are times when He does not. We are not God's plan; we are *part* of God's plan, remember? We know He has provided and will provide for everything He intends for us to accomplish.

Finally, we are peacefully elated to have learned that by abandoning fundraising, we have experienced *faith raising* as we have watched Him be true to His every word. He *is* truth, so how could He do any less?

Day by day, we have watched life get even better!

CHAPTER 16

NOT ALL FUN AND GAMES

I am told it is the most common expression in the Australian vocabulary. It is used in situations of minor importance to issues of major concern. We hear it in movies and advertisements in a way that is intended to instill reassurance in the listener. Without a doubt, all of us would like for "No worries" to actually be our state of mind. But it is an ideal that is as elusive as the expression is common.

All people aspire to an existence free of worry and stress, but even believers who claim being at peace in Jesus Christ would have to confess it seems impossible this side of heaven. However, that state of mind is exactly what the people of God are told to experience.

Notice I did not say we are told to *pursue* a worry-free character. We are told to *possess* a worry-free character. In John 14:1, Jesus did not say, "Try not to let your heart be troubled." He said, "Do not let your heart be troubled."

No matter what translation of the New Testament you may read, you cannot escape the clear directive of the opening phrase of Philippians 4:6. The King James Bible reads, "Be careful [full of care] for nothing," while other versions say, "Do not worry about anything" (NLT), "Be anxious for nothing" (NASB), and, "Do not fret or worry" (MSG). This does not sound like a suggestion, does it?

Jesus said quite plainly in the Sermon on the Mount, "do not be worried about your life." Then He asked the supporting question, "Who of you by being worried can add a single hour to his life?" (Matthew 6:25, 27). He completed His comments in this section of Scripture by reiterating, "Do not worry then," and, "So do not worry" (Mark 6:31, 34). Therefore as they say, "any way you slice it," we are instructed in the Word of God to be free of worry and stress.

Being free of worry is quite a challenge. Causes for worry are abundant. Some are with us continuously and others appear unannounced. How are we to deal with it? The Bible contains many directives that may seem completely unreasonable and even irrational. But we can rest assured that God is not cruel, making demands He knows we cannot follow, so He can watch us squirm in guilt and failure.

Paul offers help in Philippians 4:6: "but in everything by prayer and supplication with thanksgiving let your requests be made known unto God." This is not news to most of us, but if we're honest, we will admit our worry seems to overtake our minds before our praying gets very far. Our prayers end, but our stress remains.

What is the answer? Somehow we have to be brought to the point where the abundant *causes* of worry no longer *result* in worry. How? Let me offer the following illustration.

I suppose I will always vividly recall Valentine's Day of 1979. My wife and I were in seminary about three hundred miles from our hometown, when I was called to the registrar's office and given devastating news. My father had just died suddenly of a heart attack. He was fifty-eight. My sister, brothers, and I rushed to our mother's side, all reeling from the life-altering loss.

The next morning, it was time to view his body and make funeral arrangements. I had attended many funerals and had seen many families deal with loss, but never anyone so close to home. As his widow and adult children stood over him, weeping uncontrollably, this man, who had always been so responsive to our needs, did nothing. He was a career military man, tough and tender. On this morning, he was neither.

On the day of his funeral, just before the service, we gathered to have one final look at the man nicknamed "Jake." With tears flowing freely once again, I recall saying, "Be seeing you, Jake." The quick-witted father whose retort would have normally reduced everyone to laughter… said nothing. He made no response to his widow's heartache. He had no comment for his children's pain. The reason why is obvious. Our father was dead, utterly lifeless. That which had previously enabled him to be capable of normal reactions was gone, never to return. It had been eliminated, ruthlessly to be sure, by death.

The elimination of the reactions of stress and worry in believers also requires a death. Physical death will certainly accomplish the goal, but God has something else in mind that will preserve a more mature, effective, and *living* witness in the world. Specifically, a spiritual crucifixion must occur and nothing less. Paul said in Galatians 2:20, "I have been crucified with Christ; and it is no longer I who live, but Christ lives in me."

Dead people do not react. They cannot react. Dead people feel nothing. When the part of us that reacts to life situations with preoccupying and unproductive worry is put to death, we will no longer be characterized by that behavior. We will not be unaware of difficulties, but our attitude will not be determined by difficulties. Reasons for stress will not be gone, but the stress will be gone.

Being crucified with Christ is imperative, but it is not something we will likely bring about voluntarily. Though He submitted to crucifixion, Jesus did not place Himself on the cross, drive the nails into His own hands and feet, and then raise His cross for all to see. His execution was orchestrated by the Father but was carried out by the hands of godless and unbelieving men.

If you and I are serious about dying to *self*, which is the ultimate issue in worry, we need to be, "crucified with Christ." This means we must be ready to welcome and submit to the Father's plan for our crucifixion. It will involve a painful process. As I described regarding my own experience early in our time together, and as Jesus suffered to an immeasurably greater extent, we must be stripped of our confidence, competence, and capability. We must be left with nothing but the heavenly Father, who crucified us. Only then can He shape us and use us according to His pleasure, which we will quickly find to be our own pleasure.

Let us face a fact. While we all want to claim crucifixion with Christ and desire to be used greatly by Him, the line at the crucifixion recruitment office is not very long. In fact, there is no line. It is actively avoided.

Crucifixion is excruciating. However, waiting on the other side is a resurrection to greater life and usefulness, with the tendency for stress and worry left behind. Crucifixion is excruciating but necessary. We must consider, "Jesus, the author and finisher of our faith, who for the joy set before Him endured the cross" (Hebrews 12:2). For years I enjoyed ministry, enjoyed being active, enjoyed Christian relationships. But until I experienced the horrors of a crucifixion, I had no idea of the level of joy, fullness, and freedom that lay on the other side. In His omniscience, Jesus saw the joy waiting after the crucifixion and endured it willingly. In my faith, I should have but did not. God's desire for me to have all that was possible in Christ caused Him to crucify me anyway. Now I cannot thank Him enough.

Why have I given such emphasis to this subject? My description of the wonderful events since our dark time of crucifixion may have given you the idea that difficulties and hardships have been withheld from our lives. Not so. These years have often included experiences that have been simultaneously joyful and trying. The difference now is the frustration and stress that once pilfered our joy and blessing are virtually nonexistent.

For example, I shared with you the wonderful way in which God took us to Romania to assist in the construction of the children's camp. I have not told you of the day when a power planer caught the edge of my work glove, snatching my left hand into its blade. The tip of my ring finger was instantly mutilated. I was rushed to the hospital in Fagaras, where the emergency staff was waiting to do all they could with antiquated equipment. The less than sanitary conditions and the cough of the older gentleman lying beside me caused me to wonder if I would leave with something worse. Though much of the fingertip and the entire fingernail were missing, the doctor was relieved to determine there was no bone damage. After mercifully administering a numbing agent, the nurse went to work sewing up the end of my finger with suture material that looked like kite string. I was released with pain medication and instructions to return every morning to have the wound cleaned and the dressing changed.

That seemed like a simple plan, until I was reminded each morning for the next seven days that the bandage had fused with the wound. I became educated as to the extensive number of nerves located in the human fingertip each time the dressing was pulled from the injury. The level of pain from such a small part of the body was unexpected.

On the morning before my return home, it was decided the stitches should be removed and an antiseptic applied to fight infection during the three-day wait before seeing my doctor. For some reason I will never understand, I did not insist on having my hand numbed. The kite string was not cooperative in being removed from its home. The pressure required to pull the sutures from my finger brought unavoidable cries of pain that echoed through the halls of the Romanian hospital.

I suppose I should have surmised that if a bandage could seal itself to a wound so thoroughly in one day, the seal made over three days would be powerful indeed. I did not. As my American nurse worked to remove the bandage, the final layer that had attached itself to the wound appeared to be there for good. Any pressure applied to remove it was unbearable. My hand was soaked in a solution for thirty minutes in hopes of coaxing the stubborn gauze to loosen its grip, but the effort was futile.

Finally, my doctor sprayed my finger with a freezing substance that was supposed to dull the ensuing pain. However, as he began to pull the bandage from my hand, I concluded that a frozen finger hurts just as badly as a warm one. His facial reaction to the exposed wound let me know he was not happy with what he saw, and he immediately recommended I see a plastic surgeon. The end of my finger was visually disgusting. It looked as if it had been continuously gnawed upon since my last visit at the Romania hospital.

Fortunately, a plastic surgeon made room in his schedule to see me the next day. Though he questioned the quality of care I had received, he simply advised keeping the area clean and dry to allow for healing. The wound did begin to clear, and in a few weeks, the hint of a fingernail miraculously appeared. Today, the end of my finger is only slightly misshapen, and the full fingernail renders any former damage almost unnoticeable.

Though we have returned many times with additional construction teams, I have kept a safe distance between me and the power planer.

You know the rewarding results of our multiple journeys to Africa, but there have also been experiences when unprecedented challenges accompanied the rewards. Our 2009 spring project seemed to be unusually fraught with peculiarities. That was the trip where we dealt with cobras and scorpions. On the same project, Roy and Sammy were moving from their vehicle to a canoe that was to take them to a village across the river. Almost immediately after stepping on the ground, both of them were covered from head to toe by large ants. They were forced to strip to their underclothes to be rid of the invading pests. Fortunately, that particular species of ant did not bite.

The peculiarities did not end there, particularly for me. On the same night I had been surrounded by scorpions during the film, I awoke from my sleep with growing discomfort in my digestive tract. A fever developed, and I was disappointed to be unable to participate in our final day and evening of ministry. During the next night I awoke to find the fever had broken, and I seemed to be improving in every way. Morning came, and as our team was preparing to return to the airport, I felt fine and also relieved to know that whatever bug I had was temporary… or so I thought. The trip home included a day in Germany, and I energetically enjoyed myself with little memory of my recent discomfort.

As we often do on my return home, Lynne and I went directly from the airport to a favorite restaurant. As we were nearing the end of our meal, a couple and an elderly mother were seated at the table beside us. Not long after they arrived, I heard an unusual sound and turned to see the older woman's head resting on the table. It was soon determined that she had died suddenly on the spot. Perhaps this should have been some indication to me that the peculiar nature of our Africa experiences was going to continue closer to home. However, it did not cross my mind.

In a few days, I received a phone call informing me Roy had to be taken to the hospital with some unexplained neurological symptoms. Tests revealed no detectable cause, and he was finally allowed to return home with specific answers not forthcoming. *This project has had its ups and downs during and after,* I thought, but I entertained no idea that anything further might yet be in store for me.

I had been home for just over a week, when Lynne and I began preparing for our Sunday morning. While getting ready, I commented, "I feel a bit strange, like I don't have the energy I should." I went to lead the worship at our church's early service, which that morning included a selection by our choir. As I led, my energy level seemed to decrease by the minute. I actually leaned against the heavy pulpit to brace myself. By the time I went to the Wilora Lake Lodge service, a discomfort in my digestive tract was developing, very similar to what I had experienced recently in Africa. I managed to fulfill my duties but went home and soon found myself in bed—with the fever and other symptoms I thought I had left behind.

Following an uncomfortable afternoon and night, I was able to see my doctor on Monday. He prescribed some typical medications to treat what he thought to be common problems following travel abroad, though it was strange they reappeared after several asymptomatic days. That afternoon some of the symptoms eased slightly, but the fever and lack of energy remained.

Later that evening, the real adventure commenced. I began to have cramps in my midsection that grew increasingly uncomfortable. These lasted for about two hours and then seemed as if they would subside. The pause was the lull before the storm.

Soon the cramping returned with a vengeance, rapidly growing more severe. My abdominal area began to inflate like a balloon, becoming larger and harder by the minute. The growing pain was approaching unbearable, and nothing I could do produced the slightest relief. I was reduced to moans and muffled cries as I writhed on the floor of our den. Lynne insisted, "We are going to the emergency room!" I was bereft of any independent masculinity and cooperated immediately. She helped me into our car and my discomfort increased as she drove. To our delight, we found the emergency room virtually unoccupied. To our dismay, we discovered the speed with which one receives attention was apparently not based on that condition.

I was finally taken to an initial examination room and then immediately to have a CAT scan. In addition to the pain I became acutely nauseated, and the ensuing sounds and sights were unprecedented and disturbing, both to me and those charged with my care. Back in the examination room, pain medication was at last mercifully administered. I euphorically drifted into welcome sleep. I recall awaking briefly as I was being positioned in a regular room and hearing my wife say it was approaching four o'clock in the morning. My final memory of the night was another injection that rendered me comfortably unconscious once again.

After the light of day, I awoke to see my wife and daughter settled in at my side. I also saw the intravenous connections common to a hospital stay. I was free of the previous evening's pain but immediately desired information that would explain the reason for my current predicament. Soon a dignified-looking doctor appeared at my door. He introduced himself as not just a doctor but specifically a surgeon. "Mr. Andler, you appeared on my rounds this morning, but I am not sure why."

Alert enough to make an attempt at humor, I replied, "Well I can assure you I am not sure why, either. What do you say we not schedule anything until we both are sure?"

"Oh, of course. I need go to the nurses' station and read your medical chart. It should explain why I have been assigned to you."

He quickly reappeared and began sharing his interesting discovery. "Your CAT scan reveals you have air in the venous portal system of your colon." Undoubtedly noticing the bewildered look on each of our faces, he continued. "There is never supposed to be air in the venous portal system. If there is, it is an indication that something is very wrong."

"Like what?" I asked.

"Well in your case, it appears that part, or possibly all, of your colon has died."

"What does that mean?" I asked, "And what do we do about it?"

"The sections that are dead have to be removed," he said, at which point he instantly captured my rapt attention.

"Remove my colon? We're talking a life-altering situation, aren't we doctor?"

"We aren't ready to draw any conclusions yet. You have been assigned a gastrointestinal specialist. He and I need to discuss your situation and then get back to you."

He left me, Lynne, and Lyndsey to our inevitable discussion, but I remember being calmly at ease as we waited. "I'm not going to get concerned until there is a reason," I said. "Right now we do not know anything, so let's not manufacture scenarios that may or may not materialize."

No worries, remember?

After several hours the surgeon and the specialist finally returned with interesting but reassuring news. "On close examination of your CAT scan results, we see no sections of your colon that have died, but there *are* three areas that have stopped working. That is good news, but it is still a dangerous situation. You cannot go home until the entire colon has returned to normal function."

Having been informed by my wife of my recent travel, they suspected a parasite had hitched a ride in my body, supposing to find a permanent home in the United States. "We know of your trip to Africa and of your brief problem there," the specialist said. "An intestinal parasite would cause the problems you are having, so we are bringing a tropical disease specialist in on your case. If she agrees, you will be treated for parasitic invasion, which involves heavy doses of anti-amoebic drugs. Even so, you will remain here until the process restores your colon to normal."

I was so pleased to hear that a drastic surgery was unnecessary, the thought of an extended stay in the hospital was not troubling. The next morning, a young African American woman entered my room. She introduced herself as the tropical disease specialist the doctors had called. Sensing a familiarity in her accent, I asked, "Where are you from?"

"I know you have been to my country," she answered cheerfully. She revealed being born and raised in the Ghanaian capital of Accra. I was also pleased to find she was a faithful believer, and actively involved in a well-known church in our city. She explained that a parasite can appear, be dormant, and then reappear, which clarified the mystery of the time between my problem in Africa and the resurgence days later. We began the intravenous treatment discussed by the previous doctors.

Just five days after my admission, I was ready for another CAT scan to determine if I could be released. On the sixth day, I was sent home with instructions to continue oral medication for an additional three weeks, and with an appointment for a follow-up test. A total recovery was realized, and one month after my release from the hospital, I was permitted to make another scheduled ministry trip abroad.

"You need to stay closer to home where it is safer," I heard from well-intended observers. "This was a close call," others warned. "Maybe you should reconsider these places where you travel." All humanly reasonable concerns to be sure, but what about the worth of a soul? Are we to avoid places that are wide open to the gospel after one bout of sickness amid dozens of trips without incident? To use the words of Job 2:10, when his immense sufferings had just begun, "Shall we indeed accept good from God and not accept adversity?"

The preceding would not be the end of our challenges in 2009. My mother was in her mid-eighties and had been struggling with the increasing symptoms of congestive heart failure. By this time, she was on continuous oxygen and moved slowly with the use of a walker. On the first Saturday in June, her family reunion was to be held as always in northwest Florida. She, her two remaining siblings and almost all of our cousins lived in the area, so the activities had been conveniently reduced to a midday meal and a brief visitation.

Because of the distance from North Carolina and Sunday responsibilities, Lynne and I rarely attended. We did not plan to participate this year either, but my mother's deteriorating condition motivated me to make a last minute attempt. I knew it would mean a lot to her for us to join her family environment. We departed on Thursday evening, surprised my unsuspecting mother on Friday, attended the reunion on Saturday, and drove all the way home after its early afternoon conclusion. I was glad we did, and I would be even more so later.

By summer's end, my mother's condition worsened. Arrangements were in place for our September mission to Africa, but I questioned whether I should stay closer to home. Despite the struggle, I knew she of all people would understand whatever decision I made. Though not totally sure of myself, I decided to continue with my travel plans, hoping she would survive until I returned. While there, we had unusually sufficient cell phone service, which enabled me to speak to her every two or three days. Her decreasing respiratory capacity was obvious. I could tell it was an effort for her to engage in conversation, but her typical determination kept her as involved and spirited as possible.

It Gets Even Better

At the close of our project, I was grateful for the success of our ministry *and* the fact that my mom was still hanging on. On my return to Charlotte, I made plans to travel to her Florida home, feeling sure it would likely be the final visit. The night before my flight, I received a call from my now-deceased brother John, informing me our mom had taken a distinct turn for the worse and may not last until I arrived. "My flight is tomorrow," I said. "I'll get there as soon as I can."

My sister and both my brothers were waiting, all surrounding our mother, who was seated as usual in her favorite chair. She did not appear to be totally aware of her surroundings, but when I sat beside her and said, "Mom, it's Jeff," she responded immediately and as enthusiastically as she could. Her body's intense need for oxygen was manifested not only in the expected gasps but also in the unusual grasping motions of her hands. My siblings informed me the hospice nurse had told them earlier to expect such actions, as the body was instinctively groping in every way for the elusive life-giving air.

I cannot know this, of course, but once all her children were present, it was almost as if our mother was ready to call it a life. Within mere minutes it was necessary for us to call hospice, have a hospital bed brought to the house, and to have them administer final care and comfort to one stepping into death's doorway. It was Wednesday night, and she lingered until early Friday morning, when with her final breath, she was "absent from the body and present with the Lord" (2 Corinthians 5:8).

"When I pass on, I want Jeffery Paul to speak at the service," she had said many times. I knew I would naturally be grieving, but I always felt like I would be able to grant her desire. We also invited her church pastor and longtime friend to participate, and his words were appropriate and powerful. In the two hours prior to the service, we received friends and guests. It was touching and rewarding to see those whose lives she had influenced through the years gather to bid a grateful farewell. The church building was filled to capacity with those who had benefitted from her sacrifice and service. The atmosphere was one of glad reunion as much as of a sad departure.

When my time came to memorialize our mother, I represented our family as best I could in verbally expressing the life of the woman who remains alive in us today. I expressed our grief at her passing, our gladness for the end of her suffering, and our gratitude for the example she left for everyone.

Admittedly, at times like that I suppose we always wonder, *Should I have made an extra visit during those last few months? Could I have gotten to her side a day sooner?* And the big one, *Should I have canceled my trip to Africa when I knew she was weakening and not likely to rebound?*

I decided not to allow unanswerable questions to dominate my thinking and, therefore, fill me with crippling regret. I credited the Spirit within with keeping His promise to "bring to your remembrance all that I said to you" (John 14:26) when my mind was reminded, "If anyone comes to Me, and does not hate his own father and mother and wife and children and brothers and sisters, yes, and even his own life, he cannot be my disciple" (Luke 14:26). Jesus was obviously not telling us to literally hate anyone but that our love for this life should be as hatred when compared to our love for Him.

This life will often give us the opportunity to exemplify the requirements of genuine discipleship. When it does, we all too often rationalize whether those requirements really apply to the situation in which we find ourselves. The true question is when do they *not* apply? Following Christ's directives is usually not the most comfortable path to choose. In fact, it is often the most difficult. Said another way, following Christ's directives will not always be fun and games. But believers who have been "crucified with Christ" follow Him with peace rather than anxiety, with confidence rather than doubt, with determination rather than reluctance. Believers who are dead to self realize God works in every circumstance. He can also work in the hearts and minds of those who do not always understand their choices.

The natural course of life suggests to us from our youth that we will watch parents age and pass from this life ahead of us. However, the sudden departure of one closer to our own age is always shocking. I had always looked up to my brother John in many ways. He was talented and especially humorous, which usually made him the life of any gathering where he happened to be present. I'm sure he did not always like the idea, but as the little brother, I typically got to tag along in his escapades.

Both being prone to mischief and provoking laughter in others, our time together could often get interesting. This was no less true when we found ourselves in the same graduate school classes as it was when we sang in the same church children's choir. Before life took us in different directions, we often sang duets in church services, revival meetings, and entertained at special events. In regard to the latter, you could always count on some comedy being included with the music, and most of that was impromptu. Not that we ever planned it this way, but we both trusted Christ on the same Saturday night in our Chateauroux, France, church. We both were baptized on the same night soon after, and we both walked across the same graduation stage at the seminary in New Orleans, Louisiana, in 1979.

My marriage, our ministry paths, and life in general logically put distance between us. Additional differences also developed. At this point, I beg your indulgence if you think I am being too revealing, but I am not one who seeks to paint situations in a way they are not. It is also my hope that honesty may serve in some way to help you or someone you love, as we loved our brother.

As time passed, we suspected John was beginning to make choices that might lead to self-destructive patterns. His career in vocational ministry was short-lived, though he remained involved in church activities. However, with time, even this became irregular. Though we could not substantiate our suspicions, we sensed his deviation from the standards we had learned was progressing to deeper levels. Any attempt to engage him in concerned conversations was met with a closed mind and mouth, and to push further often resulted in a defensive conclusion. Unfortunately, his chosen direction remained unaltered, and we watched regretfully as his life seemed to trudge along in unfulfilled potential and unrealized dreams. As this continued through adulthood, everyone who loved him realized that any chance of past promise and opportunity was likely forever gone.

Though he strayed from his family in practice, he never strayed from us in consciousness and caring. His loved ones could expect a birthday call before rising from bed, which may or may not have preceded the gift that was in the mail. His aesthetic creativity endured, so any gift was nothing short of a visual adventure. Because the consequences of poor choices continued to haunt every area of his life, the contents of each gift reflected economic creativity more than financial prosperity.

Physical evidence of poor choices also became increasingly visible as the years passed. But caring curiosity on the part of family faced the same closed response as always. We watched as each visit revealed further deterioration of energy, personality, humor, and appearance. The one who was once the life of every party, the instigator around every meal, the creative wit on every family trip, sat quietly and lethargically amid our gatherings. More than once I commented to my wife, "I know John is not well, but I also know that he will not reveal any information if I ask questions." I finally added, "I fear that one day someone will just find John dead and alone."

Shortly thereafter, I did make an attempt at one more private conversation with John. My tone was guarded, and I was pleased to find he did not respond with defensiveness. He revealed nothing informative, however, and assured me all was well. I was not at all convinced, but I had done all I knew to do. I had long since learned we cannot force a genuine attitude or action upon any fellow human being.

In March 2012, our team concluded our usual spring evangelism project in Ghana. Roy and I were waiting in the Accra airport to board our flight to Washington, DC on Sunday night. I called Lynne to let her know all was well, and I would contact her again after our safe arrival on American soil. Only twenty minutes had passed when Roy said, "Jeff, Lynne just sent me an e-mail and wants you to call her."

"I just spoke to her," I said. "Did the e-mail come since then? I wonder what's up?"

I simply pushed the redial button to reconnect with Lynne. Accustomed to her various vocal inflections after thirty-five years of marriage, I recognized the presence of a problem as soon as she answered. "Hey, baby, did you want me to call?" I asked curiously.

"Yes," she answered as tears obviously challenged her speech.

"What's going on?"

"Your sister called," she continued with difficultly. "They found your brother John dead in his apartment today."

It Gets Even Better

In an unbelieving whispered tone I reacted, "What?" My free hand simultaneously grasped Roy's arm, and he could tell immediately by my entire demeanor that something was not right.

Lynne continued as best she could. "Phyllis said she had seen John about a week ago. He wasn't feeling well. She took him food and medicine. She began calling to check on him about midweek, but her repeated efforts received no answers and no returned calls. Instead of going to church this morning, she and Jim drove across town to John's apartment. His truck was there, but he did not come to the door. She called the police, who contacted the landlord. When the police entered his apartment, they found him lying across his bed. Jeff, I'm so sorry."

The sadness of my brother's demise did not end there. He had never married and lived alone. His job was such that it was common for him to work a few days and then be off for a few days. Adding to our heartbreak, we would learn his death had taken place several days before his body was discovered. Any possibility of viewing him one last time was eliminated, and our only choice in the preparation for his burial was cremation.

The circumstances rendered the entire situation surreal, and I somehow knew immediately that our adjustment to the loss would never have the normal closure we had experienced in the passing of other loved ones. Over two years have passed, and so far my assessment has been right. It almost seems like he should be out there somewhere, and only the absence of the phone calls, birthday contacts, and holiday visits convince me he is not.

The return trip from Africa seemed even longer than usual. Fewer than twenty-four hours after my return home, I was on a plane to Atlanta. I joined my sister, brother-in-law, and nephew in removing John's belongings from his apartment.

Our brother Mike is in the funeral business in the North Florida area where many relatives reside. John loved visiting there, and we agreed it would be the site of his final resting place. I served as the presiding minister at the memorial service, as I had for our mother just two and one-half years earlier. It was more difficult, but God gave grace as we did our best to honor John in a way I believe would have pleased him.

As family and friends were leaving the graveside service, I knelt as if to get a closer look at his headstone and somehow have one last touch with John. I recall being simultaneously overcome with grief, loss, disbelief, and a touch of anger. I contemplated the probability of a totally different day had John made different life choices. I missed my brother. I still do.

John and I were in our favorite department store the day after his last Thanksgiving when I introduced him to Sue, a dear senior friend who works there. During their conversation, she sweetly said to John, "You have a very nice brother." With a remaining spark of character and wit, he spontaneously replied, "So does he." I have no argument with you on that point, John, but I sure wish things could have ended differently for you—and for us all.

No life—not a better life, not even the best life—is all fun and games. Ours is a fallen and corrupt world, and, therefore, unavoidably inherent with unpleasant problems and challenges. For those who permit, these will absolutely dictate a victimized life, plagued by worry, doubt, confusion, discouragement, and ultimately defeat. Jesus said, "In the world you have tribulation [not "may have" or "might have"], but take courage; I have overcome the world" (John 16:33).

Try as we might, we will never control all that happens to us. And God does not always accompany the difficulty He allows with an explanation as to why. That's because His main concern is not the trial or its cause but the results it brings in us.

Christ's promise that tribulation is a part of our lives was followed with two key words: "courage" and "I." Telling us to "take courage" means courage is possible and expected, but bringing Himself into the equation means the courage required is found only in Him. How do we appropriate His courage? By following His example of courage. Where did His courage take Him? It took Him to a cross. Knowingly, willingly, purposefully, it took Him to a crucifixion and death.

So we are back where we began a few pages ago. It is inevitable. We all desire to be done with the weariness of worry and stress, but are we willing to go to the cross and be crucified in order to see it happen? Nothing that follows a crucifixion can ever equal the trauma of that crucifixion. Therefore, we will be left with the necessary attitude that keeps trials and their potential impact in peaceful perspective. We will have an unprecedented confidence that the One who took us through the crucifixion is the same One who is with us in every ensuing difficulty. The former experience of anxiety will be rendered a fading memory.

Whether personal injury or illness, the loss of loved ones to old age or senseless living, the inconvenience of computer crashes and car troubles, returning home to the loss of a beloved pet, my chronically uncomfortable spinal issues, or Lynne's daily monitoring of a diabetic condition, reminders of life's trials abound. They will not stop. They will likely increase. Will we have increased peace in the face of it all? Will we genuinely say with Paul, "We are afflicted in every way, but not crushed; perplexed, but not despairing; persecuted, but not forsaken; struck down, but not destroyed" (2 Corinthians 4:8–9)?

One last time, to reach such a point will require a crucifixion of self. It will be life's most difficult experience to be sure. But may I encourage you, assure you, promise you, urge you that the better life that waits should cause you to cease the typical avoidance of your crucifixion and to desire it with all your heart.

CHAPTER 17

FULL CIRCLE

Anything of significance that has happened in my life has been since the time we spent in Europe. I had a life before then, but it was a young life and not yet very eventful—as far as I can remember. I do have limited visions of the days before our move to European soil, but they are just images mostly. For example, the Valdosta, Georgia, trailer park and the silver mobile home where our family of six resided. There was a short fence that enclosed our yard, with a gate through which our father appeared at the end of each day. When he arrived, my brother John and I, the youngest and smallest of our brood, were hoisted to his shoulders and carried to the porch. I'm glad I remember that.

I still have the foggy memory of our dad crowding us into the living room of that mobile home to tell us of our coming relocation to a place called France. I seem to recall our parents being fairly serious in it all, but as a four-year-old, I didn't share their concerns. The next thing I remember was the trip in a propeller-driven airplane that took us across the ocean. It was noisy and bumpy, but not enough to prevent me from sleeping in my mother's lap.

I promised you more news was coming in regard to Chateauroux, France and the church our parents helped to form there. We arrived in July 1959, but the church was not officially established until October 1960. Other than images of the temporary barracks where our family lived and then our transfer to base housing, I remember little of what happened in between. However, once we began going to Sunday school and worship services through the narrow doorway on a cobblestone street, the impressions on my memory became increasingly clear and detailed.

I have many memories of that church. Our Sunday school classes in the attic; the small backyard surrounded by the usual stone wall; the cherry tree in the corner of that yard, which made it a temptation to skip Sunday school when the cherries were ripe; the echoes of our laughter bouncing between the wall-to-wall homes on the narrow street.

The memory that is foremost, the event that changed my life, changed my eternity, was the one that occurred on Saturday night, August 26, 1961. As I shared briefly with you earlier, that was the time this energetic, mischievous clown of a young boy was serious long enough to realize a need for Christ. At the close of a revival service, I confessed my sinfulness and received Jesus as my Savior. Four nights later, I was baptized, along with my brother John and others. I remember that event well also, especially the fact the water in the baptistery was freezing.

Less than a year later, our family returned to the United States. My father was stationed in Panama City, Florida, for the second time. Life rolled on, along with the years and decades. You know how our involvement in the First Baptist Church of Chateauroux resurfaced over forty years later and brought us together with Cristi Hodoroaba in Romania. Now let me share with you how our relationship with that little church was miraculously resurrected again, this time after more than fifty years had passed.

It was the first weekend of December 2012 when our JAMin. Christmas singers were participating in prison crusades, once again near Columbia, South Carolina. We led a service on Saturday night and were assigned to a rural facility on Sunday morning, located about thirty-five miles outside of the city. We were to lead two services, at seven and eight o'clock. We were instructed to arrive at the prison an hour earlier. "You should be met by Chaplain Bob," we were told on Saturday night by the event coordinator. "He's an eighty-four-year-old prison chaplain. You'll love him."

Perhaps you have been where we went that morning. The middle of nowhere, the boondocks, one of those places that convince you that you are lost although you are following directions precisely. Not yet daylight when we arrived, Chaplain Bob met us as expected. He was a kind man who seemed to be made confident yet unassuming by a lifetime of experience. He escorted us to the chapel area, we went through the required security procedures, and began our various preparations for the service. In order to make correct introductions, Chaplain Bob asked me to remind him of my name as the inmates began to arrive.

He began the first service by stepping forward to introduce me and our team. It is true that Andler is not a common name, but I don't think it could be considered a strange name. However, I have heard it mispronounced all my life. I have been called Angler, Angley, Adler (okay, that's close), and more often than any, my personal favorite, Antler (maybe that's one reason I love Christmas so much). I don't actually recall what the chaplain called me, but it was not very similar to Andler. Being accustomed to the mishap, I did not mind and gave it no further thought. As the first congregation was leaving and the second arriving, Chaplain Bob approached me once again. "Please tell me your name again," he requested.

"Andler," I replied. In an attempt to reassure him in the situation, I added, "But don't worry about it. Like my dad used to say, 'I don't mind what you call me just so it's not late for dinner!'"

As he began the second service, Andler again was not the name the group heard. Again I did not mind. Our singers shared Christmas music, and I shared a gospel message, which caused the allotted hour to pass quickly. After gathering our belongings, we waited at the security gate to be escorted to our vehicle. The chaplain joined us and stood at my side. "I apologize for mispronouncing your name," he said. "I don't know why I had a problem with it. The name Andler is not unfamiliar to me. I knew an Andler family when I lived in France in the 1960s."

He immediately seized my attention.

"Excuse me?" I said, feeling my facial expression reflect my immediate intrigue with the conversation. "*My* family lived in France during the 1960s. We were there from 1959 until 1962."

"Yes, I was there at that time," he confirmed.

By this time, our exchange had the rapt attention of the entire ministry team. "May I ask why you were there?" I inquired.

"I was a chaplain in the US Air Force," he revealed.

An amazed and excited realization began growing within me. "My father was in the Air Force. That's why we were there. Where were you stationed?"

"In a town called Chateauroux."

"LaMatinerie and Deols Air Force Bases!" I declared.

"Yes." He paused, smiled amiably, and said pleasantly, "I know who you are Jeff. I helped your parents start the First Baptist Church of Chateauroux."

As our ministry team looked on with mouths and eyes gaping, Chaplain Bob and I shook hands and embraced as two friends who had been unexpectedly reunited after a lifetime. "I became a Christian in that church!" I said excitedly.

We shared memories as time allowed. Though not generally permitted to take pictures on prison property, the officer assisting us was apparently moved by what he had just witnessed and granted approval. Before departing, we made several photographs together; the military chaplain and the impish kid, sharing this moment in the middle of nowhere. Two who shared a history in another middle of nowhere, halfway around the world, more than fifty years prior.

Amazing as the morning had been, I would find that this experience was just beginning. Once aboard our van, I immediately called my friend and assistant coordinator of the prison assignments and described the morning to him. "That *is* amazing," he said, "but there's even more to it than that."

He explained, "When you told me you saw Chaplain Bob, I knew he must have been back to work today. He's been sick for over a week. This morning was his first day back. If you had been there yesterday, you would not have seen him."

He went on. "That's not all. Last Tuesday we were reviewing the assignments for this weekend. Another singing team has traditionally been assigned to that prison, but for this weekend, we felt compelled to send them elsewhere and put you in their place. It looks like the Lord just meant for you to be there." I did not dispute his conclusion.

Our ride home was characterized by moments of quiet contemplation and amazed conversation about the experience. For years I considered a return trip to Europe in hopes of retracing the steps our family made there. But I never seriously pursued a plan. The discovery at the backwoods prison rekindled those thoughts, though the determination to see them materialize was not immediately born. It was enough, however, to send me to the Internet the next evening where I curiously began a search based on the word "Chateauroux." The effort was not fruitless.

Almost instantly, a title appeared that represented a Facebook group of people living in America who shared ties to the French city. As I read, I learned the group members maintained contact with each other and even made occasional visits to the place of my childhood. My eyes finally fell on a name I recognized. She was a few years older than I, and her family lived across the street from us in Brassioux, our base housing area. They also happened to be members of the First Baptist Church of Chateauroux.

I contacted her and was fortunate to have her immediately respond. She remembered me and my family, and we spent much of that evening comparing memories. She offered to send old black-and-white photos of their time in Chateauroux, and I enthusiastically accepted. In a matter of minutes, many pictures arrived via e-mail. I sat nostalgically looking at them, suddenly transported over fifty years into the past.

Several of the pictures were of a church fellowship event held in the Andler's early 1960s home. There was my young mother, eating at a table with the women. There was my young father, pouring coffee and laughing with the men. There was my teenage sister, hanging around with, well, a few guys. There were the Casanovas, the French couple whose farm we often visited and who had come to know Christ through my parents and the ministry of the church. Another picture featured my eldest brother, standing beside our 1956 Pontiac, which was parked at the church entrance.

My mind was racing with the sudden flood of memories. I could feel my longtime consideration of a return to the obscure French city quickly hinting at determination. It certainly seemed as if circumstances were being orchestrated for a reason. But I knew to be careful not to take it on myself to fill in the gaps. At any rate, hold on because it gets even better!

My friend and I continued to communicate over the next few days, and I appreciated the valuable input she had learned from multiple return trips with her group. I knew my schedule would not permit me to participate in their next visit, so I saved all her e-mail information to use in the event of a trip of my own. During this time, I also informed Chaplain Bob of the developments taking place since our incredible meeting several weeks earlier.

Two more weeks had passed when yet another surprise waited for me on my morning arrival at the computer. There was a Facebook friend request from someone with an obviously French name. In light of my recent experiences, I readily accepted. As she began to communicate in fluent English, she informed me her name was Michelle. She and her now late husband had retired to their hometown of Chateauroux after a career with an American company in northern Africa. Then she revealed, "I was Chaplain Bob's secretary at the American Air Force base when you all lived here. If you ever want to visit Chateauroux, I will be glad to meet you at the train station and show you all that you want to see."

It should not be surprising by this point, the spark of desire to return to that place of long ago was kindled into a fire of curiosity and resolve. So many pieces of this possibility had been presented to me without solicitation—the former air force chaplain, advice in revisiting a past culture, and a volunteer hostess and translator who shared that past. It seemed all that was left to do was make the necessary plans. But other than fulfilling a personal desire, what would be the purpose for such an excursion?

I discussed the possibility with my wife, and we agreed if I indeed intended to pursue the dream, it should be added to the end of an existing mission endeavor, due to the expense. We decided a stop in France on the way back from an Africa project might be the practical approach, since passage through Europe was usually involved anyway.

I continued to communicate with Michelle as my anticipation grew. She promised to be open and accommodating toward whatever plan we could coordinate, and I became increasingly impressed with this hospitable Chateauroux native. She informed me it would not require a great deal of time to see the desired sights, so the idea of adding just a few days onto the end of an existing trip became more sensible.

If a side trip to France was to be added to an Africa mission, my friend Roy would be affected. We enjoy traveling together, so he readily agreed with the idea of hitching a ride on his friend's special adventure. Clearly, I was becoming simultaneously filled with excitement and disbelief at the thought of the opportunity that seemed to lie just ahead.

As is so often the case, the plan we considered to be simple turned out to be nothing of the kind. I will relieve you of suffering through the details, but if you have ever had much experience with travel, particularly the airline industry, you know simple plans can quickly become complicated. Due to the unexpected cost and time added to a trip that was already quite long and expensive, we were unable to include a visit to France in either our spring or fall journeys to Africa. It became evident that a trip dedicated solely to this purpose would actually be more convenient and less time consuming. After confirming the dates with Michelle, Roy and I made our plans for the end of October 2013.

Charlotte, Munich, overnight in Paris, and finally the two-hour train ride to Chateauroux. Could it really be happening? Darkness was beginning to fall as we arrived, and Michelle Chabanet-Forest was waiting as promised.

Before you join me for our brief visit to the quaint city, I must say a word about this kind widow who opened her calendar, home, and especially her heart to her American visitors. She is rather petite and has a bright and welcoming smile. She was more than hospitable; she was more than just glad we were there. As I told her on our departure, she made us feel like she *wanted* us there and that it was as special for her to help me visit my past as it was for me to do so. During our return to Paris, Roy and I agreed we would gladly visit Chateauroux again, if for no other reason than to see Michelle. We could not have had a better host, translator, guide, and friend to make us feel at home while so far away from home.

Due to the time of day, it was decided Michelle would deliver us to our hotel, and we would begin our tour of the Chateauroux area the next morning. Roy and I were checked in quickly, but we were not ready to *settle* in. Michelle had told me the church site was only a ten-minute walk from the hotel. A visit to the church was scheduled the next day, but the temptation was too great. It was dark but not late, so Roy and I dropped our bags, looked at each other, and almost simultaneously said, "Let's find that church!"

The hotel concierge produced a map of the area and highlighted our route, which we would find to be almost no help (our fault, not hers). The old and narrow city streets and alleys just behind our hotel seemed to have twists and turns that were not obvious on the map. We had no success in finding anyone who spoke enough English who could help. Finally, we resorted to the time-tested tactic of any good Boy Scout—the global positioning systems in our smart phones. At first it appeared the lady in our phones had never been to Chateauroux, but after a few backtracks and U-turns, we found the large and very old church that was indicated on our map as being a block away from our destination. As we passed that sizable and ancient landmark, I immediately wondered why I had absolutely no memory of it. It was apparent we had to pass it every Sunday on the one-way street to our worship facility of the past.

With a few more steps, we found ourselves at the beginning of the short street where our church had met over fifty years before. Looking down the slight hill, I recognized it immediately. The old cobblestone was now just a decorative edging on each side of the street. The main portion had been paved with asphalt. Other than that, it was as I remembered.

Because of the address being displayed in one of the old pictures I had received, there was no guesswork in determining which door was the one for which we searched. In a few seconds, we were standing at 10 Rue Basse, now a residence but once the site of a small church facility, where the youngest child of John and Vada Andler first placed his trust in Jesus Christ.

As I said, it was not very late, but on this damp and chilly night in the old part of Chareauroux, the residents along Rue Basse had retreated into their homes with shutters fastened. The streets in the area were generally not well lit, so Roy and I found it interesting that a lone but bright streetlight was mounted on a wall directly across from the old church site. I am not one who looks for special meaning in everything, but it could be argued the light was deliberately positioned to illuminate the face of the long past First Baptist Church. Probably not, of course, but of all the doors on Rue Basse, the one for which we searched was rendered brighter than all the rest. And for that, I was grateful.

I would soon be grateful for another reason. Michelle had told us the family who lived there would be out of the country, so we were never able to enter the old church building. That was understandably disappointing. However, prior to our trip, I was reminded when the church was founded in 1960, the leaders placed a fairly large cross above the entrance, between the windows of the second floor. I did not recall that detail from my childhood, but on this night, over fifty-two years later, in the brightness of a lone streetlamp, there it was. The cross is still there! I learned no family who had lived in the house after the church left was willing to remove a cross. They feared it would bring misfortune upon them. I have no idea of the materials of which that cross was made, but as I stood and looked, I was thankful it had weathered the decades as well as it had.

I doubt the presence of that cross brings many firsthand memories to the minds of the Rue Basse neighbors of the church that once met under its watch. I do hope it brings to many minds the One that cross most importantly represents. Not the church, not a local church, but the One who died on the cross to give birth to His church, Jesus Christ, the only hope of the world.

You do not likely have to be told I will say more in regard to the cross, but first let me share with you the remainder of our brief return to the past. Michelle met us as planned the next morning, and our tour began. We returned to the church site first, and though it was the light of day, it did not look that much different than it had in the brightness of the streetlight.

Michelle drove us in the direction of the old air force base called LaMatinerie and the airfield Deols. Both were deserted by the Americans at the request of Charles de Gaulle in 1965. We saw the site of the old commissary, the high school my sister attended, and the military hospital. Though I had frequently visited that facility due to recurring pneumonia and upper respiratory ailments, I did not recognize the outside of the building. I did recognize the base snack bar building, where the Andler kids were thrilled to be taken every time our parents were so inclined.

As we approached the Deols airfield, I immediately recognized the white buildings, hangars, and the vast, open airstrips behind them as "the place where my daddy worked." From there it was on to Brassioux, the main housing area built for US Air Force personnel and their families in the late 1950s. In those days, the streets bore the names of American states. Brassioux is now logically a French neighborhood, and the street names are no longer American. With helpful information from my Facebook friend, I was able stand in front of the Andler home of a lifetime before. It was still white with the red-tile roof. I got the idea Europeans do not stay at home very much, as this house was also locked and sealed shut by the rolling window covers that had become common to the area.

There was actually just one remaining place for me to see that was significant to my childhood. It was the school where I attended the first and second grades, located in an area of Chateauroux called Touvent. The school shared the same name.

Sunset was approaching and Michelle wanted us to see something not included in my list of memories. "I want to take you to Deols Cemetery," she said. It was very old, with some areas approaching ancient. We passed between rows of headstones until we stood before a large group of small graves. On the wall above was a marble plaque that read, *"Aux Enfants Americains Decedes a Deols* 1953–1965," which is roughly translated, "For the American Infants Who Died at Deols 1953–1965."

We were looking at the graves of American military children who had died while their families were stationed in this foreign land, post–World War 2. "Many were stillborn," Michelle said, "and many died due to other reasons."

The sight reminded me that even in a peacekeeping environment, there were those who paid a high price for freedom. Young parents who dutifully followed orders to assist in a recently war-torn land, only to return home while leaving a once bright promise resting alone in a faraway grave. I have no doubt the innocent children are resting in peace. I pray their bereft parents found rest also, and still do.

As we made our way back into Chateauroux at twilight, I surprised myself and Michelle when I recognized an open area beside a small river as the site where we had enjoyed weekend carnivals and flea markets over fifty years before. "It is still used for that purpose," she said. The sight disappeared from my rearview mirror as night fell, and this much anticipated return to my past was coming quickly to an end. Michelle had said it would not take long to see what I wanted to see, and she was right.

We were deposited at our hotel for the final time with Michelle's word to arrive the next morning in time to board our train to Paris. Once at the train station, we said our appreciative and heartfelt good-byes to Michelle, and in mere moments, my new experiences in the town of Chateauroux, France, became a new set of memories.

You may possibly consider the beginning of this journey to be much more interesting and fascinating than the end. If so, we share the same mind in that regard. Was there supposed to be a distinctively special reason for all this? Is one yet to be revealed? I cannot say at this point. But as I earlier implied, if full meaning and significance are not readily understood, I do not make it my business to manufacture them or look for them.

It is enough for me that the unexpected meeting with Chaplain Bob resulted in returning me briefly to the old backstreets and surrounding countryside of Chateauroux, taking my life full circle. Back to the place of my oldest, clearly recorded memories. Back to the place of my earliest spiritual awareness. Back to the place of my soul's rebirth, which has impacted my life ever since. Back to a place where a cross still marks the spot, reminding me *the* cross will always mark my life.

So what do I leave with you in all this? I obviously am not encouraging anyone to expect or even desire a similar experience. To do so would probably result in fruitless frustration. I did not seek the special ingredients of the recipe that made the year 2013 one of the most memorable of my life. They came to me. But may I remind you of what I have been reminded in this and so many other experiences? I'm pretty sure I at least hinted at this a long while back, but perhaps your memory can become clouded like mine. Future opportunities and experiences come to us when we're busily obedient in present opportunities. If I had not been involved in prison ministry in early December 2012, going where I was directed by God's Word and by human authority, doing what I was to do, and using my God-given abilities along with others, the inclusion of this chapter would have been very unlikely.

Given the experiences of the last dozen years, we may find this particular adventure has not ended after all. But for now, as promised, let us stand once again at the door of 10 Rue Basse. Whether by the light of day or an abundantly luminous nightlight, you cannot miss it. Look up just a bit, and see a simple, man-made cross that remains after more than one-half century. More than that, however, may we always be reminded and encouraged to see the superlative God-made cross that remains after two millennia. I am not referring to the rough-hewn and cruel instrument of agonizing death that stood on a skull-shaped hill just outside of old Jerusalem. That piece of wood was indeed fashioned by the hands of men. The cross to which we fix our gaze is far different and so much more.

That for which the cross stands, what it represents, what it accomplished and still accomplishes—all of this and infinitely more was God-made, God-ordained, God-orchestrated. The *blood* of that cross—the age-old and unchanging requirement of God for the forgiveness of sin (Hebrews 9:22). The *redemption* of that cross—the price paid to purchase the freedom of a slave (Romans 6:17; Ephesians 1:7; 1 Corinthians 6:20). The *salvation* of that cross—our rescue from the penalty, power, and ultimately the presence of sin (Acts 4:12; Ephesians 2:8–9). The *peace* of that cross—knowing we have been reconciled to our Creator and have restored fellowship with Him (Isaiah 59:2; Ephesians 2:14; 2 Corinthians 5:18). I could easily go on… and on… and on… but I will not.

However, I must mention one more—the *Christ* of that cross. It is He who shed His perfect and precious blood to pay the required price for our redemption. In Him is the salvation that has rescued us from the eternal doom of sin and made our peace with God (Romans 5:1). It is He who died on that cross to pay for sin, left the grave to conquer sin, and enters the hearts of repentant sinners to empower them to live above sin.

Oh yes, may we ever look to the cross. Have you been to the cross? It is still there to take away your sin and all it implies. Come to the cross, and join the hordes who have received its peace and purpose. It still stands firm, weathering our challenges, our doubts, our difficulties. It has overcome and therefore cannot *be* overcome.

Are we joyful? Look to the cross, the source of our joy. Are we downtrodden? Look to the cross, for joy is on the other side (Hebrews 12:2). Visit the cross often. Come full circle. It is where life begins. *Not* above the door at Rue Basse, *not* hanging in gold or silver from our necks, *not* even at the point of a spire towering above a house of worship. Look to Jesus. The cross is Jesus, and Jesus is the cross.

Each time Michelle met us at the hotel for another segment of our tour, I presented her with a small gift. I saved the best and most meaningful for last, which was presented to her on the morning of our departure. I had been encouraged to take a gift that would represent the area where I live. In the weeks prior to our trip, I struggled to find something that was distinctively North Carolinian. Since our area produces a good deal of pottery, it was suggested something of this nature might be the answer.

My wife made me aware that just a few blocks from our home is a small pottery studio. There was an impressive variety of vases, trays, jewelry, and more unusual creations. But nothing really touched me as uniquely appropriate. I literally had reached the last display booth when, there it was: a pottery birdhouse. But not just a house. It was a church, and there above its door was a cross, with another one perched on the steeple above. I knew immediately I had found the special gift for this special occasion. It was carefully wrapped and hand-carried to our kind and gentle hostess.

I have no way of knowing if she is keeping it indoors or out, but either would be acceptable as far as that birdhouse is concerned. I do hope that its cross is in clear view, and all who see it will somehow be touched beyond the mere level of witnessing an unusual work of North Carolina pottery. I hope it will remind Michelle of a former little church on Rue Basse, where lives were touched and a young boy was changed. I hope it will remind all of an eternal Savior, who came to change a world.

As I contemplate it all and how I was privileged to be taken full circle to that place where for me it all began… my, how life has gotten even better.

IT GETS EVEN BETTER

First Baptist Church Chateauroux, France
1960 (Chaplain Bob Taylor, left)

Jeff Andler and Chaplain Bob Taylor, December, 2012

Andler home, October 2013 with Michelle Chabanet-Forest

Jeff Andler and First Baptist Church of
Chateauroux France site, October, 2013

CHAPTER 18

NOT FINISHED UNTIL HE IS

Testifying to the fact that I have come full circle would suggest it is time to wrap up this endeavor, at least for now. I recall saying when we began it was time for me to get started. Now, months later, it is about time I close. Not that there is no more to tell. Quite the contrary; much has been omitted. The experience reminds me of the closing line of an old gospel hymn I first heard by the crusade choir on a Billy Graham telecast. I have loved it ever since: "The half has never been told."[1]

I am also reminded of the apostle John's closing commentary regarding the Lord Jesus: "And there are also many other things which Jesus did, which if they were written in detail, I suppose that the world itself would not contain the books that would be written" (John 21:25). I am certainly not applying this high standard to myself or our ministry, but rather to Jesus, in whose work we will continue to participate.

As I begin this ending, I do so enthusiastically confessing that anyone who has embarked on a totally consumed walk with Christ will draw the following twofold conclusion. Due to His eternal and fathomless nature and our human limitations, we will never be able to fully communicate all He has *done*. Nor will we imagine or anticipate all He will *do*.

There is no end to His story, so there is no end to the story of those who receive Him, know Him, and follow Him. Because He is eternal, He will never be finished with us, and we will never be finished with Him. As long as I am taking breath, my earthly usefulness to Him is still active.

Like many of the elderly I see every week, I may reach the point that I no longer understand how I can be useful to Him. But if I am breathing, He is at work in me, if for no other reason than to be the object of the love and obedience of one younger and stronger. The same principle will apply then that has applied throughout my entire walk with Christ. It is not imperative that I always know and understand what He is doing; I just always need to know *Him*. I have learned… I am learning, that if I know Him, I will trust Him, and therein lay all the satisfaction and peace that is necessary.

One day He will be finished with me on this earth, and you and I will have no doubt when that time comes. I will cease to breathe, cease to speak, cease to physically exist. I will have been invisibly and mysteriously transported to meet Him face-to-face. Yes, one day I will be finished on this earth, but not until He is finished with me.

I will reach my conclusion in this temporal world, but I will continue in another realm. There will be no more souls for me to reach, no more lives to touch, no more earthly service of the gospel to perform. That will be left to those who follow as I begin thriving elsewhere. Unhindered by physical limitations, temptations, and distractions, my praise, worship, and service will soar to heights as yet unimagined. On this earth I am not finished until He is finished with me, but there I will never be finished! The words of yet another old hymn come to mind.

> I love to tell the story, for those who know it best
> Seem hungering and thirsting to hear it like the rest
> And when in scenes of glory I sing the new, new song
> Twill be the old, old story that I have loved so long.[2]

There have indeed been other priceless experiences. I'll hint at some final examples, but I must avoid verbosity. I received an e-mail during my first trip to Africa, asking me to pray for a university student. While handcuffed in his eleventh-story room under suspicion of drug possession, he suddenly broke from his captors and dove through the window. He fell to the bushes over one hundred feet below. Somehow he survived, though he spent the next few months hospitalized, undergoing treatments and surgeries that involved almost every part of his body. I initiated a relationship with Adam and his traumatized parents, which resulted in him receiving Christ as Savior, along with a Bible and a new basketball. He was finally transported to his northern home to complete his recovery. About two years later, I received a letter that included a picture of him waterskiing and his thanks for the time we spent together.

In 2008 Roy and I spent a weekend in Sand Point, Alaska, on the Aleutian Islands. We worked with the thirty-member congregation of the First Baptist Church on an island where only a few hundred people reside. We saw twenty-six profess Christ as Savior. The endlessness of the sea in every direction was intimidating, and Roy and I agreed we felt farther from home there than any other place on earth. Yet, it was not remote enough to escape the working of God's presence (Psalm 139:7).

Soon after my 2009 hospital stay we spent two weeks in the communist nation of Vietnam. Four hundred converts were baptized in the dirtiest water we had ever seen in the Mekong Delta, and also in the waves of the China Sea.

I can share the tales of our experiences in India, a land overrun with false religions, enslaving the hearts and souls of those who desire to find God. Despite that hindrance, we were allowed into many schools, where over eight thousand students responded to the gospel of the one true God. We also had the privilege of baptizing many converts in multiple locations.

Christmas is a special season for the Andlers, so it naturally extends into our ministry. I must mention our Neighborhood Noel, an annual event held in our subdivision. I decorate extensively during the season, but my friend Whitey, around the block, goes all-out. He's a fellow believer, so a few years back we decided to take advantage of the fact many visitors are drawn to our neighborhood to see the sights. For three hours on the Saturday evening before Christmas, our JAMin singers present live music in front of his cul-de-sac residence. Volunteers distribute hot chocolate, candy, and Christmas gospel tracts to the visitors who have joined the party. When the crowd seems to be the greatest, the gospel is presented verbally, and it is common to see a dozen or so respond.

We were also impressed to initiate the Neighborhood Nativity Project, an Internet effort to encourage believers everywhere to make a statement of their faith by displaying a visible nativity scene in front of their residences. With all the worldly opposition to Christmas we hear about recently, this to us is a believer's opportunity for a positive, peaceful, and practical reaction.

So much of our story has been drawn from past years, but much has continued to happen even in the months I have been writing. You'll remember it was the unusual loss of my voice that set me on this path. I am happy to report that after extended therapy, and guarding the progress with the use of a personal amplification system, my voice has made a full recovery. I have resumed my regular vocal activities, including the full schedule of our busy Christmas music ministry. To relive the blessings of the past dozen years through this written record has been worth the interruption. My time without a voice doesn't seem like such an inconvenience after all.

On a more solemn note, we have recently said good-bye to one with whom we have partnered in ministry. Perhaps you recall our early prison experience, when our friend Terry had to rein in my absentminded exuberance. Just days ago she passed away due to complications from an illness. She was a mother and grandmother, but not that old. Now she will never be old. Her parting comment at the end of any visit or conversation was always, "Be blessed." Through her life many were, especially women with a prison past in whom she poured herself. Now she is forever blessed by the One who bestows upon the faithful their eternal reward.

Why do I include these final thoughts? Primarily to emphasize that life is moving, so life moves on. For good or bad, it moves on. With or without us, it moves on. God is moving in this life. His purposes are being performed continuously. He deeply desires to include us in His dealings, but so great is His sovereignty that our inclusion is in no way requisite to His success. It is a prerequisite, however, to our success in experiencing a truly joyful, fulfilling, and rewarding life. All of this is without question. The consideration for you and me is, am I moving with Him and in Him as life passes so quickly? Do I experience the unprecedented and incomparable quality of life that comes only through denial of self and emphasis on others? Am I enjoying the sweetest blessing of a believer's life, or is that something I occasionally see in someone else and hope to experience one day for myself?

If the time arrives when we answer those questions with a humble yet confident affirmative, the resulting quality of life will be accompanied by a gentle determination never to regress. We may be as busy as the proverbial bee in church business, our business, or other "important" business. Or we may busy ourselves in what is truly "the Father's business." One leaves us weary and wanting something more. The other leaves us energized and receiving more. My prayer is that more and more of His children will traverse the bridge from one to the other.

You know what that bridge was for me. We have no need to revisit that time. In fact, it feels like even my earlier communication about that experience was an eternity ago, much less the experience itself. But isn't that exactly the point? God wants to bring the believer into a consistent existence, where the inevitable trials fade while the ensuing blessings flourish. If this is not the testimony of your life, ask Him to give you the desire to have all He desires for you, and be genuinely willing to submit to the procedure in which He chooses to bring it about.

I must admonish us all to avoid the idea we are talking about the erroneously shallow "name it, claim it, confess it, possess it" perpetual feel-good, wealth, and prosperity Christianity sweeping the world. No, this is something from God's heart to yours that is infinitely more valuable, eternal, and biblical. It is for everyone, not a select few or only the obviously gifted or talented.

Everyone's journey will not be the same in appearance, expression, or involvement. But it will be in joyful and peaceful satisfaction. All believers will not be wealthy or prosperous, all will not be well known or widely influential, but all may experience this ultimate in Christian living. It will come to pass, not when we seek our own good, but the good of others as we exemplify the directive of our Lord (John 13:15).

If you have endured until now, I thank you. I am also glad you have been diligent because I have saved what I consider to be the most exciting news for last.

Perhaps you recall my early concern that a new and unfamiliar approach to ministry would somehow weaken the priority of evangelism in my life. Perhaps I am being merciful to myself in calling that assumption uninformed rather than foolish, as it has been totally unsubstantiated by our experience. What do I mean? I am humbled to share with you that since our ministry began in June 2002, we are approaching 700,000 indicated professions of faith at home and around the world!

I am not usually around to see how many of those who *prayed for* salvation have actually come to *practice* salvation, but I am thankful for the opportunity to share and the openness I have seen. Since salvation is the work of God, I am peacefully trusting in Him to complete the work He has begun in the hearts of those who are genuine in their desire (Philippians 1:6).

That final, exciting fact being shared, it is now time to bring this end to an end.

On that night in October 2009, when the Andler children gathered around our dying mother, we needed to lift her from her reclining chair so she could be moved to a hospice bed. My eldest brother, Mike, positioned himself in front of her, so he could achieve the best leverage possible as he led our effort. Though barely able to breathe and completely helpless, our mother still managed to express her disapproval of being so uncharacteristically manhandled. With her familiar wit and determined independence, we heard her whisper, "I'm not dead yet!" We could not contain our smiles at the sound of such strong words from one who had become so weak. But we had no doubt that our mom was not quite finished. Very close, yes, but not quite.

I do not know how close I am, but I know as long as I breathe, whether heartily or laboriously, I am not finished, for He is not finished with me. As we move along, there will be delightful moments, there will be difficult moments. It's taking a lifetime to learn about life, but through it all, I continue to learn that I will be able to genuinely and continuously declare as I have declared, "It gets even better!" And live or die, it will get better still (Philippians 1:21)!

For now…

NOTES

Chapter 1
1. Palmer Hartsough, 1844–1932, "I Am Resolved." Public domain.

Chapter 3
1. Clement Clarke Moore, 1779–1863, *A Visit from St. Nicholas.* The New York Book of Poetry, Charles Fenno Hoffman, editor, 1837.

Chapter 8
1. Jeffery P. Andler, 1954–, "He Became What I Am." Copyright 1992.

Chapter 13
1. Jesse Stone (aka Charles Calhoun), 1901–1999, "Shake, Rattle, and Roll."

Chapter 14
1. Anonymous, traditional African melody.

Chapter 18
1. Lelia N. Morris, 1862–1929, "'Tis Marvelous and Wonderful." Public domain.
2. Katherine Hankey, 1834–1911, "I Love to Tell the Story." Public domain.